CORPORATE GOVERNANCE

CORPORATE GOVERNANCE

theory and practice

CAROL PADGETT

palgrave
macmillan

First published 2012 by
PALGRAVE MACMILLAN

Palgrave Macmillan in the is an imprint of Macmillan Publishers Limited,
registered in England, company number 785998, of Houndmills, Basingstoke,
Hampshire RG21 6XS.

Palgrave Macmillan in the US is a division of St Martin's Press LLC,
175 Fifth Avenue, New York, NY 10010.

Palgrave Macmillan is the global academic imprint of the above companies
and has companies and representatives throughout the world.

Palgrave® and Macmillan® are registered trademarks in the United States,
the United Kingdom, Europe and other countries.

ISBN 978–0–230–22999–0   paperback

This book is printed on paper suitable for recycling and made from fully
managed and sustained forest sources. Logging, pulping and manufacturing
processes are expected to conform to the environmental regulations of the
country of origin.

A catalogue record for this book is available from the British Library.

A catalog record for this book is available from the Library of Congress.

The Palgrave Finance series has been developed in association with
ICMA Centre, Henley Business School, University of Reading

Series editors:
Professor Adrian Bell
Professor John Board
Professor Charles Sutcliffe
Professor Charles Ward

10 9 8 7 6 5 4 3 2 1
21 20 19 18 17 16 15 14 13 12

Printed in China

to Paul, Catriona and Lorna

CONTENTS

FIGURE, BOXES AND TABLES

FIGURE

BOXES

TABLES

PREFACE

Everyone loves a scandal – until it affects them. In the UK, those of us who had never worked for Mirror Group Newspapers were able in 1991 to express shock at the misappropriation of money from its pension fund, but at the same time to watch the unfolding story of Robert Maxwell as we would watch a soap opera. Ten years later, Americans probably felt the same about the Enron debacle until it was closely followed by WorldCom, and it began to appear as if corporate America was facing a systemic crisis. Today, regardless of where we live, we have felt the aftershocks of the global financial crisis which began in the American sub-prime mortgage market and quickly spread throughout the world, leading to bank failures and bail-outs and restricting the flow of funds to businesses. This has led us to question the way in which companies are and should be run, which is exactly what corporate governance is all about.

When I decided to write this book I realised that I would need incentives to keep me going – as you will soon see, incentives are an important part of governance. I decided that I should tell my friends about the book, because then they would ask me how it was going and I would be forced to make progress to avoid becoming another failed author. This was useful, because it kept me on track, but also gave me insights into the way people think about companies. As someone with a background in economics I am comfortable with the idea that companies exist to make their shareholders better off. In today's economy companies are run by professional managers who may not always succeed in creating shareholder value, so they need a mixture of incentives and oversight in order to do their job well. Yet as I spoke to my friends I realised that many people see companies as the means by which more people get jobs and access to new products. For them, even though they contribute to pension funds which hold shares, shareholders are a remote group whose interests are secondary to those of the wider community. For others, companies are personified by their founders or management – Richard Branson is Virgin, Steve Jobs is Apple – and so corporate success or failure rest firmly in the hands of a few individuals. This makes it easy to blame greedy bankers for the financial crisis.

These popular views of companies are grounded in a variety of academic disciplines, each of which has contributed to the development of corporate governance. In this book I will draw on insights from economics, finance, management and law in order to explain how corporate governance has evolved both as an academic subject and as a system of corporate practices. Thinking of corporate governance as a system implies recognising it as something which develops over time as a result of the interplay between historical, cultural and geographic factors.

All too often corporate governance textbooks focus on the US or the UK, as if their systems are representative of those found in the rest of the world. They are not; in fact in some respects they are outliers, the exception rather than the rule, so in this book I will offer insights into corporate governance practices outside these countries through an exploration of regulation and empirical evidence, as well as case studies about companies in Australia, Brazil, France, India and Japan as well the UK and the US.

Chapter 1 sets the scene for what follows by exploring the scope of corporate governance and considering the way in which law, culture and more recently globalisation have affected the systems that have emerged around the world. In chapters 2–5 I will go on to consider a set of corporate characteristics that shape governance, looking at ownership, the board of directors, stakeholders and management remuneration. While each company is free to pay its managers as it chooses, the managerial labour market sets norms which cannot be ignored. This means that chapter 5 offers a bridge between what could be thought of as 'internal' or firm-level governance measures and 'external' or market measures. External factors are considered in chapters 6–8 in which I discuss the implications for governance of the market for corporate control, regulation and corporate communication. Chapter 9 is different from the others in that it considers a particular set of countries rather than a feature of governance. In it I look at the governance challenges faced by companies in emerging markets. One of the key features of the book is that it discusses a great deal of empirical evidence on the effectiveness or otherwise of specific governance practices. In chapter 10 I will consider the reliability of some of the evidence offered by looking at the problems involved in modelling corporate governance, before making my concluding remarks. As you read the book you will notice that some words appear in italics. These are terms that may be new to you, so they are further explained in the glossary at the end of the book.

While each chapter covers a particular topic, some themes inevitably recur throughout the book. Many people describe the board of directors as the cornerstone of corporate governance. Chapter 3 is devoted to the board, considering its historical development, the legal duties of directors and the different board structures observed in practice. Given the importance of the board, regulators have made far-reaching recommendations on board structure, which are described in chapter 7. As corporate governance has developed there has been considerable controversy over the place of shareholders and stakeholders in the system. I devote a separate chapter to each group in order to consider the variety of people and organisations which make up the two broad groups. Of course, these groups affect and are affected by all corporate decision-making, so they are considered in a different light in chapter 6 on the market for corporate control and chapter 8 on communication and financial disclosure. This means that while each chapter will give you insights into specific governance topics, you need to read the whole book to see the bigger picture. To keep you interested, I include many examples, both within the text and in a series of boxes, that highlight particular aspects of governance. Each of chapters 1–9 ends with a case study illustrating the theme of that chapter; I hope that these examples will help you to recognise both corporate governance problems and solutions as you interact with companies, whether as a customer, as an employee or as a shareholder.

I have been teaching corporate governance for longer than I care to remember, so I have benefited from lively debates with many students over the years. I would like specifically to mention Simon Forsyth, Suranjita Mukherjee and Amama Shaukat. Working with Suranjita and Amama made me stop and think about governance more deeply than I had done before, and Simon gave me valuable insights into how students really read textbooks. The quality of this book has been improved by the insightful comments of the anonymous reviewers who have read it at various stages in its development. I am grateful to them and to Aléta Bezuidenhout and Martin Drewe of Palgrave Macmillan for their support throughout the process. All errors and omissions are my sole responsibility.

THE SCOPE AND NATURE OF CORPORATE GOVERNANCE

LEARNING OBJECTIVES

- To appreciate why different definitions of corporate governance have emerged since it was first recognised as an academic subject
- To understand why specific governance systems may be appropriate in some geographical areas but not in others
- To understand how global markets and competitive pressures can lead to the dissemination of governance practices around the world
- To appreciate why academic researchers and corporate information providers are so interested in measuring the strength of corporate governance within countries and individual companies

INTRODUCTION

Companies are an important part of our daily lives. Every purchase we make has been influenced by a company and in turn influences it. Even if we do not buy its products each business we encounter has an impact. We may appreciate the architecture of its headquarters building or cover our faces to avoid inhaling its pollutants. Advertising billboards may make us smile or frown. The news that a company's share price has risen has a positive impact if our pension fund or unit trust is holding it, or may cause concern if we know that the company is profitable because it exploits child labour.

In today's economy we are bound together through a myriad of relationships with companies. We are their customers, their employees and their shareholders and in addition our bank deposits become their loans. We are their *stakeholders* with the power to augment or reduce their profits through our purchasing decisions, to improve or diminish their efficiency by the way we work, to change their boards of directors through our votes and to increase or curtail their supply of funds through our savings.

We are all important to companies. For this reason every company strives to find the best way to manage its relationships with its stakeholders, or to put it another way, to find the best methods of corporate governance. This definition of corporate governance as a way of managing relationships between corporate stakeholders would not be recognised by everyone. In the next section we will consider how the study of corporate governance has changed over the years and why some people choose to define governance as we have here, while others prefer to narrow down the list of stakeholders, in some cases so that it includes only shareholders. While definitions of governance are influenced by theory emanating from a variety of academic disciplines, the practice of governance is affected by national characteristics including, law, politics and culture. The section on corporate governance systems will discuss why different countries have different views of governance and therefore why corporate governance systems vary between nations. The answer is based on *path-dependency*, the idea that on any journey your destination is affected by your starting point.

We live in a global economy in which companies are linked through international *supply chains* and global markets. This can have the effect of diluting national culture and making countries more and more alike. Some authors argue that for these reasons corporate governance systems are converging. We will examine this idea in the next section of this chapter. We then go on to offer a plan of the book explaining how the themes already introduced will be developed later. The conclusion summarises the chapter, highlighting why governance has become so important to investors and to companies. This theme is taken up in the case study at the end of the chapter. It considers how the strength of corporate governance is measured by information providers who sell their measures to investors. Academic research which uses these metrics shows that they are not perfect substitutes for each other, so must be handled with care.

THE DEFINITION AND SCOPE OF CORPORATE GOVERNANCE

In 2001 Diane Denis published a paper entitled 'Twenty-five Years of Corporate Governance Research ... and Counting'. That title marks 1976, if not as the year in which corporate governance was born, at least as the year when it became a subject for serious academic study. For students of finance 1976 is significant in that it was the year when Jensen and Meckling published their seminal paper on *agency theory*. In their paper they look at the problems that arise when an individual who owns all the shares in a business and is its chief decision-maker sells a proportion of those shares to an outsider who cannot influence day-to-day decision-making within the firm. They show that this changes the manager's spending habits, making them less likely to invest in projects that increase the value of the firm. If this can happen in a situation involving one owner-manager and one external owner, the likelihood of sub-optimal decision-making becomes much higher in real-world situations where companies are owned by many absentee shareholders and run by a small team of professional managers. These observations have led to the idea that corporate governance is about finding solutions to this problem, that is, ensuring that management teams act so as to improve the wealth of shareholders.

According to this shareholder-centred view of corporate governance, it is important to find effective ways of monitoring the actions of management teams or of aligning their incentives with those of the shareholders on whose behalf they work. This can be done in a variety of ways; monitoring can be undertaken by *boards of directors* and by *auditors*. Boards can align the interests of managers and shareholders by paying managers in ways that encourage them to pursue profitable projects, since the pursuit of profit leads to improvements in shareholder value. The stock market can punish errant managers by acting as a market for corporate control, facilitating the takeover of poorly performing companies by others which are better run. Like the other mechanisms already mentioned, the threat of takeover should encourage managers to act in the best interests of shareholders.

This classic interpretation of Jensen and Meckling (1976) is over-simplistic because in addition to discussing the tensions that exist between managers and shareholders, they also examine the potential for conflicts between shareholders and lenders. This prompted later authors like Shleifer and Vishny (1997) to expand the definition of corporate governance to include practices that protect all suppliers of finance, not just shareholders. Once we think of governance as a process that supports lenders, we have to consider the rating agencies that quantify the risk of corporate debt, together with the legal protection offered to lenders as part of the corporate governance system.

While finance theorists tend to think of firms as coalitions of providers of finance and people who make decisions about how that finance is used, other subject specialists consider broader coalitions. Sociologists, organisation theorists and management specialists include employees as an important interest group within the firm. Ethicists are concerned that companies can affect wider society and the environment. This has led to an even broader approach espoused by the OECD (1999) which characterises corporate governance as a set of mechanisms designed to regulate the relationship between a company and all its stakeholders. This approach to corporate governance leads us to consider the legal rights of employees, the relationships between companies in a supply chain and corporate communications with customers as part of the governance system.

Some readers may be dismayed at the lack of a single, agreed definition of the subject matter of this book. Others will be excited at the idea of exploring different approaches and deciding for themselves which is more useful. The author hopes that most readers will fall into the second category, because in this book we will consider a variety of theories from different disciplines, each of which can add something to our understanding of the nature of the problems that exist when we start to think about companies as coalitions of interest groups rather than as single decision-makers, as economists traditionally do.

CORPORATE GOVERNANCE SYSTEMS

In the previous section we saw that different approaches to corporate governance lead us to include various different activities and institutions as part of the corporate governance system. Over the years a variety of different taxonomies of governance systems have been offered. These include shareholder and stakeholder, inside ownership and outside ownership, market-based and bank-based and market and network systems. Regardless of which of these we look at, each classification puts English-speaking countries into one category and continental European countries into another, which they often share with Japan.

The shareholder/stakeholder distinction characterises countries according to whether their laws and practices tend to favour shareholders or a broader group of stakeholders in the company. One key indicator of this is the composition of the *board of directors*. If the board includes representatives of the company's employees or its bank, then it is deemed to have a stakeholder orientation. Given that boards in continental Europe may include both these groups, and Japanese boards may include bankers, these two regions are deemed to have a stakeholder orientation. The UK, US, Australia and New Zealand, on the other hand, are classified as being shareholder-oriented because in those countries boards are deemed to represent the interests of shareholders only.

The inside-ownership and outside-ownership classification distinguishes between countries in which shareholders are involved in the running of the business and those in which shareholders cannot take control. A shareholder may be classified as an insider because they sit on the board or hold a large proportion of equity, otherwise known as a blockholding, which gives them easy access to board members. An outside shareholder cannot influence management thinking because they hold little equity and therefore have few votes. Blockholdings of equity are common in continental Europe and some Asian countries, which means that they can be characterised as inside systems, while share ownership is more widely dispersed in English-speaking countries, which are therefore known as outside systems.

The bank/market distinction refers to the way in which companies are financed. In a bank-based system companies tend to borrow in order to expand their activities. This may involve a close relationship with a particular bank which may even offer personnel to sit on the boards of the companies to which they lend. This type of relationship gives the bank a key monitoring role which is beneficial for any minority shareholders who do not have the time, expertise or incentive to monitor the company's activities. Germany and Japan are often described as bank-based governance systems. In a market-based system companies choose to issue securities on the stock market when they need funds. This means that the stock market monitors their behaviour through the mechanism of the hostile takeover which is almost exclusively associated with the UK and the US.

Weimer and Pape (1999) offer a variant of this taxonomy in their classification of countries as either market-oriented or network-oriented. As we have already seen, in a market-oriented company shareholders are the key stakeholding group to which the company is accountable. The stock market is important as a conduit of funds and also acts to discipline companies through the threat of a hostile takeover. They go on to argue that in a system like this managers are likely to be rewarded in a way that is highly sensitive to corporate performance. You have probably already guessed that this is the category into which the English-speaking countries fall. In countries which are network-oriented lenders and blockholders are the key stakeholders, which means that the stock market does not have a corporate control function and there is little pressure to reward managers according to shareholder wealth. Weimer and Pape (1999) go on to make distinctions between three geographical regions which it includes within the board grouping of network-centred countries. The Germanic group[1] is distinct from the other regions in that banks and employees are the key stakeholders. This is in contrast to the Latin group,[2] where families and the state are key blockholders, and Japan, where city banks, other financial institutions and employees are the most important stakeholders.

In a series of influential papers La Porta *et al.*, often known as LLSV, offer a rather different classification of countries according to their legal tradition. Legal systems are often classified according to their basis in either common or civil law. In a *common law* system tradition and precedent are very important. Judges make rulings based on the outcome of earlier cases with similar facts. In contrast, *civil law* systems, based on Roman law, rely far more on the content of written laws and codes. Each case is judged in relation to statute rather than in relation to previous rulings by judges. La Porta *et al.* (1996) offer a finer classification of civil law countries according to whether they have French, German or Scandinavian origins. As you can imagine, these legal systems, along with the common law that is associated with the UK, have spread across the world thanks to colonisation. The French commercial code dates back to 1807 and was developed under Napoleon. The Germanic code came rather later, in 1897, when Bismarck reunited Germany. The Scandinavian codes originated earlier than the others but were subject to more change. La Porta *et al.* (1996) show that investors enjoy the greatest protection under common law, so it is not surprising that equity finance is so important in English-speaking countries (La Porta *et al.*, 1997). Civil law countries offer less protection to investors, with the French system offering the least legal protection, and therefore being associated with the least developed stock markets.

Other authors have used the LLSV classification to make connections between political systems (Pagano and Volpin, 2005) and cultural influences (Licht *et al.*, 2005) on corporate governance. Pagano and Volpin (2005) argue that the legal system is not exogenously given; instead it develops from political processes, and specifically from the voting system. They examine two types of voting systems, the proportional system, in which seats are awarded on the basis of the proportion of all votes cast in favour of each party, and the *majoritarian system*, in which candidates are elected according to the votes cast in a particular region. In the proportional approach all votes are important, so political outcomes are determined by groups with similar preferences. Pagano and Volpin (2005) argue that this is a good description of entrepreneurs and employees, since each of these two groups is associated with specific aims. In contrast, when voting is regional, particular geographic areas can tip the national balance between parties. This means that voters in specific regions are important, and within this group of voters those with unusual preferences can hold the balance of power and encourage the passing of laws that are of less benefit to other groups like employees and entrepreneurs. When they apply their model to data from 45 countries they find that proportional voting systems lead to strong protection of employees' rights, while shareholders are better protected in majoritarian systems like the one in the UK.

Licht *et al.* (2005) question the importance of legal tradition as a determinant of corporate governance on the grounds that recent attempts to implement laws on investor protection in some former communist countries have not improved financing in those countries. This leads them to suggest that a legal system can be successfully transplanted in another country only when it is consistent with that country's culture. This explains why both culture and law are similar in Australia, Canada, New Zealand and the US. When the British colonised these countries, significant numbers of British people settled in them, affecting their culture and easing the adoption of UK legal norms. Those former communist countries that adopted western laws on investor protection found they made no difference because the existing culture was at odds with those new laws, so day-to-day practices did not change. This discussion implies that corporate governance systems are path-dependent. In other words, they evolve from a set of pre-existing conditions; given that each country has its own starting point, it will move towards its own governance system. However, some authors have argued that the forces of competition and globalisation are leading to a convergence of governance systems, an argument to which we turn in the next section.

ARE GOVERNANCE SYSTEMS CONVERGING?

We have already seen that corporate governance systems are heavily influenced by financial markets and institutions, law and culture as well as by the type of tensions that exist between the stakeholders in companies. Stock markets are increasingly seen as global rather than local marketplaces. Neither investors nor companies restrict their activities to their local markets. Investors increasingly seek to diversify their portfolios by including the shares of overseas companies, and companies themselves 'shop around' to find the best exchange on which to list, rather than simply listing on their domestic exchange. An *institutional investor* that maintains close relationships with investee companies in one country will attempt to do the same thing with investee companies abroad. In this way it will encourage convergence in reporting and governance practice around the world. Similarly if a company decides to list its shares overseas, it will have to meet listing and reporting requirements that are different from those to which its local competitors are subject. This will affect the way it collects and processes data, which may in turn affect the way that it communicates with other stakeholding groups. If it is able to provide more useful information to customers as a result of this, it will gain a competitive advantage in its product market. If other companies are to compete with this one, they may have to change their own practices so that they become consistent with overseas regulation, despite the fact that they are not bound by it.

For multinational companies the idea of a local market is hazy at best. Multinational companies may be listed on more than one exchange; they certainly operate in many countries and so are subject to a range of different laws and regulations in financial, labour and product markets. In such a case it is easiest to stick to the strictest regulations encountered. If this means offering product information and guarantees that are better than those offered by rivals in some markets, those competing companies will have to change their own practices in order to retain market share. In this way they find themselves behaving as if they were subject to stricter regulation than in fact applies.

In cases such as these practices are diffused across national boundaries without any interference by regulators. Some corporate governance practices may be disseminated by more explicit intervention by regulators. Three examples spring to mind, all of which will be discussed in more detail later in this book. In the UK the Financial Reporting Council recently published a Stewardship Code (Financial Reporting Council, 2010) designed to encourage institutional investors to use their votes and to engage in other forms of dialogue with the companies whose shares they hold. The Code explicitly states that it expects British institutions to take the same approach to dealing with all investee companies regardless of where they are domiciled. This implies that British investors may encourage overseas companies to change their practices in line with what is done in the UK.

Earlier in this chapter we saw that the OECD takes a broad view of corporate governance as the means by which relationships between a company and all its stakeholders are managed. It issued a set of Principles of Corporate Governance in 1999, which it then updated in 2004. It encourages countries to adopt their own set of governance rules based on the guidelines. While the OECD is at pains to say that each country should adopt rules that are consistent with its own situation, it is inevitable that some convergence will occur as countries implement a single set of principles.

We have already seen that legal systems have a significant effect on the rights of investors and so can encourage or discourage the growth of stock markets as a means of financing companies. Legal systems have also affected the way in which companies report their activities to shareholders, so countries developed their own generally accepted accounting principles. As globalisation developed it became increasingly important for investors to have access to comparable information on all the companies in their now global investment universe. This prompted the development of International Financial Reporting Standards which are now mandatory within the European Union, gaining ground in the US and recommended by the World Bank for use in developing nations.

Developments like these add to the pressure for companies around the world to adopt practices that originated outside their own economy. We can see this in the way that certain features of board organisation and structure have become established as best practice in countries as diverse as the UK, Sweden, Turkey, South Korea, Bahrain and South Africa. Regulators in each of these countries, and many more besides, have introduced codes of corporate governance which lay down an ideal standard for governance practices at the level of the firm. Companies are required to either comply with the content of the code or to explain to their investors why they choose to use an alternative practice. In each of these countries, it has become normal to organise the board of directors so that the chair of the board is not the most senior management figure within the company. This has been done so as to avoid concentrating too much power in the hands of a single person. This wariness of power is also seen in the way in which companies in all these countries are encouraged to ensure that the majority of directors are *non-executives*, that is, they are not employed in the companies on whose boards they sit. Instead they work in other businesses and bring an independent perspective to bear on the issues faced by other companies. In addition certain key board functions such as succession planning, board remuneration, management of the audit process and relationships with auditors are being considered in small board sub-committees staffed by non-executive directors. This both recognises the importance of these functions and ensures that they do not become mired in company-specific norms.

Of course, it is one thing to introduce regulations of the kind described in the previous paragraph, and quite another to observe that the regulations are being implemented. Companies can choose whether or not to act in accordance with the regulations, so these examples of best practice may differ markedly from observed practice. Khanna *et al.* (2006) examine the extent to which governance systems are converging by looking at the relationships between firm-level governance measures supplied by Crédit Lyonnais Securities Asia, and the LLSV legal origins data. They find that countries that are trading partners adopt very similar corporate governance laws, supporting the idea that globalisation and competition lead to convergence. However, when they examine the relationship between corporate practices used in countries that trade less frequently, they find that the similarities disappear. In other words, the regulation has changed the appearance of governance but not the practices chosen by companies.

This supports an argument put forward by Gilson (2001). He distinguishes between form and function in corporate governance, where form is the mechanisms chosen, and function is the activity facilitated by those mechanisms. He argues that forms are path-dependent and therefore unlikely to converge rapidly, while functions are more likely to be similar in different parts of the world. For example monitoring is a function that all shareholders would agree is necessary, so we would expect to see monitoring all over the world. This is a convergence of function. However, in some countries monitoring may be done by banks, in others by boards and in others by a controlling shareholder, so the forms remain very different.

PLAN OF THE BOOK

The rest of the book will elaborate on the themes we have identified in this chapter. The next four chapters will consider the implications for governance of certain features that are specific to a company. These are its owners, its board, its stakeholders and the way it rewards its management team. We have already seen that shareholders are at the centre of some governance systems, but not others. While we often think of shareholders as the owners of companies, in fact they own a particular class of security issued by companies. This is a subtle yet important distinction which, as we will see in chapter 2, is important in defining the rights and responsibilities of shareholders in comparison to the rights and responsibilities of the owners of other assets. Finance theory is based on the assumption that all shareholders are rational and risk-averse. That is, they want to get the best possible return available given the level of risk they are willing to bear. This description may be accurate for some types of shareholders but not for others. We will consider the motivations of different types of shareholders and the extent to which they see themselves as owners of companies or owners of securities. Their viewpoint is likely to affect their relationship with the company's management team and therefore the extent to which they allow the managers to take control of the company. When managers take control they may, as we have already seen, make decisions that are not in the shareholders' best interests. When a dominant shareholder is able to maintain control of a company they may act in a self-serving way, using the company to fulfil their own ambitions rather than to create wealth for the other shareholders whose holdings are not large enough to give them control over decision-making. By examining the rather different shareholding patterns observed in different countries we will see that corporate governance problems and therefore systems vary in line with the idea of path-dependency introduced earlier in this chapter. In addition we will look at a range of empirical evidence on the relationship between corporate value and share ownership by different groups to see if some ownership structures encourage greater value creation than others.

Voting is one of the key ways in which shareholders can exercise control over the company. Perhaps the most important issue on which shareholders vote is the election of directors. The board of directors has a unique role in both setting corporate strategy and in monitoring decisions so as to ensure that they are beneficial for shareholders. In chapter 3 we will consider the tensions between the two roles and look at how they can be relieved through the addition of *independent directors* to a *unitary board* or through the *dual board* system in which each company has two boards: one in charge of strategy and the other which has a specific monitoring function. We will also consider an increasingly important feature of board organisation, the use of subcommittees to oversee particular functions; again we will consider a range of empirical evidence that attempts to find out whether particular board structures are associated with better value creation than are other structures.

Just as the organisation of the board varies between countries, so does its role, depending on the extent to which the company acknowledges a responsibility to stakeholders as well as to shareholders. In chapter 4 we will consider what it means to be a stakeholder in a company and how companies might change their behaviour in response to pressure from stakeholders. We will specifically consider the ways in which lenders, employees, customers and other companies become involved in governance. In considering the role of employees there will be some overlap with chapter 3, because employees and their representatives sit on *supervisory boards* in some continental European countries.

In chapter 5 we will turn to the question of how boards of directors are rewarded for their work. The area of executive pay is a controversial one, especially in the wake of the recent banking crisis. While the Walker Review (HM Treasury, 2009) has introduced new rules concerning the disclosure of the earnings of what they term 'high-end' employees, in non-banking companies the only information that must be revealed relates to the remuneration of board members. For this reason the discussion of remuneration will be limited to the payments received by directors. One key role of the remuneration system is to motivate directors, so we will begin by considering three rather different theoretical approaches to motivation. Maslow's hierarchy of needs implies that money should not be important to board members; in contrast, according to equity theory, people decide how much effort to expend based on how much money they earn relative to their peers. This approach gains some credibility given that in practice salaries are based on industry norms. However, it is the agency-theoretic view that holds sway in determining how remuneration packages are constructed. According to this view directors must be paid in ways which align their interests with those of shareholders. This means that compensation packages include several elements related in sometimes complicated ways to the gains received by shareholders. An examination of the evidence will help to establish whether or not these packages do lead to greater value creation.

In the next three chapters we will turn to external influences on corporate governance. In chapter 6 we will see how an active stock market can trade control of companies through takeovers. This is important if we accept that corporate governance is about protecting the interests of shareholders. In theory the threat of a takeover should be enough to encourage directors to make decisions in the best interests of their shareholders and therefore substitute for monitoring by the board or for remuneration schemes that align managerial and shareholders' interests. However, we must recognise path-dependency again here. In some countries ownership patterns and legal systems discourage takeovers, so we will use empirical evidence on the takeover market to consider whether or not it works as theory suggests it should.

It would be impossible to write a book on corporate governance without mentioning regulation. The last 20 years have witnessed a proliferation of corporate governance regulation around the world. Much of it has been in the form of codes which require companies to either comply with a set of rules or explain why they have adopted a different procedure. This approach has the advantage that it lays down a clear set of expectations but still allows companies to choose alternative practices if they are better suited to their situation. We will look in some detail at the development of codes in the UK. The Cadbury Code was one of the earliest corporate governance codes and was also highly influential. In a comparison of codes of corporate governance around the world we will see that many of the prominent features of UK regulation can also be found in other codes. Of course we must recall the work of Khanna *et al.* (2006), who show that while it may appear that governance systems are converging, companies do not always choose to adopt what regulators recommend. While directors' associations in the US have been writing codes for years, the legislature has shown a preference for law over voluntary codes in passing the Sarbanes-Oxley Act in 2002. We will consider the costs and benefits associated with this wide-ranging piece of legislation and look at the evidence on its effect on American companies.

A common feature of regulation around the world is an emphasis on transparency so that shareholders and stakeholders can easily see what the company is doing and appreciate its implications for them. In chapter 8 we will look at the many ways in which companies communicate with both shareholders and stakeholders. Before the advent of the internet it made more sense that in does now to differentiate between communications with shareholders and communications with stakeholders. Today anyone can gain access to the investor relations section of a corporate website and see the annual reports of companies, which were previously sent only to shareholders, although they were available on request to others. In addition they can see other reports and presentations given to analysts and other stakeholders. In this chapter we will consider how reporting has changed over time and look at companies' incentives to both disclose additional information not required by regulation, yet also to manipulate some information so as to mask or amplify its significance. This leads into a discussion of why auditors do not always recognise the kind of manipulation that characterises fraud cases. We will also look at forms of communication that target specific groups of stakeholders and consider how certain forms of communication can enable companies to gain or enhance a good reputation.

Chapter 9 is rather different from the earlier chapters in that it focuses on a particular governance context. It looks at the issues faced in emerging or developing markets. While western economies have become interested in corporate governance many years after industrialisation has been achieved and they have gained the status of 'developed nations', emerging markets are being encouraged to consider governance issues as they develop. The World Bank and the OECD see corporate governance as part of the development process because it has the potential to attract foreign investors whose activities will encourage stock market development which will, in turn, facilitate economic growth. In chapter 9 we will see how initiatives by the World Bank and the OECD have influenced corporate governance in emerging markets, looking in particular at the OECD's 'Principles of Corporate Governance'. Finally we will summarise the empirical evidence which shows that improvements in corporate governance are having a beneficial effect on shareholder wealth, and thereby encouraging growth in emerging markets.

Chapter 10 concludes the book by summarising the important developments in corporate governance since 1976 and by looking in a little more detail at some of the technical issues involved in interpreting the empirical evidence on those developments. You must have noticed that the phrase 'empirical evidence' has appeared many times in this section. There is a vast empirical literature on the relationship between governance mechanisms and corporate performance. Much of it is based on the underlying view that corporate performance is determined by governance, or to use a more technical phrase, that governance is given *exogenously*. However, this is not necessarily the case. Given that companies can choose which governance mechanisms to adopt they may make the choice based on performance. For example a company might react to falling profitability by inviting non-executive directors to join the board and offer a fresh viewpoint on strategy. If the new members join during a year in which profitability falls, a conventional model would treat the new directors as the cause of the falling profit. In fact they may be a reaction to it, in other words, the board structure is determined *endogenously* rather than given exogenously. This and similar modelling problems will be considered in the final chapter.

CONCLUSION

We have seen in this introductory chapter that corporate governance is a relatively new field of academic study. It attracts interest from scholars from many disciplines including finance, sociology, management and ethics. Each offers a distinct theoretical perspective on how to solve the problems that arise due to conflicts between the various stakeholders who make up the company. Regulators too are keen to find solutions to governance problems. They are inevitably informed by existing laws and practices, so it is not surprising that different systems have evolved in different countries. Yet we must not forget that today economies are bound together by strong trade and financing links, which encourage the spread of good practice across national boundaries. Some practices can be adopted worldwide, but others rely on a specific set of national characteristics to work properly. Regulators and companies must think carefully before recommending or implementing practices that work well in other contexts.

While every type of organisation has its own governance structures the emphasis in this book will be on the governance of companies that are listed on stock markets. This is due in the main to the fact that listed companies have to produce more information than private ones, so their governance practices are more transparent and therefore offer the possibility of being tested for their effectiveness. In addition, regulators are keen to introduce new codes and laws to affect corporate governance in listed companies, and it is important to consider the effects this has on the companies themselves as well as on the economies in which they operate.

- Corporate governance is a relatively new area of academic study which searches for solutions to the problems that arise in companies made up of stakeholders whose objectives differ. Its development has been shaped by theoretical insights from a variety of disciplines, including finance, sociology, management and ethics.
- The corporate governance system found in any particular country must be compatible with that country's existing laws, culture and political system.
- Some governance practices can and have been transplanted from one county to others through competitive forces and the operation of the global capital market.
- There is widespread interest in measuring the effectiveness of corporate governance systems at both the corporate and the country level. Academic researchers and information providers have contributed to this endeavour, and throughout this book we will use their metrics to consider the usefulness of specific aspects of corporate governance.

CASE STUDY   Measuring the strength of corporate governance

Around the world regulators are encouraging better corporate governance through the publication of codes and laws, companies are providing more information on their own practices and investors are showing a willingness to pay more for equity in companies that have sound governance practices (McKinsey & Co., 2002). With such an interest in what constitutes good governance, it is not surprising that academics have attempted to quantify governance practices in order to undertake empirical research into its relationship with corporate performance and information providers have developed their own proprietary measures for sale to clients.

Corporate governance ratings are calculated by awarding points to companies which display certain governance characteristics, such as independent boards and remuneration packages based on stock market performance. Academic measures like the Gompers *et al.* (2003) G-score based on 24 indicators of shareholder rights and the slimmed-down version including just six indicators, the E-index created by Bebchuk *et al.* (2009), usually treat all characteristics equally, while commercial measures may weight certain types of characteristic more heavily than others. The fact that Yahoo! Finance includes one such rating (CGQ®, provided by RiskMetrics) in its corporate profiles indicates just how mainstream corporate governance rankings have become.

The Corporate Governance Quotient CGQ® is based on eight categories of information, each of which can be used to calculate a sub-index as well as the overall measure. The sub-indices are based on the characteristics of the board, the audit, the company's bylaws or charter, its anti-takeover provisions, director compensation scheme, progressive practices, ownership and director education. Clearly some of these characteristics are based on local laws and regulation, so the precise components vary according to where the company is based. RiskMetrics takes a rather broad-brush approach by listing one set of characteristics for American companies and another set for the rest of the world. The major differences are in the way that anti-takeover and charter provisions are handled.

Other corporate governance ratings like GMI and TCL are based on very similar information. Until 2010 these ratings were provided by GovernanceMetrics International and the Corporate Library, respectively. Then these two companies merged and were joined later that year by Audit Integrity. The merged company now operates as GovernanceMetrics International, Inc. At the time of the merger the company committed itself to continue to produce the full range of products previously offered by the three independent companies, but also unveiled plans for a new rating incorporating environmental social and governance factors, to be launched in July 2011.

GMI and TCL contain fewer categories than CGQ®, but use overlapping characteristics. GMI rates companies according to board accountability, financial disclosure and internal controls, shareholder rights, executive compensation, the market for control and ownership and corporate social responsibility. TCL includes board compensation and succession planning, CEO compensation, the takeover defences used and accounting concerns at board level. It then rates companies on a scale from A to F, where an A-rated company is free of any problems in all four areas and shows superior qualities in two areas while an F-rated firm is completely controlled by management, shows little or no regard for its shareholders and potentially faces bankruptcy.

As its name implied, Audit Integrity took a particular interest in accounting measurements in order to produce its measure of accounting and governance risk, AGR®. It is based on over one hundred accounting and governance variables and is used to give companies scores ranging from zero to 100. The companies are then classified along a spectrum ranging from very aggressive to conservative. A very aggressive company is one which is likely to face class action suits from investors and to have to restate its accounts at some time, while a conservative company has proved itself to be trustworthy.

Academic researchers have recently become interested in these commercial measures and have investigated the extent to which they can explain or predict corporate value. Daines et al. (2010) note the similarities between CGQ®, GMI and TCL but find no cross-sectional correlation between the three indices, indicating either that they are measuring rather different ideas of what constitutes good governance or that they are subject to measurement error. Certain indices have some predictive power in the case of firms that have to restate accounting earnings (AGR®, GMI and TCL) and are faced by class action lawsuits (AGR® and GMI). AGR® is also positively related to future operating performance and market outperformance and TCL is positively related to future company value. Only CGQ®

has no predictive ability. Further Epps and Cereola (2008) find that it is not related to current accounting performance. Looking only at GMI, Bauer *et al.* (2008) find that GMI is a useful tool for portfolio selection, because companies which it labels as well-governed produce higher market returns that those it labels as poorly governed, while Spellman and Watson (2009) find that it can help to explain future returns.

These results indicate that investors should be careful when they choose among commercial governance ratings. Some ratings are useful as a negative screening device to identify companies that should be avoided because of their dubious accounting practices or vulnerability to litigation. Others can be used to predict performance. As companies realise that their governance scores are being taken seriously by investors they may change their governance practices in order to improve their ratings. On the face of it this is positive, but it can lead to what many people have called a 'box-ticking' mentality. In other words companies may introduce subcommittees, separate the role of CEO and chair of the board or drop their anti-takeover devices to improve their ranking on paper rather than because they believe it will improve their working practices or lead to greater investor protection (Sonnenfeld, 2004). In this case the companies will look stronger even though they are unchanged and the ratings will lose their association with performance or their ability to predict business failures. This highlights the fact that good governance is not just about introducing new procedures or doing what other successful companies do. It is about maintaining effective relationships with stakeholders that enable the company to attain its objectives.

Case-study questions

1 Why are investors willing to pay for corporate governance ratings given that they are based on publicly available information?
2 Why does RiskMetrics use different sets of characteristics for companies depending on their location?
3 Why might the use of commercial indices of corporate governance lead to a change in corporate behaviour?

REVISION QUESTIONS

1 Why might a country's laws affect the development of its corporate governance system?
2 Thinking about the culture of your own home country, which aspects of culture have affected your corporate governance system?
3 What factors could lead corporate governance systems around the world to become more similar?

REFERENCES

Bauer, R., Frijins, B. and Otten, R. (2008) 'The Impact of Corporate Governance on Corporate Performance: Evidence From Japan' *Pacific-Basin Finance Journal* 16 (3) 236–251

Bebchuk, L., Cohen, A. and Ferrell, A. (2009) 'What Matters in Corporate Governance?' *Review of Financial Studies* 22(2) 783–827

Daines, R.M., Gow, I.D. and Larcker, D.F. (2010) 'Rating the Ratings: How Good are Commercial Governance Ratings?' *Journal of Financial Economics* 98(3) 439–461

Denis, D. (2001) 'Twenty-five Years of Corporate Governance Research … and Counting' *Review of Financial Economics* 10 (3) 191–212

Epps, R.W. and Cereola, S.J. (2008) 'Do Institutional Shareholder Services (ISS) Corporate Governance Ratings Reflect a Company's Operating Performance?' *Critical Perspectives on Accounting* 19, 1135–1148

Financial Reporting Council (2010) 'The UK Stewardship Code' FRC

Gilson, R.J. (2001) 'Globalizing Corporate Governance: Convergence of Form or Function' *American Journal of Comparative Law* 49 (2) 329–357

Gompers, P.A., Ishii, J.L. and Metrick, A. (2003) 'Corporate Governance and Equity Prices' *Quarterly Journal of Economics* 118 (1) 107–155

HM Treasury (2009) 'A Review of Corporate Governance in UK Banks and other Financial Industry Entities Final Recommendations' HM Treasury

Jensen, M.C. and Meckling, W. (1976) 'Theory of the Firm: Managerial Behavior, Agency Costs and Ownership Structure' *Journal of Financial Economics* 3 (4) 305–360

Khanna, T., Kogan, J. and Palepu, K. (2006) 'Globalization and Similarities in Corporate Governance: A Cross-Country Analysis' *Review of Economics and Statistics* 88 (1) 69–90

La Porta, R., Lopez-Silanes, F., Shleifer, A. and Vishny, R. (1996) 'Law and Finance' NBER Working Paper 5661

La Porta, R., Lopez-Silanes, F., Shleifer, A. and Vishny, R. (1997) 'Legal Determinants of External Finance' *Journal of Finance* 52 (3) 1131–1150

Licht, A.N., Goldschmidt, C. and Schwartz, S.H. (2005) 'Culture, Law and Corporate Governance' *International Review of Law and Economics* 25, 229–255

McKinsey & Co. (2002) 'Global Investor Opinion Survey: Key findings' McKinsey & Co.

OECD (1999) 'OCED Principles of Corporate Governance' OECD

Pagano, M. and Volpin, P.F. (2005) 'The Political Economy of Corporate Governance' *American Economic Review* 95 (4) 1005–1030

Shleifer, A. and Vishny, R. W. (1997) 'A Survey of Corporate Governance' *Journal of Finance* 52 (2) 737–783

Sonnenfeld, J. (2004) 'Good Governance and the Misleading Myths of Bad Metrics' *Academy of Management Executive* 18 (1) 108–113

Spellman, G.K. and Watson, R. (2009) 'Corporate Governance Ratings and Corporate Performance: An Analysis of GovernanceMetrics International (GMI) Ratings of US Firms, 2003 to 2008' http://ssrn.com/abstract=1392313

Weimer, J. and Pape, J.C. (1999) 'A Taxonomy of Systems of Corporate Governance' *Corporate Governance: An International Review* 7 (2) 152–166

SUGGESTIONS FOR FURTHER READING

Denis, D.K. and McConnell, J.J. (2003) 'International Corporate Governance' *Journal of Financial and Quantitative Analysis* 38 (1) 1–36. The authors review what they call two generations of governance research; the second emphasises the impact of the legal system as discussed in this chapter.

Doidge, C., Karolyi, G.A. and Stulz, R.M. (2007) 'Why Do Countries Matter So Much For Corporate Governance?' *Journal of Financial Economics* 86 (1) 1–39. This empirical paper shows that country level governance has more impact than firm characteristics on corporate governance rankings.

http://www.icgn.org/ The website of the International Corporate Governance Network provides links to a useful publications, including advice on best practice.

2 OWNERSHIP

LEARNING OBJECTIVES

- To understand the nature of shareholders' rights
- To understand the difference between ownership and control of companies
- To appreciate different patterns of ownership around the world
- To see how different ownership structures can lead to different governance issues
- To comprehend why different groups of shareholders may have different aims for the company
- To appreciate the empirical literature on the effects of owner characteristics on corporate performance

INTRODUCTION

Businesses come in all shapes and sizes and several legal forms. An individual who operates as a *sole trader* can be thought of as the company because they are both the owner and the decision-maker. The situation is similar in a *partnership*, with the slight complication that the partners must either agree all decisions or determine a division of labour in which each has responsibility over a particular area. In both cases the owners of the business are able to control it. The same cannot always be said in a *limited liability company*. Some small business owners choose to form companies so as to create a legal separation between themselves and the company and to take advantage of limited liability. In this case a single person might own all the shares and run the firm in exactly the same way they would run a sole tradership. The key difference is that if the company goes bankrupt the shareholder can only lose the value of the shares because he owns securities rather than the company itself. A sole trader or partner remains personally liable for all the company's debts because they are not legally separate from it.

When the company has several shareholders they can all enjoy limited liability, but their ownership is diluted and they cannot think of the firm as their own in the way a sole owner can. While some may work in the company, others will not; those who do not will have no day-to-day control; they are *principals* who must rely on agents – the firm's managers – to take decisions on their behalf. This agency relationship can impose costs on the principals as the management team uses the firm's resources in ways that the shareholders do not condone. Agency problems become more likely once a company is listed on a stock market. Some companies may have loyal shareholders who keep their shares as a long-term investment and use their voting rights; others will trade regularly so as to make short-term gains; for them the company itself is hardly relevant to their decisions.

Shareholders, as the name indicates, own shares not companies. In the next section we will explore the rights and responsibilities that go with ownership of financial securities as opposed to ownership of other assets, using company law in the UK as a reference point. Given the potential for the separation of ownership and control that we have already noted, we will then explore this in more detail; looking not only at how shareholders may lose control to managers, but also at how some shareholders may be able to secure greater control than seems commensurate with the size of their shareholding. In the next section we will present data on the ownership of shares in the UK, US and continental Europe. The data show that while financial institutions are the dominant shareholding group in the US and the UK they are much less important in the rest of Europe, where non-financial institutions and the state play a more significant ownership role. Having identified key shareholder groups we will then consider what motivates the different types of shareholder, presenting relevant empirical results on the relationship between ownership structure and company value. The case study that accompanies this chapter is about L'Oréal. This French company has an interesting ownership structure, with two blockholders who can together outvote all other shareholders, which clearly has control implications for the minority owners.

THE RIGHTS AND RESPONSIBILITIES OF SHAREHOLDERS

In general terms the owner of an asset has the right to use it, to modify it, to exclude others from using it and, if desired, to sell it. They have the responsibility to make sure that the asset does not cause harm to anyone else. Taking a car as an example, the owner can use it as a means of transport or as a storage space, if they choose. They can respray it if they don't like the colour; add tinted windows, spoilers or any other feature they want. They can lend it a friend (as long as one of them has the relevant insurance) or they can refuse to let anyone else sit in it. They can enjoy all these rights exactly as they please as long as they do not injure anyone else.

A shareholder's rights are very different. Interestingly, the word 'shareholder' does not appear in the UK Companies Act 2006. Instead the Act refers to 'members'. The members are individuals or organisations that hold shares. The law recognises that some members hold shares for others' benefit, for example when a pension fund holds shares on behalf of its contributors. In this case it is the pension fund that is the member. Members have the right to receive information on specific issues, to vote on *resolutions* put forward by directors and to raise resolutions if certain conditions are met. Authors usually refer to these as *control rights*, but clearly the practical extent of your control depends on whether you own sufficient equity to raise resolutions, and if not, on the type of resolutions raised by the directors.

Under UK law, members have the right to vote in person or by proxy on resolutions concerning the appointment of directors (s.160); directors' service contracts (s.188); substantial property transactions involving directors (s.190); loans offered to (s.197) and credit transactions with (s.201) directors; severance payments made to directors (s.217); the directors' remuneration report (s.429) and the acceptance of the annual report and accounts (s.424). All these resolutions are classed as ordinary, which means that a simple majority of over 50 per cent is sufficient to pass them. Members can add a resolution at a meeting, provided that the request comes from 100 members or members representing 5 per cent of the shares. Shareholders representing 10 per cent of the shares can call a general meeting. Decisions on mergers with other companies and to divide a company, for example through de-merger, are also subject to shareholder approval (sections 907 and 911, respectively) but in this case a majority of 75 per cent is required to pass this special resolution.

The details of corporate law vary from country to country, but there is general agreement that the kind of rights described in the Companies Act 2006 should be available worldwide. The OECD Principles of Corporate Governance (which will be discussed in more detail in chapter 9) give a prominent place to shareholder rights. The OECD encourages all countries to, where necessary, amend legislation to ensure that shareholders have secure rights of ownership and transfer of their equity, that they receive sufficient information to be able to vote at general meetings, to elect and dismiss board members and to judge the implications of proposed takeovers. If shareholders do not have these rights they cannot contribute to corporate governance.

Shareholders also have *cash-flow rights*. In other words, they have the right to receive dividends if the board decides that it is appropriate to distribute profits in this way. In the UK and US control and cash-flow rights usually go hand-in-hand because the one-share-one-vote system dominates. However, there are notable exceptions. When Google went public in 2004 it issued class A shares with one vote each and class B shares with ten votes each. The Class B shares were only available to the founders and current management team. Swisher (2006) estimates that their 33 per cent share holding gave the founders, Eric Schmidt and Larry Page, 80 per cent of the votes. This is rare in the US where Gompers *et al.* (2003) estimate that just 6 per cent of companies have *dual-class shares*, but more common in continental Europe. Faccio and Lang (2002) report that 66 per cent of Swedish, 51 per cent of Swiss and 41 per cent of Italian companies have dual-class shares. This creates the potential for the shareholders with superior voting rights to pass resolutions that are beneficial for themselves but not for other shareholders. This problem is exacerbated in cases of *pyramid ownership*. This occurs when one company owns shares in another. Suppose A owns half the shares in B. An individual who owns half the shares in A owns a quarter of B and hence has rights over a quarter of B's dividends. In the extreme case that A owns all the voting shares in B, the half-owner of A also enjoys half the control rights in B. This is one of the issues that are raised in the L'Oréal case study that accompanies this chapter. In some companies *voting caps* are used to ease the problems associated with a dominant shareholder. A voting cap limits the proportion of votes a single shareholder can cast. For example, until 2008 a 20 per cent voting cap was in place at Volkswagen which meant that Porsche, which at that time held 31 per cent of the equity, had greater cash flow than voting rights.

While the control and cash-flow rights discussed so far are clearly important to shareholders, they are limited in that they stem from decisions already made by the board of directors. It is the board that is responsible for producing the annual report and accounts, the remuneration report, proposals for mergers and de-mergers and the board that decides what level of dividend to pay. In other words, the board decides what resolutions to put forward and hence what choices are available for the shareholders. It is as if the shareholders have made a very loosely worded deal with the board. They have said, 'you get on with running the business, at the end of the year tell us what you have done and we will vote to let you know whether we like it or not'. In legal terms this is a *relational contract*; in economics it is known as an incompletely specified contract. In other words, the board has a duty to manage the business on behalf of the shareholders, but it is impossible to specify how this should be done because no one can know in advance what opportunities and challenges will arise. An incompletely specified contract cannot provide complete protection to the parties involved because it does not cover all contingencies. The law attempts to meet these contingencies through the concept of *fiduciary duty*.

A fiduciary duty arises when one party is given control of another's assets in order to use them to make that other better off. This can happen when property is held 'in trust' for a child until they reach adulthood or when members of a pension fund allow a trustee to invest their money. The fiduciary has discretion over decision-making and must choose actions characterised by candour, care and loyalty. Candour is simply honesty. The fiduciary must reveal all relevant information (as long as he does not breach commercial confidentiality) so that their decisions can be judged. They should take the same level of care of the principal's assets as they would of their own, and they should display loyalty by forgoing opportunities to make profit as a result of the relationship. This does not mean that the fiduciary gets nothing from the deal, rather that they only receive agreed rewards.

This sounds like an excellent description of the relationship between the shareholders and the board of directors; indeed it has been used to justify shareholder primacy in corporate governance. The argument goes that directors owe a fiduciary duty to the shareholders. The directors must seek to maximise profits so as to maximise the market value of the company. If all companies do this, resources are used efficiently, shareholders become wealthy and can increase their spending leading to economic growth. The situation in UK company law is not quite this clear-cut. Directors owe duties to the company, not its members, but their duty is to contribute to the success of the company so as to benefit its members. In bringing benefits to the members directors are also required to consider employees' interests, to foster good business relationships and to consider the wider environment. To what extent does this consideration of other stakeholders threaten the supremacy of shareholders in governance terms? This is a big question and one which has fuelled much debate in the academic literature as people have argued over the relative merits of the shareholder and stakeholder approaches to the subject. We will defer further discussion of this question until chapter 4. At this stage we will offer two related reasons why in practice it makes sense to say that shareholders should be the main beneficiaries of the fiduciary duty owed by the directors.

The first reason is that shareholders are the only group whose contract with the company is relational. Other providers of finance have detailed contracts stating how much interest they should be paid and when they will receive the payments. If the company fails to maintain the payments the law allows creditors to force the liquidation of the company so that assets are sold in order to repay the creditors. The shareholders have no guaranteed payments because the directors have discretion over the level of dividends, and capital market movements decide whether or not it will be possible to make a capital gain by selling shares. The shareholders need a fiduciary duty to fill the gaps in their contract with the company. The second reason is related to the first in that it stems from the fact that creditors can force the liquidation of the company. In the event of liquidation the law sets out a 'pecking order' of creditors which shows who is entitled to be repaid first. While there are international differences at the top of the pecking order, there is universal agreement over who is at the bottom: it is the shareholders. This means that shareholders bear residual risk in the firm. If the company ceases to exist they lose their entire stake. This makes them different from other providers of funds and hence special in governance terms. They need the protection of the fiduciary duty.

Clearly the word 'ownership' in the context of a financial security has rather different connotations than in most other situations. It implies both cash-flow and control rights, but not necessarily in equal measures. Control in this context means the right to vote on particular issues dictated by company law, or to raise issues at a general meeting if the shareholder represents sufficient votes. If shares are widely held by a group of dispersed shareholders they may be unable to influence the agenda at a general meeting and so control will cede to the managers who dictate the agenda. If voting shares are concentrated in the hands of a few owners they can have greater influence over both meetings and management, and may indeed be said to control the business.

So far we have considered the rights of shareholders but said nothing about their responsibilities. Returning to the example of the owner of a real asset, we saw that our car owner can do what they like with the vehicle as long as they do not injure anyone else. In addition to legal rights the owner of a real asset has responsibilities to other people. To what extent do shareholders have similar responsibilities? Just as a car can damage people and property if driven recklessly, a company can cause injury and loss to others if its decision-makers act without due care. The shareholders are not held responsible for the reckless decisions of managers, but they may bear the costs of those decisions when they lead to consequences such as fines for environmental damage. It could be argued that shareholders should pay more attention to managerial decision-making when corporate actions could hurt others. After all, it is in their interests to ensure that the company's cash flows are not used to settle legal disputes. Regulators are becoming increasingly keen that major shareholders should treat their right to vote as a responsibility to vote. In 2010 the UK's Financial Reporting Council issued a Stewardship Code addressed to financial institutions. We will describe it in more detail in chapter 7, but at this point it is important to note that an increased emphasis on the responsibility to vote and become engaged with corporate issues could lead to a shift in the balance of power between shareholders and boards of directors.

OWNERSHIP AND CONTROL

In the introduction to this chapter we saw how in simple organisations like sole traders and partnerships, ownership and control are vested in the same people. For the sole trader there can be no conflict of interest between the roles of owner and manager because it is clear that if, as an owner they want to maximise profit, and by extension the value of the firm, this can only be done through hard work and efficiency. If they do not feel like working that way then there is no one else to blame when profits slide. Tensions may be more evident in partnerships where the individuals may disagree over aims, but the fact that both or all are working together means that they have to reach agreement in order to keep the partnership going. It is in the limited liability form of organisation that tensions between ownership and control become important.

The reasons for the introduction of the limited liability form are well known. Technological change made production more capital-intensive, to the extent that individuals and small groups could no longer afford to finance businesses without outside help. The concept of limited liability was introduced to safeguard the interests of external investors who did not have the time or expertise to be involved in day-to-day management, ensuring that if things went wrong they could only lose their initial stake in the business. As capital markets matured the number of outside investors rose, and the relationship between equity holders and managers became more and more arm's-length.

The dangers inherent in this arm's-length relationship between managers and shareholders were clear even in the eighteenth century when Adam Smith expressed concern that company directors would be less careful with shareholders' money than they would be with their own (Smith, 1976). The mid-twentieth century saw an explosion of interest in the problems resulting from this development. Berle and Means (1932) wrote about the separation of ownership and control in the context of big business in the US. Economists recognised that the traditional emphasis on profit maximisation is misplaced when decision-makers do not reap the full benefits of their choices. They offered alternative approaches to the theory of the firm by looking at the implications of goals such as *revenue maximisation* (Baumol, 1958), *managerial utility maximisation* (Williamson, 1963) and *satisficing* (Simon, 1959), which simply means working hard enough to achieve 'acceptable' rather than maximum profit levels. Box 2.1 explains the implications for the company of these alternative goals.

The common theme underlying all this research activity is the premise that managers are a small, coherent group while shareholders are widely dispersed individuals or possibly financial institutions who own equity as part of a diversified portfolio. They have no emotional ties to any particular firm and seek only to maximise their own wealth. As portfolio investors, shareholders own only a small fraction of the total equity in any one business, so each is 'small' in that sense. Given the anonymity of stock markets the small shareholders find it hard to get together to influence decisions, so there is a classic *free-rider* problem in which, if shareholders are dissatisfied with a particular company, they wait for others to do something about the issue. In the event that no one acts, the dissatisfied shareholders simply sell their equity to other portfolio investors or potentially to a company making a takeover bid.

Box 2.1 Alternative theories of the firm

Economics is based on the idea that all economic agents are optimisers. Firms are assumed to maximise their profits, which, if markets work efficiently, should lead to the maximisation of the firm's stock market value. Maximisation of profit implies producing additional output as long as the revenue received is greater than the costs of producing the output. From the 1950s onwards economists started to analyse reasons why managers might choose not to act optimally. These approaches became known as alternative theories of the firm. These theories recognise that managers can choose strategies that bring them personal benefits from their position within the firm. Given that salaries are higher in larger firms, managers might encourage growth through maximising sales revenue, which can only be done by producing more than a profit-maximiser would. They might instead consider other workplace benefits like perks and prestige and maximise the satisfaction or utility gained from a package of benefits. Once again this would encourage growth strategies. Finally, optimisation might be too much like hard work and they might simply satisfice; that is, work hard enough to make a reasonable profit that is big enough to keep shareholders quiet, if not entirely satisfied.

In a development that was hugely important, Jensen and Meckling (1976) worked through the implications of widely dispersed ownership and concentrated management in their seminal paper on agency theory. Given that agency theory has had a significant impact on the direction of research in corporate governance, it is worth spending some time considering it here.

Jensen and Meckling (1976) tell the story of what happens when a utility-maximising owner-manager sells part of the equity in their business to an outsider who has no decision-making power. The manager becomes an *agent* acting on behalf of an absentee *principal*. The decision-maker is shown making a simple choice over how to use the firm's resources. They can spend money either on activities that raise the value of the business, or on activities that give them a personal benefit that does not extend to the business. This latter category of spending could be thought of as perks, non-pecuniary benefits such as a plush office, company car, etc. As an owner-manager they know that both types of spending bring them a benefit, so they make the choice according to their preferences, and are, by definition, happy with the outcome. When they sell part of the equity to an outsider their preferences remain the same, but they face a rather different constraint. Now they can keep all the benefits of spending on perks, but only a proportion of any increase in the value of the firm. Not surprisingly the decision-maker increases spending on perks, which leads to a reduction in investment that could improve the value of the company. This means that the outside equity holder now holds shares whose value is lower than when they were purchased. The size of the problem increases as the owner-managers sells more of their equity. In other words, when managers own few shares they have little incentive to strive to raise the value of the company.

Jensen and Meckling (1976) analyse the agency problem in a one-period model in which the outside equity holder has no voting rights. The problem they identify can also occur if outside equity has voting rights but is dispersed among many owners. In this case each shareholder has control over a tiny proportion of the total voting rights and so feels that their vote is irrelevant. They either do not vote at all or hand their proxy to the board of directors, thus placing control squarely in the hands of management.

This insight has led to the search for mechanisms to overcome the principal-agent problem through *monitoring* and *bonding*. Monitoring activities, as the name implies, are ways of overseeing managers. A key feature of such activity is that it is costly to shareholders. Bonding, on the other hand, represents managers' attempts to overcome the problem because they recognise that it will be difficult to obtain future injections of capital if outside investors feel they have been cheated in earlier financing rounds. Managers thus become willing to incur costs in order to maintain access to new funds.

Much of the corporate governance literature, and indeed this book, is devoted to discussions of how to overcome this problem, that Villalonga and Amit (2006) call the Type I agency problem. Monitoring may be performed by independent boards of directors and auditors, while managers may use dividend payments, which reduce the amount of cash flow available for discretionary spending, or debt issues which open up the possibility of monitoring by lenders, to bond themselves to shareholders. An alternative or indeed complementary approach is to ensure that both managers and owners have the same aims, by paying remuneration based on equity value.

This emphasis is all well and good if the Type I agency problem is significant. The central premise that managers hold few, if any, shares in the businesses they run, and that owners are a widely dispersed group has been challenged by, among others, Holderness *et al.* (1999) for the US and La Porta *et al.* (1999) for the rest of the world. Holderness *et al.* (1999) compare managerial shareholdings in 1935, just after Berle and Means published their influential book, with managerial share-holding 60 years later. They found that the proportion of equity owned had not fallen; indeed on some measures it had increased, suggesting that the incentives of the two groups differ to a lesser extent than suggested by the conventional wisdom. La Porta *et al.* (1999) showed that while dispersed ownership of the largest companies is observed in the US, UK and Japan, the situation is significantly different in other parts of the world. In countries as diverse as Austria, Singapore, Israel and Italy the state is a significant shareholder in many of the largest companies. If shares are held in concentrated blocks it is difficult for managers to retain effective control. The blockholder can vote against the board at a general meeting or simply exert pressure behind the scenes, threatening to replace a management team that doesn't do the blockholder's bidding. While this means that the Type I agency problem is not important, it doesn't mean that there is no problem at all. Instead, blockholders may promote decision-making that is good for them, but is inconsistent with the objectives of smaller shareholders. This is often known as *entrenchment*, but was dubbed the Type II agency problem by Villalonga and Amit (2006).

If all shareholders have the same objective, the maximisation of the value of the firm, then the Type II problem cannot exist. However, there are sound reasons to suppose that the dominant shareholders identified in the literature may have rather different aims from smaller, portfolio investors. The state may use companies for political ends, for example to keep up employment levels or to retain a national defence industry. A dominant family shareholder may see the family business as an asset to be handed on from one generation to the next or as a source of employment for family members. Earlier we saw that dual-class shares impact on the control rights enjoyed by shareholders. States and families are exactly the type of owners with an incentive to issue dual-class shares when they float companies. If they retain all or most of the voting rights they can use the firm exactly as they choose, potentially to the detriment of other shareholders. Solutions to Type I agency problems may have a part to play in type II problems, for instance independent boards should safeguard all shareholders. However, government regulation in the form of shareholder protection laws may also be necessary when shareholders have different objectives.

SHAREHOLDING PATTERNS AROUND THE WORLD

Commentators have coined the phrase 'Anglo-Saxon governance' to describe corporate governance in the UK and other English-speaking countries, or more specifically the UK and US. The fact that people mention the two countries in the same breath, as it were; indicates that they believe the two countries are identical in governance terms. In terms of equity ownership, the two countries have both been characterised by a decline in the relative importance of households as owners, while at the same time financial institutions have grown in importance. On the other hand, there are differences in respect of public ownership and more importantly overseas ownership of equity. Tables 2.1 and 2.2 show how the proportion of equity held by different groups has evolved over the period 1963–2006. In these tables 2006 is chosen as the latest date because at the time of writing this was the most recent year for which comparable data were available for all the countries discussed in this chapter. More recent data would reflect the state reaction to the recent banking crisis. Governments around the world have taken equity stakes in banks in order to aid their recovery. The data presented here pre-date the financial crisis and so represent a 'normal' situation in which some states hold no equity while others have ideological reasons for being shareholders.

While the patterns in the data on ownership by individuals and financial institutions shown in tables 2.1 and 2.2 are similar, the numbers involved are very different. Share ownership by individuals has declined in importance in both countries, but during the time period shown, individuals were a far more important ownership group in the US than they were in the UK. In 1963 individuals owned 84 per cent of equity in American companies, but only 54 per cent of equity in British companies. By 1969 individuals owned less than half of UK equity, but it was only in the twenty-first century that the figure dipped below one-half in the US. Throughout the twentieth century financial institutions in the UK owned a much larger proportion of the equity in British firms than their American counterparts owned in American firms. However, the trend in the US was upwards throughout the period shown in the tables, and by 2006 American institutions' proportionate ownership of corporate America had outstripped the equivalent British figures. Foreign ownership is far more important to the UK than it is to the

US. In 2006 overseas investors owned 40 per cent of shares traded in UK firms, only just behind financial institutions. The proportion of overseas ownership of American companies has grown since 1975 but remains small, reaching just 12 per cent by 2006. Some ownership categories are so unimportant in the US that their holdings are not large enough to appear in the table. Banks, charities and non-financial institutions are absent, while the public sector makes just one appearance.

Table 2.1 Ownership of equity in UK companies (%)

	1963	1969	1975	1981	1989	1998	2006
Individuals	54	47	38	28	21	17	13
Financial institutions	29	34	47	58	58	49	41
Banks	1	2	1	0	1	1	3
Charities	2	2	2	2	2	1	1
Private non-financial institutions	5	5	3	5	4	1	2
Public sector	2	3	4	3	2	0	0
Rest of the world	7	7	6	4	13	31	40

Source: Office for National Statistics (2007) 'Share ownership: A report on ownership of UK shares as at 31st December 2006' HMSO

Table 2.2 Ownership of equity in US companies (%)

	1963	1969	1975	1981	1989	1998	2006
Individuals	84	79	70	65	56	50	30
Financial institutions	13	18	24	27	35	41	59
Public sector	0	0	0	0	0	1	0
Rest of the world	2	3	4	5	7	7	12

Source: Board of Governors of the Federal Reserve System (2008) 'Federal Reserve Statistical Release Z.1, Flow of Funds Account of the United States'

Table 2.3 provides a snapshot of equity holding in continental Europe in 2006. The picture that emerges is rather different from the one in the UK and the US. Financial institutions are the most important equity holders in the UK and US, but in the continental European countries shown here, they play a modest role, with Sweden having the highest proportion of equity held by non-bank financial institutions, at 25 per cent, but this is still lower than the comparable figures for the UK and US. Only three other countries have financial institutions holding 20 or more per cent of shares: Denmark, France and Poland. Banks play a more important role than in the Anglo-Saxon countries, but even so, the largest proportionate holding is 13 per cent, occurring in both Austria and Lithuania. Germany is often described as a bank-based financial system, which indeed it may be, but its banks own a smaller proportion of shares that do its other financial institutions. The results for the public sector may come as a surprise. Given that privatisation has come only recently to some of the countries shown, it is interesting to see that Norway has by the far the highest public-sector ownership, at 32 per cent. Its nearest rival in this respect is Slovenia, while France and Greece have higher public ownership than Estonia and the Slovak Republic, which registers only 1 per cent.

Foreign ownership is very important in continental Europe, with the highest proportions appearing in the Netherlands (79 per cent) and Hungary (78 per cent), two countries with very different economic histories.

The category 'non-financial institutions' does not appear in the American data, yet it is important in many of the European countries listed in table 2.3. This category includes non-financial companies and trusts. Only 9 of the 21 countries in the table have equity ownership by non-financial institutions of less than 20 per cent. It is over 30 per cent in Denmark, Estonia and Germany. This is important in governance terms because, as was discussed earlier, when individuals hold shares in a company which itself owns shares in another, those individuals are able to wield disproportionate power over the corporate sector. Thus, while none of these countries reaches the 30 per cent individual ownership seen in the US, some may in fact have higher figures once the pyramid structures are taken into account. The level of control held by particular individuals may also be high in cases of differential voting rights. Even ignoring the non-financial institutions column, individuals hold 20 or more per cent of shares in 5 of the 21 countries and 13 of these countries have higher individual ownership than the UK, indicating very different shareholding patterns within Europe.

Table 2.3 Ownership of equity in continental Europe in 2006 (%)

Country	Individuals	Financial institutions	Banks	Non-financial institutions	Public sector	Rest of the world
Austria	8	9	13	20	4	45
Belgium	20	18[1]	n/a	22	3	38
Denmark	18	23[1]	n/a	31	1	27
Estonia	5	1	1	37	10	47
France	6	20	9	12	13	41
Germany	14	17	11	36	2	20
Greece	23	4	3	8	15	47
Hungary	4	6[1]	n/a	9	4	78
Iceland	11	16	7	29	0	38
Italy	27	18	5	27	10	14
Lithuania	11	4	13	14	21	38
Malta	21	8	1	28	5	37
Netherlands	5	6	3	0	0	79
Norway	4	6	1	18	32	40
Poland	17	22	0	11	16	35
Portugal	11	16	5	25	1	43
Slovakia	4	4	0	20	1	63
Slovenia	16	11	5	28	24	15
Spain	24	10	9	24	0	33
Sweden	17	25	3	9	8	37
Switzerland	16	12	3	9	0	60

Notes:
1 this figure includes shares held by banks
n/a = not available

Source: Federation of European Securities Exchanges (2008) 'Share Ownership Structure in Europe'

SHAREHOLDERS' MOTIVATION

The previous section showed that in the UK and the US, financial institutions are the key owners of equity. Overseas owners have replaced British individuals as important shareholders, while in the US, individuals are still more significant than overseas investors. The picture is very different in continental Europe, where non-financial institutions and, in some countries, the public sector play a much more important role. When it considers the motivation of shareholders, finance theory rarely takes account of identity. It may distinguish between informed (usually institutional) and uninformed (usually individual) investors, but it relies on the assumption that all investors are *rational* and *risk-averse*. In other words, they create diversified portfolios with the aim of maximising wealth given the level of risk they are willing to take.

We have already hinted that there may be some investors who hold shares for very different reasons. Football fans may buy shares in their clubs to show their loyalty, for example. In this section we will consider how identity may affect shareholders' objectives and, if they can exercise control, the performance of companies. The groups we will consider are families, financial institutions, the state and management. In terms of the data presented in the previous section, both families and managers are included under individuals. We are treating them as distinct groups because families are often important as founders of companies and managers are often blamed for behaving as selfish agents. Given their importance as equity holders, financial institutions are a potentially important part of the corporate governance system in the UK and US. Finally, the state plays an important role as a shareholder in many of the European countries shown in table 2.3 as well as in parts of Asia, so its distinctive objectives should be considered.

Families

For many people the term 'family business' conjures a mental picture of a small business, probably organised as a sole trader or partnership with two generations of the family working together. Evidence indicates that this is a flawed view. The family firm is hugely important the world over, accounting for over 70 per cent of all business in Indonesia, Korea and Malaysia (Driffield *et al.*, 2007), 44 per cent in Western Europe (Faccio and Lang, 2002), 36 per cent in Japan (Saito, 2008) and perhaps most surprisingly, 37 per cent of Fortune 500 firms (Villalonga and Amit, 2006). These figures call into question the way in which family firms are often discussed as something special in the governance literature. Perhaps we should instead consider non-family firms as different or special. However, in keeping with the literature, we ask 'what is different about listed family firms?'

Family firms are usually classified as such because the founding family still owns a proportion of the equity and supplies members of the board and possibly other members of the management team. According to this definition J. Sainsbury, the Ford Motor Company and L'Oréal are all family firms. In any organisation, an individual can play a number of roles. They could be simultaneously an employee, a director and a shareholder. *Executive directors* in all types of business would fit this picture. The complicating feature in a family business is that in addition to the three roles already identified, the individual is also a family member. As we all know, each family is unique; it has its own set of affiliations and rivalries which can affect business as well as pleasure. Those of us who are old enough to remember the 1980s TV series *Dallas*, discussed in box 2.2, will know that the business dealings depicted were all the more intriguing given that the company was run by two brothers with very different personalities and ideas of what constitutes family loyalty.

Box 2.2 *Dallas*

Dallas was a hugely successful American TV series that ran from 1978 to 1991 and was shown in 90 countries, illustrating the international appeal of its story of business and family rivalries. The main characters were J.R. and Bobby Ewing, brothers who ran Ewing Oil following the retirement of their father, who had founded the business. J.R. was a ruthless businessman who was happy to use any tactics to benefit the company at the expense of his rivals, especially the Barnes family, which owned a firm with which Ewing Oil had a long-running dispute. J.R. found it hard to work alongside the mild-mannered Bobby, who took a more ethical approach to business and who, to complicate matters further, was married to a member of the Barnes family. The extended Ewing family lived together at Southfork Ranch, which meant that their business and family lives were completely entwined, making for great viewing, but poor corporate governance. It is hard to see how any non-family investors or managers could have any input in decision-making within Ewing Oil.

I would hesitate to compare any real family businesses with Ewing Oil, but the potential for business problems to affect family life and vice versa is always there, which is why in some countries, regulators treat family firms as a special case, advising that they introduce family councils to work alongside the board of directors in order to maintain a clear separation between the interests of the family and the interests of the business.

If we compare two decision-makers, one who is an executive director in a non-family firm, and another who is a family member and an executive director in a family firm, both will have multiple objectives. As employees they will seek good working conditions and rewards. As directors they will aim to achieve a successful strategy for the company so that it can achieve good returns for all its shareholders, themselves included. While the potential conflicts between the two viewpoints are often highlighted in the literature, as Zellweger and Nason (2008) point out, different performance outcomes can often satisfy a number of stakeholders. Enhanced profitability is good for shareholders and implies that the firm has sufficient resources to pay good salaries and provide congenial working conditions which, in turn, make employees happier and more productive, achieving further profit gains. However, there will be some cases when outcomes are substitutes for one another, and there may be more cases of this in family than in other types of business.

Our non-family executive director will, for example, encourage employment practices that attract and retain the most efficient employees. Our family director would probably say that this is their aim, but there may be occasions when this is not the case, because the family pressurises them to employ family members who may be unsuited to their roles. There is a wealth of business history literature that documents the decline in the fortunes of family businesses as they are handed down from the entrepreneurial founder through the generations of less and less able or motivated family members. This should not be too much of an issue in a one-share-one-vote system where outside shareholders can prevent such abuses of power, but when control and cash-flow rights diverge, as they often do in family firms, the family can increase its utility at the expense of returns to non-family owners. Given that families hold their shares over the long term, there are few opportunities for other groups to gain control through simple stock market transactions.

Given these observations it is surprising that family firms get outsiders to invest in them at all, but of course they do, or they would not be as numerous as research shows them to be. Family firms have the advantage of having a stable base of loyal shareholders who will not sell their equity in response to a short-term decline in performance. The family maintains a long-term perspective which implies a willingness to maintain investment levels. In short, a family is likely to be a good steward of its own and outside shareholders' investment in the business. So, should investors avoid or seek out family businesses?

We can consider this question using a theoretical framework developed by Miller and Le Breton-Miller (2006). They argue that there is an inverted U-shaped relationship between firm value and family ownership. Over a range of values, increasing family ownership has a positive effect on value thanks to a reduction in type I agency costs and an emphasis on good stewardship of the company's assets. At some stage a turning point is reached, family management becomes entrenched and the incentives to expropriate wealth from other groups become too great to resist. Corporate governance is important in that it can affect the position of the turning point. The negative effects of managerial entrenchment could be mitigated by the influence of strong directors. Miller and Le Breton-Miller (2006) argue that these strong directors could be either other family members bringing distinct skills to the business or independent directors who are not afraid to challenge the incumbent management. On the other hand, expropriation is more likely when control rights far exceed voting rights. This reasoning implies that the turning point will come at relatively high levels of family control when the company has multiple family directors or strong independent directors; and at low levels when the company has dual-class shares or is part of a pyramid structure.

Unfortunately for us, the hypothesis of the inverted U-shaped relation between family ownership and firm value has not been empirically tested. However, researchers have examined the influence of independent directors and differential voting rights on the value of family firms, but reach conflicting conclusions. Yeh *et al.* (2001) find that in Taiwan the best-performing family firms are those with the lowest family representation on the board. In contrast, Mishra *et al.* (2001) find that the presence of independent directors depresses the market value of family firms in Norway, while Villalonga and Amit (2006) find that the proportion of independent directors has no impact on the market value of American family firms. The influence of independent directors is one of the issues we will discuss further in chapter 3. However, it is worth mentioning here that the evidence on the relationship between firm value and board independence is mixed even before we start considering specific types of company. Anderson and Reeb (2003) and Villalonga and Amit (2006) ask whether the presence of a family CEO raises the market value of family firms in the US. This would support the idea that a family CEO is a good steward. Anderson and Reeb (2003) provide evidence in favour of this view but Villalonga and Amit (2006) find no statistically significant relationship between value and the presence of a family CEO. Maury (2006) addresses the same question using data from Western Europe and finds that the presence of a family CEO raises value. Driffield *et al.* (2007) look at a related issue, the impact of a *cronyman* on firm value. A cronyman is a CEO, chair or vice-chair of the board who is also a controlling owner. They find that the presence of a cronyman is associated with higher market value in Indonesia, Malaysia and Thailand. Taking these papers together we can say that at the very least value is not damaged by the presence of a family CEO, and may be enhanced by it.

International evidence on the impact of differential voting rights is mixed. For the US and Norway, respectively, Villalonga and Amit (2006) agree with Mishra *et al.* (2001) that family firms that issue dual-class shares underperform those with a single class of shares. Bozec and Laurin (2008) find that for the majority of family firms in Canada differential voting rights are unrelated to performance. The exception is those firms with the highest free cash flows; within this group performance is better when cash and control rights are equal. This makes sense in that high free cash flow is in itself a temptation to spend on unnecessary projects, and so exacerbates the potential problems associated with differential voting rights. In contrast Driffield *et al.* (2007) find that in Indonesia, Korea and Malaysia market value is higher in companies with dual-class shares than in those with equal cash and control rights.

At first sight the conflicting evidence on the effect of dual-class shares on value is frustrating. However, one of the issues that will come up time and again in this book is the idea that effective corporate governance is about introducing a set of measures which together lead to the desired outcome. Some measures will be chosen by individual companies; others will be imposed by law. Clearly companies will be constrained in their choices by the regulations they have to meet and by the culture in which they operate. This means that companies in different parts of the world will choose different solutions to their governance problems. A measure which in one part of the world apparently encourages expropriation of wealth may in another concentrate control in the hands of those who will make the best use of it.

Management

Managerial share-ownership is the obvious answer to the type I agency problem. If managers become owners of the companies for which they work, then they will make decisions that raise the share price, thereby making themselves and other shareholders better off. This logic has been extended to other employees, and employee share-ownership schemes are now common in the US and Western Europe. In the UK many listed companies require their executive directors to hold a certain amount of equity, usually expressed as a multiple of their basic salary.

Since company directors have to disclose their shareholdings and dealings, much empirical work has been done, particularly in the US, on the relationship between firm value and board or CEO holdings of equity rather than on shareholding by more junior management. There is agreement that the relationship is non-linear. That is, market value increases as board ownership rises over some levels of shareholding, thereafter it falls (Holderness *et al.*, 1999; McConnell and Servaes, 1990; Morck *et al.*, 1988). While this general result has been observed in all studies, there is no agreement over where the turning point occurs. This finding implies that there is a trade-off between the incentive and entrenchment effects of ownership. Up to a point managers are motivated to make better decisions and work hard to increase their own wealth; thereafter they become complacent and do not improve shareholder value. As with many areas of empirical research on governance questions, these findings have been queried on the grounds that causation between managerial ownership and value could run in both directions. Not only might value increase as managers hold more equity and agency costs are reduced, but as the market value rises equity becomes a more attractive investment, so the management team buys more. Models like the ones reported here that use levels of ownership and value may pick up this endogeneity in the relationship. McConnell *et al.* (2008) respond to this criticism by looking at the impact of changes in the proportion of shares owned by officers and members of the board on abnormal returns around the announcement of a change in holdings. Their results confirm previous findings that value depends on ownership, and the relationship is non-linear.

Banks

Equity ownership by banks varies tremendously around the world. Banks do not feature as owners in the US and hold negligible amounts of equity in the UK. As table 2.3 shows, they are important owners in some parts of continental Europe. In 2006 banks held more equity than individuals in Austria, France and Lithuania, and had greater holdings than non-bank financial institutions in those same countries. Some readers may be surprised to see that in Germany both individuals and non-bank financial institutions held more equity than banks in 2006, despite the fact that Germany's financial system is often described as bank-based. German banks are able to play a disproportionate role in corporate control because they hold and vote shares on behalf of individuals. Japan is also known as a bank-based system. There, banks are central to the operation of business groups, called *keiretsus*. A keiretsu is a group of companies organised around a main bank which both lends to, and holds shares in the members' companies.

Clearly a bank which is both an owner and a lender has access to very rich information about its client companies. This enables it to be an excellent monitor, able not only to observe the potential for conflicts between shareholders and managers, but also to resolve agency problems between shareholders and lenders. This type of agency problem is discussed in some detail in chapter 4, so here we will offer a very brief outline of the problem. Shares and debt offer very different returns to their holders. Debt holders can expect regular payments of interest together with the return of the principal when the debt matures. As long as the borrowing company has sufficient cash flows to make the payments, they can be regarded as certain. Shareholders have rights over an uncertain stream of cash flows. They have no guarantee that the board will decide to pay a cash dividend, and while they hope that the share price will rise in the market, they cannot be sure of receiving a capital gain. This may lead the shareholders to attempt to transfer some of the risk they face to the debt holders, for example by using borrowed funds to invest in risky projects. Most lenders have limited access to company information and so would be unaware that this was being done, however, a bank which both holds equity and makes loans to the company would be in a better position to observe such behaviour and prevent it in the future. In this way the bank protects not only itself, but also other lenders. Flath (1993) provides evidence that Japanese banks hold more equity in keiretsu companies that face higher agency costs of debt than in those with lower agency costs, indicating that equity holding increases the security of banks' lending activities.

Banks can use the information they gain as lenders and owners in order to obtain a broad picture of the needs of particular industries. Franks and Mayer (1996) examine the role of German banks in takeover activity. As we saw earlier in this section, German banks are able to vote their own shares and those they hold for individuals, giving them an important decision-making role in battles over corporate control. They find that banks vote in favour of mergers when they can see the industry in question needs to be restructured. This explains their voting behaviour in takeovers in the tyre and steel industries during the 1980s.

The evidence from Germany and Japan indicates that shareholding banks are in a unique monitoring position. They have access to information on a range of client companies, giving them insights into a variety of industries as well as the strategies used by individual firms. As they safeguard their own interests by monitoring corporate behaviour, banks provide a valuable service to other shareholders.

Non-bank financial institutions

Non-bank financial institutions are probably those investors who conform most closely to the picture of the rational, risk-averse shareholder depicted in finance theory. Insurance companies, pension funds and other mutual funds hold diversified portfolios in order to meet their liabilities and satisfy their investors. The judgement of fund managers should not be clouded by sentiment. Indeed fund managers, although they control large amounts of equity, probably do not see themselves as owners of corporate resources at all. Equities are just another security to be traded for gain so as to raise the value of the portfolio. This explains the interest in the type I agency problem in countries like the US and UK where disinterested fund managers control large amounts of equity, allowing managers to use corporate resources as they see fit, unchecked by shareholders. This does not necessarily mean that financial institutions are acting negligently by taking this approach. If it becomes known that a fund manager is in dialogue with corporate management this may alert the market to the problems in the company and depress the share price, making the fund worse off. Potentially more damaging is the possibility of becoming privy to inside information during the course of the dialogue. If this happens the fund manager cannot trade the shares for fear of being accused of insider dealing.

Regulators, at least in the UK have been keen to change the trading mentality of fund managers and encourage financial institutions to take an interventionist stance towards equity ownership. The Financial Reporting Council, like some academic writers, argues that shareholder engagement is a natural part of the responsibilities of financial institutions. Fund managers have a fiduciary duty towards their investors. They must safeguard investors' resources and do all they can to ensure that the fund's aims are met, which includes voting on issues that affect value and, if necessary, intervening with management to encourage improved performance.

Of course some institutional investors have taken an active interest in the companies whose shares they own. Probably the most famous example is CalPERS, the pension fund for state employees in California. It targets underperforming companies and intervenes in management to encourage a change in policy and governance practices. A number of researchers have reported that the strategy yields good returns for CalPERS, but more recent evidence from English *et al.* (2004) suggests that the gains are only short-term. In the UK the Hermes Focus Fund uses a similar strategy, buying equity in poorly performing companies then engaging with the CEO and chair of the board through letters and meetings. The strategy has been successful; between 1998 and 2004 the fund made abnormal returns (net of fees) of 4.9 per cent a year (Becht *et al.*, 2009). Other investors may not advertise their interventions but do work with companies to encourage change. In a survey of British unit trust managers, Solomon and Solomon (1999) found that 84 per cent had used private meetings with management to bring about a change in policy, and the same percentage had joined forces with other institutions to help companies in a crisis situation.

Unlike the funds discussed so far, hedge funds do not have an obligation to diversify their portfolios. This allows them to take large stakes in individual companies. Like other fund managers the managers of hedge funds are paid by results, but their remuneration is more sensitive to the value of the fund. Taking these two features together, the managers of hedge funds have stronger incentives than the managers of other types of funds to become actively involved in the decision-making of the firms whose shares they own. Both Brav *et al.* (2008) and Clifford (2008) find that when hedge fund managers choose to follow an interventionist strategy they are successful in creating positive abnormal returns.

Companies

Companies can come to own shares in other companies for a variety of reasons. A firm which is planning a takeover may buy a small proportion of the target's equity in the stock market (a *toe-hold*) in order to persuade it to negotiate. It may acquire shares as a purely financial investment, or as a means of exerting control without owning the business. In table 2.3 corporate ownership of equity is shown in the non-financial institutions category, which also includes private organisations and trusts and 'other'. As the table indicates, this is an important ownership category in continental Europe. In 2006 non-financial institutions were the largest equity owners in Denmark, Germany, Italy and Slovenia, and in those economies like Austria, Belgium, Estonia, Hungary, Iceland, Malta, Portugal, Slovakia and Spain, which are dominated by overseas investors, they were the largest domestic owner. While it is impossible to know how much of these proportions is accounted for by companies, anecdotal evidence suggests that companies are important equity holders in other European firms. The L'Oréal case that accompanies this chapter is a good example. Notice that non-financial institutions do not appear as a category in table 2.2, which looks at American data, and show very small proportionate holdings in table 2.1, which looks at the British case. Regulatory differences between the UK, US and continental Europe probably account for this huge difference in corporate equity ownership. In 1935 the American government introduced taxes on inter-company dividends, and in 1968 the British Takeover Panel required companies which owned 30 per cent of the equity in another company to launch a takeover bid. These measures led to the demise of inter-company shareholdings in the two countries (Enriques and Volpin, 2007).

When company A owns shares in company B this creates an ownership pyramid in which A's shareholders are the ultimate owners of B. Pyramidal ownership is often associated with both Asian and European family firms, but Faccio and Lang (2002) report that in Europe pyramid ownership is more commonly seen in cases where the ultimate owner is the state or a financial institution. The term pyramid implies a situation in which company A, which is controlled by a single blockholder, owns B, which in turn owns C, so that A could be pictured as the largest of a set of Russian dolls which, if opened up, would reveal B and then C. However, corporate ownership of other company's shares can be more complex than this.

In an earlier section we mentioned Japanese keiretsus in which a main bank owns equity in group companies. Aside from the main bank, the group is made up of industrial and commercial companies which may hold equity in one another. These types of cross-holdings are also found, along with pyramids, in Korean *chaebols*. Chaebols differ from keiretsus in two respects. The first is that by law they cannot include banks, but can include other financial institutions. The second is that the companies in a keiretsu operate independently yet are bound by *cross-shareholdings* which result in *interlocking directorships* and by trust, while the companies in a chaebol, despite being legally independent, are run as if they are part of a huge multi-divisional company.

Some of Europe's best-known companies are part of pyramids. Enriques and Volpin (2007) offer a number of examples, including Volkswagen and Louis Vuitton Moët Hennessy (LVMH). In 2005 Porsche was the largest shareholder in Volkswagen, holding 25.1 per cent of its common stock. One-half of the shares in Porsche were owned by the Porsche family, but they held all of the voting shares. This means that they had control of 25.1 per cent of the votes in Volkswagen, but only 9.44 per cent of the cash-flow rights, given the presence of preference shares and a voting cap, that is, a restriction on the percentage of votes that can be cast by a single shareholder, of 20 per cent on Volkswagen common stock. In the same year LVMH was owned by Bernard Arnault, the company's chief executive and chair of the board. He owned it through a pyramid including Christian Dior and four unlisted companies. The pyramid structure gave him 47 per cent of the voting rights in LVMH, with only 34 per cent of the cash-flow rights.

The problem with pyramid structures is that they provide an incentive for the ultimate owner at the top of the pyramid to expropriate wealth from minority shareholders further down the pyramid through *tunnelling*. Tunnelling is any activity that transfers value up the pyramid from a company in which the ultimate owner has low cash-flow rights to another in which he or she has high cash-flow rights. This can be done quite simply through activities like *transfer pricing* in which the company at the bottom of the pyramid sells goods cheaply to a company further up. This transfers profit up the pyramid, making the ultimate owner better off at the expense of shareholders who own shares in the company at the bottom of the pyramid. Bhaumik and Gregoriou (2010) review the literature on tunnelling and cite papers that find evidence of the practice in Bulgaria, Russia, Sweden, Hong Kong, South Korea and India. Perhaps the best-known example of tunnelling is the Parmalat scandal. The Tanzi family diversified the food business into areas like tourism and sport in which individual family members were particularly interested. They also diverted around $3 billion to their own use in addition to the funds they moved around the group through overpayment for asset transfers, etc.

Baek *et al.* (2006) describe several examples of tunnelling through securities issues within Korean chaebols. The LG group tunnelled funds to the controlling family by issuing shares to them in 1999, then buying them back for a higher price three years later. The Samsung group issued bonds with warrants and convertible bonds to family members at below-market prices during the 1990s. While examples like these suggest that pyramids and cross-holdings are a nightmare in governance terms because they create strong incentives for expropriation, it is worth pointing out that sometimes the controlling shareholder behaves in a more altruistic way. In 1999 Samsung Motors was on the verge of bankruptcy when the controlling shareholder Lee Kun Hee used his own funds to rescue it. This is an example of *propping*, the opposite of tunnelling. Friedman *et al.* (2003) argue that propping plays an important role in countries with weak legal protection for lenders. In some parts of Asia it is very difficult for lenders to get money out of failing firms, for example the bankruptcy process in Thailand can take up to ten years to complete. Lenders are more likely to commit funds to companies when they can expect entrepreneurs to respond to minor crises by propping.

The state

As we saw in section 2.4, state ownership of equity varies tremendously around Europe. While it is not surprising that countries like Lithuania, Poland and Slovenia had fairly high rates of public-sector ownership as recently as 2006 (at 21 per cent, 16 per cent and 24 per cent, respectively) it is interesting that in Slovenia only 1 per cent of equity was owned by the public sectors while in Greece the figure was 15 per cent and in Norway 32 per cent. The situation in the UK is noteworthy in that, following the privatisations of the 1980s, public ownership of companies all but disappeared. However, part of the government's response to the credit crisis of 2007–9 was to buy equity in the Lloyds and Royal Bank of Scotland banking group in order to protect them and their depositors. These equity purchases made the Treasury a major shareholder in the two groups, with holdings of 43 per cent in Lloyds and 70 per cent in the Royal Bank of Scotland. Following this policy move we have heard calls from individuals and the media for the government to become an active owner, intervening in matters such as lending policy and managerial remuneration. The government's refusal to become involved has angered many people. This is interesting in that it shows that the public clearly believes that ownership matters in governance issues. People expect the government to behave differently as an owner compared to financial institutions that do not try to dictate policy at the corporate level; the public wants the government to intervene in the case of banks. Clearly it would be dangerous to read too much into this situation. People are angry about the ways banks have behaved; they are afraid of losing their jobs and homes and expect the government to help. However, given that the view in both the UK and US is that state ownership is a bad thing, this gives a timely reminder that it can be used as a force for good; after all it is an important form of ownership in the rest of the world.

There are many ideological and strategic reasons for the state to own companies. These are bound to influence the way it behaves as an owner. It is usually assumed that owners seek maximum profits from the companies they own. Governments which own companies in order to ensure domestic supply of a key product may not demand efficient production. They may encourage over-employment in all companies simply to maintain popularity with voters. They may also offer top jobs in companies as a reward for political services. These behaviours all imply that government ownership leads to inefficiencies and loss of value for other shareholders. Most shareholders can expect to make money from their shareholdings in two ways, by receiving dividends or through making a capital gain on the sale of their shares. For a government, the latter is not an option, given that it has other, non-monetary reasons for maintaining its shareholding. However, it does have another way of getting money from companies, through taxation. This implies that while other owners may press for improved dividends, these are less important to the government, which automatically receives income from companies regardless of their ownership structure as long as they make a profit. This gives us a non-ideological reason to suppose that the state is less interested in shareholder returns than other owners are.

Perhaps we should pause for a moment and consider what type of returns most owners want. It is often argued that the stock market is interested only in short-term returns. Financial institutions trade often so as to make short-term abnormal gains, allowing them to make more trades in other securities in the future. This encourages corporate management to take a short-term view, potentially neglecting longer-term projects and in the extreme, hiding bad news through unethical and even illegal practices. The state has longer-term aims than other shareholders. It will not sell equity just because of bad news, so it provides some stability. It can also wield more power than any other owner, giving it the potential to be the ultimate monitor of management, reducing the impact of type I agency costs. Clearly the problem of type II agency costs remains, but in a democratic society this blockholder is accountable to other shareholders in a way that other major shareholders are not, so where blockholding is the norm, small investors may prefer to own shares in companies with a state blockholder in place of, or alongside others. This is consistent with evidence on the impact of blockholders in Egypt, Jordan, Oman and Tunisia. Solomon and Solomon (1999) find that concentrated individual ownership leads to negative return on equity, while the presence of a state blockholder brings a positive effect.

In a comprehensive survey of the literature on privatisation, Megginson and Netter (2001) find that in non-transition economies privatisation has a wholly positive impact on efficiency and profitability. However in transition economies the results are more mixed, with some evidence that these improvements occur only when another blockholder, a financial institution or sometimes a foreign investor, replaces the state. More recently there has been much interest in the nature of privatisation in China. The government has been running an extensive programme of share-issue partial privatisation since the 1990s, and researchers have been keen to see the effects of this on the companies concerned. The Chinese government controls not just the shares that it retains, but can also influence companies through the equity held by legal persons which may be other state-owned enterprises or non-bank financial institutions. Findings on these two forms of ownership vary. Sun *et al.* (2003) show that both these forms of ownership have a positive impact on the market value of companies, while Hovey *et al.* (2003) and Qi *et al.* (2000) agree that it is the blocks held by legal persons that have a positive effect on value and return on equity, respectively, while direct state ownership does not. Clearly while the majority of evidence suggests that state ownership has a negative impact of shareholder returns, there may be cases, particularly in transition situations, when some state ownership is beneficial.

CONCLUSION

The introduction of the limited liability company changed the nature of ownership and control in business. When individuals owned companies they could dictate both strategy and day-to-day practices. Shareholders can vote on resolutions tabled by the board of directors, but can only put forward their own resolutions if they can muster support from other shareholders. This is difficult if each one owns a small fraction of the total equity. In this case control passes to the management team, which may use its discretion to make decisions that make it better off at the expense of shareholders. In this situation shareholders need to be protected from managers. If shares are held in large blocks, a major shareholder can take control of the company and ensure that management runs the business in his preferred way. Some blockholders, such as families and governments, may use the company to fulfil aims that are not held in common with other shareholders. In this case minority shareholders may need to be protected from blockholders.

Patterns of shareholding vary tremendously in different parts of the world. While the British and American stock markets are dominated by non-bank financial institutions they are far less important in continental Europe, where other companies and in some cases the government own significant proportions of equity. This means that different types of governance problems will be seen in different parts of the world and therefore different combinations of governance mechanisms will be required to overcome those problems.

KEY POINTS

- Equity ownership brings cash-flow and control rights. In a one-share-one-vote system the two rights are proportional to the size of the shareholding. In a dual-class system some shareholders have disproportionate control rights.
- Control rights are in fact voting rights. Shareholders have the right but no obligation to vote on issues prescribed by company law.

- When share-ownership is widely dispersed, management can take control of the company, and may decide to pursue strategies that do not maximise shareholder value – the type I agency problem. This can be partially remedied if managers own shares.
- When shares are held in concentrated blocks the controlling owner can ensure that the management team acts in the blockholder's best interests. However, this may involve decisions that are bad for minority shareholders – the type II agency problem.
- Financial institutions hold a significant proportion of the equity traded in the UK and US. They have incentives to be passive shareholders, but when they choose to intervene they can improve corporate performance.
- Family firms make up a significant proportion of all companies worldwide. There is conflicting evidence on their performance relative to other types of business.
- The public sector is an important shareholder in parts of continental Europe and Asia. In developed countries state ownership leads to inefficiency and poor returns, but the reverse is observed in transition economies.

CASE STUDY   L'Oréal: You're worth it, at least to Nestlé

L'Oréal was founded by Eugene Schueller, a chemist who started making and selling hair dye in Paris in 1909. It was originally known as Société des Teintures Inoffensives pour Cheveux, but became the more concise L'Oréal in 1939. The company is probably best known today for its TV commercials which feature a string of well-known models and actors; indeed it has always been innovative in its approach to advertising, making the first sung radio commercial in 1931. The firm made its first acquisition in 1928 and has continued to acquire companies and brands since then. Many of you reading this book use its products perhaps without knowing, since it owns Ambre Solaire, Lancôme, Maybelline, Helena Rubinstein, Redken and the Body Shop, among others.

What is interesting about L'Oréal from the perspective of this chapter is its ownership structure. As at the end of the 2008/2009 financial year L'Oréal's equity was owned by the following groups:

Shareholder	Proportion of equity held (%)
Liliane Bettencourt and her family	31.0
Nestlé	29.8
International institutions	21.3
French institutions	9.4
Individuals	5.4
Treasury stock	2.4
Employees	0.7

Source: L'Oréal Annual Report 2009

Liliane Bettencourt is Eugene Schueller's daughter, so L'Oréal would look like a family company if it were not for the stake owned by Nestlé. In Switzerland, if a company owns 33.3 per cent of the voting rights in another firm it must make a full bid, so its holding makes Nestlé look like a potential acquirer. Indeed in autumn 2009 there was speculation that Nestlé might launch a bid for L'Oréal, but Nestlé's chief executive was quick to describe the investment in L'Oréal as financial rather than strategic.

The investment has a long history. In 1974 the Bettencourt family and Nestlé entered into an agreement designed to help L'Oréal in its bid to enter overseas markets (something Nestlé had already achieved) while at the same time adding stability to the shareholder base. Together they formed a company called Gesparal, in which the Bettencourt family held a 51 per cent stake and Nestlé held the remainder of the shares. Gesparal owned 53.8 per cent of L'Oréal's shares, which gave it 71.1 per cent of the voting rights under the dual-class share system. Each of the two shareholders could nominate three members to L'Oréal's board which, together with the differential voting rights, gave them control of the company. The current board (as at the end of 2009) includes six non-executives, three members from Nestlé, Mrs Bettencourt, her daughter and son-in-law together with the chair, Sir Lindsay Owen-Jones, who was until 2006 the CEO and executive chair, and the CEO Jean-Paul Agon. In 2004 the Bettencourt family and Nestlé agreed to a merger between L'Oréal and Gesparal, giving Nestlé a direct shareholding in L'Oréal. The two major shareholders agreed to eliminate the double voting rights that had resulted in the divergence between cash-flow and control rights in the firm and to retain their shares in L'Oréal for five years, after which the two parties would grant each other *pre-emption rights* over their shares, in other words, if one chooses to sell their holding, the other has the right to buy. This explains the speculation in the press during 2009 that Nestlé might attempt a takeover. A closer relationship could make business sense given that the two companies have two joint ventures in the form of Galderma, a company that makes treatments for skin problems and Inneov, a nutritional supplement also designed to help with skin problems.

Given the level of control held by the two blockholders, you might imagine that the individual shareholders who own 5 per cent of the equity would feel rather vulnerable. The company is at pains to make them feel involved in L'Oréal's affairs through shareholders' meetings and the shareholder panel. During 2009 L'Oréal held ten shareholder meetings in different areas of France, which attracted 7300 shareholders. At these meetings shareholders are told about new developments and have the chance to ask questions. In early 2010 the company replaced its shareholder panel with a 16-member Individual Shareholder Consultation Committee that feeds back information on L'Oréal's annual report and accounts in order to help the company to develop its financial communications.

Two additional factors add to the human interest in the L'Oréal story. The first is that Françoise Bettencourt-Meyers, a member of the L'Oréal board and granddaughter of the founder, is married to Jean-Pierre Meyers, a vice-chair of L'Oréal and a non-executive member of Nestlé's board. L'Oréal has two vice-chairs, one representing the Bettencourt family, the other representing Nestlé; but both are members of the Nestlé board. The Bettencourt–Nestlé relationship is clearly complex, having business and personal elements, but it begins to look as if L'Oréal would be a very different company if it were not for Nestlé.

The second is that following her father's death, Mrs Bettencourt-Meyers became increasingly concerned that her mother's old friend François-Marie Banier was taking advantage of her advancing age and generosity to unduly influence her to give him expensive gifts. Following preliminary enquiries French prosecutors dropped the case and Mrs Bettencourt-Meyers initiated a private prosecution in early 2010. Given that both women sit on the board of L'Oréal this dispute must affect the Bettencourt–Nestlé dynamic which is so important in determining how much L'Oréal is worth.

CASE-STUDY QUESTIONS

1 If you were an individual shareholder in L'Oréal, would you feel that the company is safeguarding your interests?

2 Would you describe the board of L'Oréal as independent?

3 Would it make sense for Nestlé to make a bid for L'Oréal?

REVISION QUESTIONS

1 What rights does the ownership of an asset usually bring, and to what extent do shareholders have these rights?

2 Under what circumstances do shareholders have control over companies?

3 What is the difference between the type I and type II agency problem?

4 Which type of agency problem would you expect to see in the UK?

5 What factors would a financial institution consider before intervening in the policy of a company whose shares it holds?

6 Should corporate governance focus on the protection of shareholders?

REFERENCES

Anderson, R.C. and Reeb, D.M. (2003) 'Founding Family Ownership and Firm Performance: Evidence from the S&P500' *Journal of Finance* 58 (3) 1301–1328

Baek, J., Kang, J. and Lee, I. (2006) 'Business Groups and Tunneling: Evidence from Private Securities Offerings by Korean Chaebols' *Journal of Finance* 61 (3) 2415–2449

Baumol, W.J. (1958) 'On the Theory of Oligopoly' *Economica* 25 (99) 187–198

Becht, M. Franks, J., Mayer, C. and Rossi, S. (2009) 'Returns to Shareholder Activism: A Clinical Study of the Hermes UK Focus Fund' *Review of Financial Studies* 22 (8) 3093–3129

Berle, A.A. and Means, G.C. (1932) *The Modern Corporation and Private Property* Harcourt, Brace & World

Bhaumik, S. and Gregoriou, A. (2010) '"Family" Ownership, Tunneling and Earnings Management; A Review of the Literature' *Journal of Economic Surveys* 24 (4) 705–730

Board of Governors of the Federal Reserve (2008) 'Federal Reserve Statistical Release Z.1, Flow of Funds Account of the United States' Board of Governors of the Federal Reserve System

Bozec, Y. and Laurin, C. (2008) 'Large Shareholder Entrenchment and Performance: Empirical Evidence from Canada' *Journal of Business Finance and Accounting* 35 (1–2) 25–49

Brav, A., Jiang, W., Thomas, R.S. and Partnoy, F. (2008) 'Hedge Fund Activism, Corporate Governance, and Firm Performance' *Journal of Finance* 63 (4) 1729–1775

Clifford, C.P. (2008) 'Value Creation or Destruction? Hedge Funds as Shareholder Activists' *Journal of Corporate Finance* 14 (4) 323–336

Driffield, N. Mahambare, V. and Pal, S. (2007) 'How Does Ownership Structure Affect Capital Structure and Firm Value?' *Economics of Transition* 15 (3) 535–573

English, P.C., Smythe, T.I., McNeil, C.R. (2004) 'The "CalPERS Effect" Revisited' *Journal of Corporate Finance* 10 (1) 157–174

Enriques, L. and Volpin, P. (2007) 'Corporate Governance Reforms in Continental Europe' *Journal of Economic Perspectives* 21 (1) 117–140

Faccio, M. and Lang, L.H.P. (2002) 'The Ultimate Ownership of Western European Corporations' *Journal of Financial Economics* 65 (3) 365–395

Federation of European Securities Exchanges (2008) 'Share Ownership Structure in Europe' FESE

Flath, D. (1993) 'Shareholding in the Keiretsu, Japan's Financial Groups' *Review of Economics and Statistics* 75 (2) 249–257

Franks, J. and Mayer, C. (1996) 'Hostile Takeovers and the Correction of Managerial Failure' *Journal of Financial Economics* 40 (1) 163–181

Friedman, E., Johnson, S. and Mitton, T. (2003) 'Propping and Tunneling' *Journal of Comparative Economics* 31 (4) 732–750

Gompers, P.A., Ishii, J.L. and Metrick, A. (2003) 'Corporate Governance and Equity Prices' *Quarterly Journal of Economics* 118 (1) 107–155

Holderness, C.G., Kroszner, R.S. and Sheehan, D.P. (1999) 'Were the Good Old days that Good? Changes in Managerial Stock Ownership Since the Great Depression' *Journal of Finance* LIV (2) 435–469

Hovey, M. Li, L. and Naughton, A. (2003) 'The Relationship between Valuation and Ownership of Listed Firms in China' *Corporate Governance: An International Review* 11 (2) 112–122

Jensen, M.C. and Meckling, W. (1976) 'Theory of the Firm: Managerial Behavior, Agency Costs and Ownership Structure' *Journal of Financial Economics* 3 (4) 305–360

La Porta, R., Lopez-de-Silanes, F. and Shleiffer, A. (1999) 'Corporate Ownership Around the World' *Journal of Finance* 54 (2) 471–517

Maury, B. (2006) 'Family Ownership and Firm Performance: Empirical Evidence from Western European Corporations' *Journal of Corporate Finance* 12 (2) 321–341

McConnell, J.J. and Servaes, H. (1990) 'Additional Evidence on Equity Ownership and Corporate Value' *Journal of Financial Economics* 27 (2) 595–612

McConnell, J.J., Servaes, H. and Lins, K.V. (2008) 'Changes in Insider Ownership and Changes in the Market Value of the Firm' *Journal of Corporate Finance* 14 (2) 92–106

Megginson, W.L. and Netter, J.M. (2001) 'From State to Market: A Survey of Empirical Studies on Privatization' *Journal of Economic Literature* 39 (2) 321–389

Miller, D. and Le Breton-Miller, I. (2006) 'Family Governance and Firm Performance: Agency, Stewardship and Capabilities' *Family Business Review* 19 (1) 73–87

Mishra, C. S., Randøy, T. and Jenssen, J. I (2001) 'The Effect of Founding Family Influence on Firm Value and Corporate Governance' *Journal of International Financial Management and Accounting* 12 (3) 235–259

Morck, R. Shleifer, A. and Vishny, R. (1988) 'Management Ownership and Market Valuation: An Empirical Analysis' *Journal of Financial Economics* 20 (1) 293–315

Office for National Statistics (2007) 'Share Ownership: A report on ownership of UK shares as at 31st December 2006' HMSO

Qi, D. Wu, W. and Zhang, H. (2000) 'Shareholding Structure and Corporate Performance of Partially Privatized Firms: Evidence from Listed Chinese Companies' *Pacific-Basin Finance Journal* 8 (5) 587–610

Saito, T. (2008) 'Family Firms and Firm Performance: Evidence From Japan' *Journal of the Japanese and International Economies* 22 (4) 620–646

Simon, H.A. (1959) 'Theories of Decision-making in Economics and Behavioral Science' *American Economic Review* 49 (3) 253–283

Smith, A. (1976) *An Inquiry into the Nature and Causes of the Wealth of Nations* ed. Campbell, R.H., Skinner, A.S. and Todd, W.B. Clarendon Press

Solomon, A. and Solomon, J.F. (1999) 'Empirical Evidence of Long-Termism and Shareholder Activism in UK Unit Trusts' *Corporate Governance: An International Review* 7 (3) 288–300

Sun, Q., Tang, W.H.S. and Tong, J. (2003) 'How Does Government Ownership Affect Firs Performance? Evidence from China's Privatization Experience' *Journal of Business Finance and Accounting* 29 (1&2) 1–27

Swisher, J. (2006) 'Dual-Class Companies: Do Inferior Voting Shares Make Inferior Investments?' *Mid-American Journal of Business* 21 (1) 40–48

UK *Companies Act* 2006, London: HMSO

Villalonga, B. and Amit, R. (2006) 'How Do Family Ownership, Control and Management Affect Firm Value?' *Journal of Financial Economics* 80 (2) 385–417

Williamson, O.E. (1963) 'Managerial Discretion and Business Behavior' *American Economic Review* 53 (5) 1032–1057

Yeh, Y. Lee, T. and Woidtke, T. (2001) 'Family Control and Corporate Governance: Evidence from Taiwan' *International Review of Finance* 2 (1/2) 21–48

Zellweger, T.M. and Nason, R.S. (2008) 'A Stakeholder Perspective on Family Firm Performance' *Family Business Review* 21 (3) 203–216

SUGGESTIONS FOR FURTHER READING

Carlsson, R.H. (2007) 'Swedish Corporate Governance and Value Creation: Owners Still in the Driver's Seat' *Corporate Governance: An International Review* 15 (6) 1038–1055. This interesting paper describes the situation in a country which rarely features in the governance literature. It discusses the fact that most households own shares, yet their combined share ownership is small. 'Spheres' or family groups are important shareholders whose control is reinforced by pyramid structures and dual class shares, yet despite this, takeover activity is strong.

Easterbrook, F.H. and Fischel, D.R. (1991) *The Economic Structure of Corporate Law* Harvard University Press. This book is written from an American perspective, but gives a very useful insight into the economic logic behind all corporate law. The first four chapters on the corporate contract, limited liability, voting and the fiduciary principle expand some of the themes discussed in this chapter.

Information on share ownership in the UK is available at http://www.stastistics.gov.uk by following the link from Economy to share ownership. Comparable information for Europe is available at http://www.fese.eu.

THE BOARD OF DIRECTORS

LEARNING OBJECTIVES

- To appreciate the role of the board, and the legal and other duties of directors
- To appreciate the difference between the role of the chief executive officer and the role of the chair of the board
- To understand the distinctions between unitary and dual boards
- To understand why independence has become such an important issue in board composition, and appreciate the empirical evidence on how performance is affected by the presence of independent directors on the board
- To comprehend the duties of board committees, and appreciate the evidence on their effectiveness

INTRODUCTION

The idea that an organisation should be headed by a board of trustees or directors pre-dates the introduction of the limited liability company. Medieval organisations recognised that it was more efficient to delegate decision-making to a small body rather than to expect all members to come together to reach a consensus decision. As the concept of limited liability grew in importance the remit of the board became wider, encompassing shareholder protection as well as ultimate decision-making authority. Today the board is viewed as the cornerstone of corporate governance. While the tasks of the board are the same the world over, boards are organised differently in different parts of the world. Boards in English-speaking countries are unitary, that is, a single board undertakes both top-level decision making and monitoring on behalf of the shareholders and possibly other stakeholders. In some Asian and European countries the two roles are separated between a *management board* and a supervisory board. In some countries, like France, regulators allow companies to choose which form they prefer.

While it is dangerous to generalise too much it is fair to say that, worldwide, boards have changed a lot over the past 20 years. The role of chairing the board is seen as important in its own right, rather than as part of the job of the CEO. In fact these days CEOs are discouraged from chairing boards. Independent directors make up a significant proportion of the board's membership and also sit on specialist subcommittees that are responsible for vital board functions. This is in stark contrast to the days when boards were filled with the CEO's colleagues and acquaintances who could be relied on to rubber-stamp decisions that had been made in advance of board meetings. While this is a caricature of the way boards used to be, it is apparent that regulators are fearful of the concentration of power in the hands of a few people. They firmly believe in the agency-theoretic view of the world which says that unless principals are protected their agents will take advantage of their decision-making power.

Of course this is not the only view of the way the world works. In this chapter, after briefly reviewing the history of boards, we will introduce *stewardship theory*. This approach contrasts with agency theory in that it assumes that decision-makers align themselves with shareholders and do not need external incentives to bring their thinking into line with that of owners. After that we will consider certain aspects of English law that affect the way boards are organised before looking in more detail at particular aspects of board organisation around the world, including unitary and dual boards, the roles of the chair and CEO, the importance of independent directors and of board subcommittees and, finally, of the need to evaluate how the board operates. The case study which accompanies this chapter is that of Marks and Spencer plc, a well-respected British company that angered its institutional shareholders when it flouted the convention that a CEO should not also chair the board.

A BRIEF HISTORY OF BOARDS

Boards of directors have a long history; indeed the practice of delegating decision-making authority to a small group of people has been common since before the advent of the limited liability company as we know it today. In the England of the Middle Ages craftsmen and traders organised themselves in guilds whose job it was to safeguard their monopoly rights to supply products and services. At first all members of the guild met together to make decisions, but after a while they decided this was inefficient, so they elected 'assistants' who would meet to make decisions binding their fellow members. The earliest record of this practice dates from 1463 when the mercers of London decided to choose 12 such assistants (O'Donnell, 1952). The term assistants continued to be used widely in a variety of organisations until the East India Company adopted the name 'committeemen'. The word 'director' was used for the first time in 1694 in the charter of the Bank of England. The word became popular and spread across the Atlantic as companies were formed for the purpose of trade with the colonies.

The corporate form of business developed over time in Britain, with companies being formed by royal charter, private Act of Parliament and letters patent until the Companies Act 1844 allowed companies to register under the Act. These different methods of incorporating businesses led to different views of the role of the board. Kessler (1959) argues that in companies with a royal charter the board became a delegated legislative body, taking over the state's normal duty of making rules. He calls this the guardian function of the board. As common law developed and the board was given power by shareholders, it became their servant.

We tend to think of features such as the *staggered board* in which a proportion of the membership is elected or re-elected each year, and the separation of the roles of chair and CEO as modern innovations prompted by recent scandals, but we would be wrong. An Act of Parliament passed in 1697 required the board of the Bank of England to be staggered, with eight new members elected each year. Until 1714 the directors of the East India Company elected a new chairman for each board meeting. After that they decided it would be preferable for the chairman to serve for one year and that the governor (more or less equivalent to the modern CEO) and deputy governor should not be eligible for the role.

While developments in the UK spread to the US, similar initiatives were being taken by organisations in continental Europe (Gevurtz, 2004). During the fifteenth century, German merchants formed associations called hanses. Each hanse was administered by a committee in the same way that English guilds were governed by assistants. When the Dutch East India Company was formed, it had a council of governors comprising 60 members representing the chambers or groups of merchants who had come together to form the company. This became unwieldy and the company subsequently established a smaller 'collegium' with 17 members – it, too, included representatives of the various chambers.

The fact that boards developed in similar ways in different countries suggests that there is an inherent logic in having a relatively small committee in place to make key decisions, to establish rules and to serve the beneficiaries of the organisation. Boards still have these three roles and others besides. As we will see later in this chapter, it can be very difficult for the board to fulfil all these roles. Different board structures may be compatible with different roles and regular evaluation is needed to ensure that boards function effectively.

STEWARDSHIP THEORY

The development of common law in England led to the idea that the board of directors is the servant of the company's shareholders. This suggests that a good board should act as an effective steward, safeguarding the resources entrusted to it by shareholders. Following the discussion of agency theory in chapter 2, the idea that any group of managers might act as good stewards might seem fanciful. However, according to stewardship theory this is exactly what the board does.

Like agency theory, stewardship theory is based on the idea that managers are rational, utility-maximising individuals. The key difference between the two approaches is that while agency theory is based on the idea that managers are motivated by *extrinsic rewards*, that is, by monetary rewards given by the firm, stewardship theory is grounded in the importance of *intrinsic rewards*. It argues that people seek personal growth and fulfilment. They can achieve this at work when they have the opportunity to be involved in decision-making and thereby feel they are making a difference to the organisation. At management level this translates to the idea that managers identify with the firm and are naturally inclined to subordinate their personal interests to those of the company, and they therefore maximise their own utility by acting as good stewards who safeguard the interests of the shareholders.

Davis *et al.* (1997) suggest that stewardship theory complements agency theory because it helps to explain why agents sometimes act in a self-seeking way and at other times behave as good stewards. Given that managers seek personal fulfilment at work they will thrive when the organisational structure gives them freedom to be fulfilled through creative thinking and decision-making. When the company is organised so that actions are controlled and decisions are closely monitored, the managers' personal aspirations are thwarted and they become inclined to rebel and take advantage of their principals instead of working to make them better off. This implies that governance structures like the board should be designed so as to empower rather than constrain managers. One implication of this is that it is beneficial to concentrate power in the hands of one individual or a small team. As we will see in this chapter, the regulatory tide has turned against this idea, yet evidence on the relationship between board structure and corporate performance provides some support for the notion.

LAW AND THE BOARD – THE UK CASE

Throughout the world a limited liability company has the status of a legal person, with its own identity distinct from the identities of the people who work for it or own its securities. Like a natural person it is subject to the laws of tort (which governs disputes between individuals over such matters as negligence) and contract, but its operation is also governed by company and securities laws. In this section we focus on how company law affects the board of directors. We concentrate here on the law in the UK, not just because this is the legal system with which the author is most familiar, but also because it gives an interesting illustration of the limitations of the law in corporate governance. The Companies Act 2006, whose implementation was completed in 2009, is the latest in a long line of Companies Acts dating back to 1844. The aim of this Act was to modernise company law in the UK. The two innovations that we will focus on here, because they are relevant to directors, are the Model *Articles of Association* and the definition of directors' duties.

Every company has to have Articles of Association, which can be thought of as an internal rulebook or constitution. A company can either write its own articles or adopt the model included in the Companies Act. The Model Articles include sections on directors, shares and shareholders. This means that they cover topics as diverse as directors' responsibilities, the capitalisation of profit and the organisation of general meetings. If a company chooses to adopt the Model Articles, its directors have the right to manage the company and use all its powers unless the members pass a special resolution that forces the directors to act in a specific way or to refrain from acting in that way. The directors must vote before taking decisions, but if a director has an interest in a particular transaction, they must declare it and are not allowed to vote. If the directors wish they can delegate their decision-making power to others, but they must retain responsibility for making decisions over the appointment of directors and how they then make decisions, and over the payment of dividends. All the directors of a newly formed company must retire at its first AGM, and at later AGMs one-half of the board's members should retire and offer themselves for re-election.

The Articles of Association form what is known as a relational contract, a contract which is characterised by its duration and its incompleteness. As discussed in chapter 2, this implies that the gaps in the contract are filled by a fiduciary duty owed to the company by its directors. The directors are obliged to act in the best interests of the company and to fulfil their responsibilities with candour, care and loyalty. Given that a company could, in principle, have an infinite life, the Articles of Association will endure forever unless 75 per cent of the members vote to change them or unless the company becomes insolvent.

While many of the rules affecting directors are laid down in the Articles of Association, some of their duties are imposed by law. The Companies Act 2006 was the first piece of corporate legislation in the UK to give a definition of directors' duties. It imposes seven duties on the directors: to act within the powers they have been given (by the Articles of Association); to promote the success of the company; to use independent judgement; to use reasonable skill, care and judgement in discharging their duties; to avoid conflicts of interest; to reject benefits from third parties and to declare any interest in the company's transactions.

The duties to promote the success of the company and to use independent judgement are particularly interesting from the point of view of corporate governance. The duty to promote the success of the company is broken down into six parts. The directors must think about the long-term impacts of their decisions, they must consider the interests of their employees, recognise the need for good relationships with suppliers and customers, consider the effects of the business on the community and environment, realise the need to maintain a good reputation and treat all members fairly. Viewed in isolation, this list of duties implies a stakeholder-oriented view of corporate governance. However, the next sub-section of the Act makes it clear that the usual purpose of a company is to bring benefits to its members. Only if it has stated that it has other aims should it act simply in accordance with this list. In other words, the usual aim of the company and hence its directors is to make its shareholders better off, but in doing so it must consider other stakeholders. This idea will reappear in chapter 4 when we consider the position of stakeholders in corporate governance and introduce the idea of *enlightened shareholder value maximisation*.

While regulation on corporate governance as embodied in the 'The UK Corporate Governance Code' (Financial Reporting Council, 2010; discussed in more detail in chapter 7) distinguishes between executive, non-executive and independent directors, the Companies Act does not mention these distinctions. All directors must use independent judgement, whether they are executives who are employed by this company, non-executives employed elsewhere or independent directors who are non-executives with no personal or business links to the firm or its shareholders. This means that executives must not be partisan or unduly deferential to their chief executive. In making day-to-day decisions the head of a division must do their best to promote the interests of the division, fighting for resources if necessary, but being willing to back down if the CEO has other ideas. If the division head is elected to the board they must forget their day-to-day allegiance to the division and loyalty to the CEO and think about the company in its entirety from an independent perspective. This is clearly very difficult, especially if it means voting to sell off the division or to replace the CEO. For a non-executive or independent director the duty to use independent judgement implies that they must not act as if representing a particular shareholder; instead they must consider the needs of all shareholders.

In judging whether or not a director uses reasonable skill, care and judgement the law imposes two tests. The first is objective: does the director have the skills, knowledge and experience that would reasonably be expected of someone in this position? The second is subjective: has the director acted as one would expect of someone with this knowledge and skill set? The latter standard is particularly important in the case of directors who are appointed because of their professional qualification, for instance an accountant who sits on the *audit committee*. The final three duties refer to the ethical standards required of company directors. They should not accept bribes or other inducements and should avoid conflicts of interest. In extreme cases this might mean resigning from the board, but in most cases would be dealt with by declaring an interest in a transaction such as a proposed merger and therefore keeping silent in discussions and abstaining in a vote.

Although it describes what directors should do, the Companies Act gives little guidance about how the board should be constituted. It lays down a minimum size of two members, but no maximum size. The 2006 Act was the first to offer an age restriction for directors, who should now be at least 16 years old. It does not require board members to hold any shares in the company. A legal board is clearly very different from the vast majority of boards that we observe in practice. Most British boards are unitary; they include a majority of independent directors who sit on a variety of subcommittees responsible for specific areas of oversight, one of them chairing the board and another the senior independent director. All these features are encouraged by the Code of Corporate Governance rather than laid down by the law. Individual companies may impose their own rules on directors' shareholdings. It is common to expect executive directors to build up holdings equal to their annual salary, and for non-executives to achieve target holdings equal to their annual fee.

THE ROLE OF THE BOARD

In considering the historical development of boards we saw that the key role of the board is to make decisions and set rules that will bind other members of the organisation. Given that companies are owned by absentee shareholders the board also has an important stewardship role with respect to the owners of the business. We can also consider the legal duties of the directors as the duties of the board as a whole; however, as we saw in the previous section, these are rather general and are not related to specific business situations. In contrast, the Business Roundtable, an organisation representing the CEOs of American companies, lists five specific roles for the board (Business Roundtable, 1990). These are to choose, evaluate and if necessary replace the CEO; this role includes succession planning and remuneration; to review the company's strategy and financing; to advise top management; to bring recommendations on new directors to shareholders and to review the company's systems and ensure that they meet regulatory requirements.

The Business Roundtable does not acknowledge the conflicts of interest that characterise the agency-theoretic view of the firm and therefore imply that monitoring is a key function of the board. Instead the roles of the board relate to running the company, ensuring that it has the right CEO with appropriate incentives and supporting that person by offering advice. It is not surprising that an organisation of chief executives should produce a list like this one. It reveals the tension that exists between the regulatory view that boards must protect shareholders and the business view that they must make strategic decisions.

These tensions are examined by Adams and Ferreira (2007) and by Linck *et al.* (2008). These authors consider the problem of choosing a board structure that allows the board to both advise the CEO or other top management and to monitor the company's decisions on behalf of the shareholders. If the board is to be an effective adviser it must understand the business and have good access to relevant information. In some cases the nature of the business makes it hard for outsiders to understand the issues it faces. Linck *et al.* (2008) suggest that in this case it makes sense to have a small board with few independent directors. Larger boards with many independent directors would waste time thinking about the nature of the problem before settling down to solve it. They find empirical support for this proposition in that smaller, less independent boards are associated with growing companies that spend heavily on research and development. Adams and Ferreira (2007) consider the incentives of the CEO to share the information that the board needs in order to be an effective adviser. They argue that the more information the CEO shares with the board, the better the advice offered. While the CEO values good advice they realise that the information they share can also be used for monitoring purposes. The CEO is assumed to dislike being monitored because they value discretion in decision-making. This means that the CEO has the incentive to withhold information from a board that is likely to be a strong monitor, in other words, an independent board. This leads Adams and Ferreira (2007) to conclude that independent boards are sub-optimal because they will receive imperfect information and hence offer poor advice. Having looked very briefly at the problems inherent in designing board structures that enable both the monitoring and advice functions, we now turn to specific issues in board design.

UNITARY VERSUS DUAL BOARDS

As we have seen, the board of directors has two broad functions: to determine strategy and to monitor decision-making. At first sight it seems odd to suggest that the same group of people can both make and monitor decisions. It therefore seems logical to split the two functions between two different groups. This is exactly what happens in many continental European countries. In these countries each listed firm has a management board that is responsible for deciding the strategic direction of the company, for implementing decisions and for publishing its annual report and accounts, and a supervisory board that monitors the management board. In this context monitoring includes appointing the members of the management board and deciding how they should be rewarded for their work. Some of this work may be organised through subcommittees established by the supervisory board. The supervisory board relies on the management board to provide it with the information it needs to perform its role, but if it feels that it is receiving insufficient information it can specify additional reports which the management board must then supply.

Adams and Ferreira (2007) extend their theory of information-sharing on the board to include consideration of dual boards. They argue that when the CEO puts a high value on having discretion over project choice they will fully reveal information to a management board in order to get good advice, knowing that the information cannot be used by the supervisory board for monitoring purposes. When corporate value is positively related to the quality of advice used in choosing projects, the dual board system is preferable as long as the interests of the supervisory board are aligned with those of the shareholders. This is not always the case.

In general terms it is shareholders who appoint non-executive members to the supervisory board. However, in countries like Germany which practise *codetermination*, some board seats are reserved for labour representatives. German companies with between 500 and 2000 employees must give one-third of board seats to labour representatives; in companies with over 2000 employees the proportion rises to one-half. In line with this, BASF, the German chemical company, has six labour representatives on its twelve-person board. Three are elected from works councils and three are delegates form a trade union, which gives it a mixture of local and national labour representation. Novo Nordisk, the Danish pharmaceutical company, also includes labour representatives on its board. In this case all four are employees rather than trade union representatives. They sit alongside seven other directors, five of whom are independent. Most countries with a dual board system seek independent supervisory board members who will represent the interests of all shareholders. An example of this practice is the board of the Dutch brewer, Heineken. Its supervisory board includes nine members, all of whom are non-executives. According to Adams and Ferreira (2007), the Heineken supervisory board structure is preferable to the system in operation at BASF and Novo Nordisk.

Other countries use the unitary board system, in which a single board has both supreme decision-making power and monitors those decisions. Unitary boards are made up of a mixture of executive directors and non-executives who work elsewhere and who therefore bring an independent perspective to the board. Non-executives usually dominate, numerically speaking, for example in the US, seven of the 9 members of the Microsoft board are non-executives as are 10 of the 13 members of the Ford Motor Company board and 8 of the 10 directors at Dell. The situation is very similar in the UK, for example 9 of the 14 members of the BP board are non-executives while both BAE Systems and GlaxoSmithKline have boards of 13 members, only 3 of whom are executives. It is tempting to suppose that the presence of both types of director leads to a division of labour within the board so that executives are responsible for strategy and non-executives for monitoring. However, this is not the case. All directors bear equal legal responsibility for both aspects of the board's work, although where they spend a lot of time in subcommittees non-executives may in practice bear the brunt of the supervisory role.

In the UK, despite the great effort that has gone into corporate governance reform in recent years, one reform that has never been seriously considered is the introduction of the two-tier system. While theoretical models of board structure have compared the two types of board, we are not aware of any literature that directly compares the effectiveness of the two types of board, so this lack of consideration is not apparently driven by empirical evidence. There is some evidence, however, that supervisory boards may suffer from certain deficiencies when it comes to monitoring the management board. These deficiencies may be caused by poor information flows, a lack of real independence on the supervisory boards or the fact that committees are not always present.

Both Davies (2000) and Maassen and Van den Bosch (1999), discussing the German and Dutch systems, respectively, highlight the potential problem of poor information flows from the management board to the supervisory board. Maassen and Van den Bosch (1999) looked at the supervisory boards of 50 of the largest Dutch companies. They found that 40 per cent had compromised the independence of their supervisory boards by recruiting members who were formerly members of the management board. Of the Supervisory board chairs they interviewed about this, 74 per cent explained that this strategy was useful because it improved information flows between the two boards. Davies (2000) notes that poor information flows, together with few meetings and lack of a committee structure, make supervisory boards ineffective monitors. However, he goes on to defend the importance of the supervisory board on the grounds that monitoring is not its sole purpose. He argues that it is a vital networking mechanism, increasing shareholder wealth by creating valuable relationships with other organisations through the members of the supervisory board.

Xiao *et al.* (2004) gained access to senior executives and members of both types of board in 21 Chinese firms in order to conduct interviews designed to assess the role undertaken by the supervisory board. They report that the supervisory board had an effective monitoring role in only four of the companies studied. In the majority of the companies its function was purely advisory, an important function in itself, while in five companies the authors classified the supervisory board as an 'honoured guest', serving a nominal function but having no real impact on the business.

While these failings have been highlighted in studies of two-tier boards we see no reason why they could not also occur in unitary boards. Demb and Neubauer (1992) interviewed executive and non-executive members of both unitary and dual boards in 11 multinational companies. Directors in both systems admitted that it was possible for executives to restrict or manipulate the flow of information to outside directors, making it harder for them to be effective monitors. The authors find many other similarities in the experience and attitudes of board members in both systems, leading them to conclude that neither is superior. Rather, board structures develop as part of a system of corporate governance in which boards, regulation, ownership patterns and society's expectations complement one another.

THE CHIEF EXECUTIVE OFFICER AND CHAIR OF THE BOARD

Every business needs a chief executive or managing director and every board needs a chair. In the US it is still common for a single person to hold both roles, a practice often referred to as *duality*, while in many other countries regulation requires that the two roles be split. One board chair interviewed by Pettigrew and McNulty (1995) gave a very simple definition of the difference between the two jobs. The

CEO runs the company and the chair runs the board. Regenersis, a British company listed on the Alternative Investment Market, publishes a summary statement of the roles of the CEO and chair. They sit quite comfortably within the definition given by the anonymous interviewee. The CEO's roles relate to corporate activity such as seeking out new business opportunities, allocating resources and managing risk. The chair's tasks centre on the board itself. They include setting the agenda, developing directors so that they can contribute to the board, making sure that the board gets information from the management team and sending decisions back to it, communicating with shareholders and providing leadership.

Both jobs are huge, so the simplest reason for separating them is to make the workload more manageable. However, fear of the consequences of giving too much power to one person lies at the heart of the separation. Recent history has given us examples of what can go wrong when decision-making power is concentrated in few hands. Robert Maxwell, the executive chair of Mirror Group Newspapers in the UK was able to use the force of his personality and his immense power in the industry to subdue debate within the board. He also acted as trustee of the company's pension fund, and when one of his fellow trustees questioned his use of pension fund assets to prop up the company, he dismissed him, and the trustee was never able to work within the newspaper industry again. Ken Lay, the CEO and chair of Enron, led a board which included an impressive array of non-executive directors and only two executives. This made it, on paper at least, a model board. The reality was that many of the non-executives were tied to Enron through its political and charitable donations, making them unlikely to question the unethical and indeed unlawful practices of the company which eventually led to Lay's conviction for fraud.

These examples give credence to the agency-theoretic view of the world in which individuals are motivated only by their own self-interest and therefore require outside monitoring or strong incentives in order to ensure that they do the 'right thing'. If this is a fair characterisation of chief executive officers then it makes perfect sense to say that no CEO should simultaneously hold the position of chair of the board. However, according to stewardship theory, CEOs are motivated in a quite different way. In this view of the world, people want to do their jobs well. Those who have risen to the upper echelons in any organisation come to equate their success with the success of the organisation, so they are motivated to produce the kind of results that will please their shareholders. This suggests that there is no problem in having a CEO who is also the chair of the board. In fact there could be advantages to this arrangement because it provides a clear, unified structure at the top of the business. The Marks and Spencer case study at the end of this chapter provides an example of a company that argued just that when it combined the roles of chair and chief executive in 2008.

Kang and Zardkoohi (2005) review 30 empirical studies of the relationship between duality and firm performance. The papers were published between 1978 and 2003; the vast majority used American data and incorporated both accounting and market-based measures of corporate performance. The picture that emerges from these papers is confused. A total of 34 per cent reveal no statistically significant relationships between duality and performance, in other words, they conclude that duality is irrelevant to performance. A total of 13 per cent find that duality adversely affects performance; 3 per cent (a single paper) indicated that duality improves performance, while the remaining 50 per cent reported mixed results dependent on the performance measure used. Taken together, these results do not provide a strong case for the practice of separating the roles of CEO and chair.

Evidence from less developed economies suggests that duality can enhance corporate performance in specific situations. Elsayed (2007) finds that in Egypt duality in itself is not relevant to corporate performance, but it becomes important when considered alongside industry characteristics. In most of the industries analysed, performance is enhanced by duality. However, in the cement industry, which at the time of the study had been recently privatised and whose ownership was dominated by overseas investors, duality had an adverse effect on performance. Peng *et al.* (2010) show that in China duality improves the performance of companies with significant state ownership but has the opposite effect on companies whose shares are more widely held. These results illustrate a principle that will come up again and again in this book; that is, the idea that each company must find the combination of corporate governance mechanisms that suits it best. By extension, while country regulators should learn from one another they must take account of local circumstances when formulating codes and laws on governance.

INDEPENDENT DIRECTORS

Not only are many boards chaired by independent directors, but they are, as we have already seen, composed largely of independent or non-executive directors. While practices vary around the world, a minimum proportion of one-third non-executives, who may or may not be independent, is common (see chapter 7 on regulation for more detail on this point). Regulation in the UK goes further, demanding that the majority of board members be independent. The distinction between a non-executive and an independent non-executive is important. While the definition of independence varies between regulators, in general terms independent directors have no business relationships with the company, its directors, officers or shareholders. Clearly it is desirable to avoid appointing directors who have a close business relationship with the company, but given the workload of an independent director, in small countries or economies with a small stock market it may be very difficult to find enough independent directors to sit on the boards of quoted companies. In this case the inclusion of *affiliated non-executives*, that is, directors who work for other businesses but are somehow linked to this one, may be the only way of avoiding dominance by insiders.

Not only are the independent directors required to bring a questioning attitude to general board meetings, they are expected to sit on specialist subcommittees too. Companies are free to have as many subcommittees as they need to function efficiently. Regulators usually demand that firms have audit committees and often remuneration and *nomination committee* as well. Most regulation requires an independent presence on each committee. Sometimes, despite regulation, companies choose to have different types of boards. Box 3.1 provides as example of one British company whose board did not respond to regulation but instead changed as its position in the market changed.

Box 3.1 The changing face of the board of Morrison Supermarkets plc

Until 2003 Morrisons was a regional supermarket chain, well known in the North of England, but not in the rest of the UK. That changed when the company made a successful bid for Safeway, which was fully acquired in March 2004. The acquisition represented a change in strategy for Morrisons, which until then had grown organically under the watchful and some would say autocratic eye of its founder Sir Kenneth Morrison. At the time of the acquisition the board was highly unusual in that it was made up entirely of executives and had no audit or remuneration committees. The board started to change following the acquisition, the 2004–5

Annual Report revealing that the company had its first non-executive director and had established audit and *remuneration committees*, of necessity dominated by executives. The following year more non-executives joined the board and took up positions on the subcommittees, but they did not become the majority as encouraged by regulation until 2008–9.

This example shows that the *'comply or explain'* approach to regulation does not impose uniform board structures; instead it offers a lot of freedom which may be curtailed by market expectations of what constitutes a good board.

The roles of the subcommittees will be discussed in the next section. For now, the key point to note is that independent directors are at the heart of many of the key activities undertaken by the board. Empirical research on the usefulness of independent directors has focused on the relationship between measures of accounting and/or stock market performance and the proportion of independent directors on the board. Given that the presence of independent directors is supposed to bring a fresh perspective and improved monitoring, the hypothesis that is tested is that there is a positive relationship between company performance and the proportion of independent directors on the board. Research in the UK and US does not support the hypothesis. For the US, a number of researchers who use different performance measures find evidence that firm performance is worsened by the presence of a larger proportion of outside directors. Agrawal and Knoeber (1996) using stock market performance as the dependent variable, Klein (1998) using both accounting and stock market returns and Coles *et al.* (2001) using a value-added measure find a significantly negative relationship between their chosen measure of performance and the proportion of outside directors on the board. For the UK, Vafeas and Theodorou (1998) find a positive but insignificant relationship between market performance and the proportion of non-executives on the board. However, before we jump to the conclusion that independent directors are unimportant, we should think more carefully about the situations in which the addition of independent directors should have an effect on performance.

Perhaps the most obvious point to raise is that it takes time for new independent directors to understand the company and its competitive situation. It would be unreasonable to expect new directors to make changes as soon as they are appointed to the board. This means that empirical studies that measure performance and board independence in the same period may be missing the point. An increase in the ratio of independent directors to board size may only affect performance with a lag. The papers cited above do not incorporate lags. The composition of the board just before changes are made is also likely to affect the impact of any new directors. To take an extreme example, if a board consisting entirely of executive directors appoints a single independent director, that new director will find it very difficult to challenge decisions. If the existing board members do not like what they hear they can dismiss the new member as being out of touch. It would be much harder to dismiss the views of several independent directors, all of whom disagree with or challenge the executive members. Once independent directors become the majority of the board, the addition of yet another is less likely to bring a new perspective, or an additional challenge. This suggests that researchers should take a 'before and after' approach to thinking about board composition, considering the change of the ratio of independent to total members and whether the change has introduced independence to the board, or simply increased it. Rosenstein and Wyatt (1990) examine the impact of announcements that additional outside directors are joining American boards. They find a significant, positive increase in stock prices following such announcements. This adds credence to the idea that changes in board structure are more significant than board structures themselves, but the study does not distinguish between large and small changes in composition. Perry and Peyer (2005) offer evidence that the composition of the board just before the announcement of the appointment of a new independent director is important in determining the impact of that appointment. They find that the addition of an independent director to a board that currently has a minority of independent members leads to larger positive gains than occur when the board is already independent. This indicates that shareholders value independent boards and believe they will serve the interests of owners.

The nature of the business environment itself may also be relevant to the impact of the introduction or inclusion of independent directors. In stable times, when ethics are not an issue, independent directors are likely to be seen as a 'good thing' but the market is unlikely to react significantly as the ratio of independent directors to board size changes. If recent scandals have shocked the business world, the reaction to a change in the ratio is likely to be much bigger as investors pin their hopes on independent directors to bring change. Finally, none of these studies consider the possible endogeneity of board structure. It is quite possible that more independent boards are associated with poorly performing companies because poor performers add non-executives to the board in an attempt to improve performance.

Clearly, evidence from just two countries cannot tell us the whole story about board independence. Interestingly, evidence from Asia and Europe paints a rather different picture. Choi *et al.* (2007) and Kiel and Nicholson (2003) look at the relationship between stock market performance and the proportion of outside directors in Korea and Australia, respectively. Both find a significantly positive relationship between performance and the proportion of outside directors. Kiel and Nicholson (2003) use an accounting measure of performance as well as a market-based measure. They find no relationship between return on assets and independence on the board. This indicates that while investors are reassured by the presence of outside directors, they do not necessarily have an impact on accounting performance. In other contexts, however, accounting performance is positively related to board independence. Krivogorsky (2006) examines the performance of a group of European companies traded on the New York Stock Exchange. She uses three performance measures, two measures of accounting returns and one of market performance, and finds that all three are significantly and positively affected by the proportion of independent directors on the board. Dahya *et al.* (2008) take a cross-country sample of companies that could be considered to be a special case. These companies all have a blockholder (holding at least 10 per cent of voting rights) in their ownership structure. As we have already seen, this situation can lead to a type II agency problem in which minority shareholders become disenfranchised. For this sample of companies coming from 22 countries in Europe, North America and Asia, the proportion of independent directors has a significantly positive effect on market performance, indicating that an independent board reassures the market that the presence of a blockholder does not have a detrimental effect on the firm.

All the statistical evidence presented here is based on the premise that an output, in this case company performance, can be explained by an input, in this case the presence of independent directors. It tells us nothing about how decisions are made by boards or how much input independent directors contribute. Clearly nobody can observe boards in action, so the next best thing is to interview directors to find out more about how they approach the job. Some of the non-executives interviewed by Roberts *et al.* (2005) confirmed the view expressed earlier that new independent directors need to work their way into the job. They explained that is necessary to listen and learn rather than to rush to express an opinion and make an impact soon after appointment. They also felt that by asking even simple questions about the organisation and its processes they made executives consider the reasons behind their accepted practices. The non-executives who were interviewed by Pettigrew and McNulty (1995) felt that they really came into their own in times of crisis. At this point they contributed more forcefully that usual, guiding the executives towards a solution before stepping back as the crisis abated.

Several authors discuss the rather unflattering names used by executives to describe their non-executive colleagues in the days before regulators increased their governance role. Interviews with both types of director reveal that there are still tensions between the two groups, even though it would be unwise to dismiss non-executives as mere 'window-dressing' or 'Christmas-tree decorations'. Pettigrew and McNulty (1995) report that non-executives feel they do not always get the information they need and Demb and Neubauer (1992) and Hill (1995) cite examples of non-executives who believe they bring qualities like the ability to resolve conflicts while the executives are more appreciative of their useful business contacts.

While the evidence on the usefulness of independent directors is mixed, corporate governance activists and regulators believe that independence is a good thing. This means that there is huge demand for non-executives with relevant experience to sit on boards, which implies a danger that certain individuals may be invited to sit on so many boards that they may become ineffective monitors. To counter this, it is often suggested that there should be limits on the number of boards on which a director can sit. In the US the National Association of Corporate Directors (NACD) recommends that a CEO should hold a maximum of three external directorships. The Council of Institutional investors (CII) goes further, advocating a single outside directorship for a CEO and two others for an individual holding an executive directorship. In the UK the Code of Corporate Governance recommends that while a full-time executive director can sit on other boards, they should only sit on the board of one FTSE100 company. Are such restrictions justified?

In recent years researchers have put some effort into considering the effects of 'busyness' on the performance of directors and the companies on whose boards they sit. A busy director is defined in terms of the number of boards on which they serve, with the number three often used as the cut-off point indicating that a director is busy. The notion of busyness is often used to measure director quality – after all, why would several boards invite an ineffective director to join their ranks? Both the director and the boards on which they sit can gain from busyness by the broadening of the individual's experience and through the networking opportunities available from multiple board appointments. On the other hand multiple board memberships might just be a perk, in which case they would not bring benefits to the firms involved. Ferris *et al.* (2003) confirm that reputation is linked to multiple board appointments. They find that when a firm performs well its executive directors can expect to receive invitations to join other boards at a later date. They further show that firms' performance is not hampered by having busy directors, and those busy directors take their fair share of committee work on the boards on which they serve. Interestingly, in their sample few directors are busy. Only 5.5 per cent hold three or more directorships, and the mean number of board seats held is 1.6. In contrast Fich and Shivdasani (2006) find that firm value is lower in firms with busy boards. However their sample is rather different in that their directors hold an average of three board seats. Jiraporn *et al.* (2009) look at a different aspect of busyness by focusing on directors' attendance at meetings. They find that as directors hold more seats they attend fewer meetings, indicating that they become less useful. However, comparing attendance before and after the passage of the Sarbanes–Oxley Act they find that attendance improved after the passage of the Act, indicating that it forced directors to take their role more seriously.

BOARD SUBCOMMITTEES

The Board of Directors increasingly delegates specific areas of decision-making to board subcommittees. Calleja (1999) examined the situation in large Australian companies at the end of 1997 when there was no legal requirement for boards to set up sub- committees. The Australian Stock Exchange listing rules had been changed the year before to incorporate the 'comply or explain' rule with respect to audit committees only. In a sample of 80 of the largest 100 companies she found 35 separate types of committee in operation. By far the most prevalent was the audit committee (present in 98 per cent of firms), followed by the remuneration committee (found in 76 per cent of firms) and the nomination committee (used by 47 per cent of firms). Some companies chose to have many more committees specialising in such areas as health and safety, compliance and the environment, but there is no evidence from this data to suggest that corporate performance can be improved by simply creating more committees.

The audit committee was commonplace in the US long before it was introduced elsewhere. The first audit committees were observed in 1939, but were not required by all companies until 1977. Of all the board subcommittees this one probably has the widest remit and certainly is the most talked about following financial scandals like those at Enron, WorldCom and Parmalat. This committee is responsible for appointing auditors and managing the relationship between them and the company, and it also reports on the integrity of the financial reporting system, even though this is, legally speaking, the responsibility of the entire board. The complexity of this role depends on the type of governance regulation in place. In the US, the Sarbanes–Oxley Act 2002 states that accounting firms may not simultaneously perform audit and other services for any company. This means that the audit committee does not have to be concerned about the independence of its auditors. In other countries where independence is deemed desirable rather than mandatory, the audit committee must consider how many other services it is appropriate to buy from its audit company, and then defend that decision in its reports to shareholders. In addition to monitoring the integrity of the external audit, this committee may also perform the same function in respect of the internal audit. In the absence of a specialist risk committee it may also have to consider the risks faced by the business, the methods used to mitigate or hedge risk and, most importantly, report this to the shareholders to ensure that the company shares the risk appetite of its owners. Perhaps predictably, the recent financial crisis and subsequent recession have brought calls for companies to establish separate risk committees rather than adding to the existing workload of the audit committee.

It is not surprising that empirical research on the effectiveness of board committees has focussed on the audit committee. Researchers have posed many different questions; here we will concentrate on those that relate to the issues discussed in this chapter. One of the key features of today's boards is independence. We have already seen the evidence on the composition of the full board: does the general conclusion that independence does not matter hold in the case of this subcommittee? Chan and Li (2008) consider the relationship between firm value and audit committee independence in American companies in the Fortune 500. They suggest two rather different measures of independence. The first and most obvious is to define a committee as independent if at least 50 per cent of its members are independent directors. The second defines a committee as independent if it includes a member who is professionally qualified in accounting or finance. This second measure could be interpreted either as a measure of expertise or as a sign of the type of independent thinking that goes with affiliation to a profession. The first measure of independence is found to be significantly and positively related to stock market performance, that is, firms that have audit committees made up of at least 50 per cent independent directors have a higher market value than firms whose audit committees are not independent. The second finding, that the presence of a finance or accounting professional has no impact on performance, flies in the face of calls to include professionals on audit committees. However, the authors investigate this point further by extending their analysis to look at the effect of having a majority independent committee that includes a financially qualified member. This practice is positively related to stock market value, implying that the value-relevance of independence is heightened by the inclusion of directors with relevant professional experience.

In the US the very real threat of litigation against companies is likely to encourage them to seek out accounting experts to sit on their audit committees. While this could lead to the presence of more accountants on audit committees, it might have the opposite effect because the accountants themselves may feel reluctant to join boards that might be sued. Krishnan and Lee (2009) investigate this tension by relating the use of experts to governance variables and to litigation risk. They find that the higher is the risk of litigation, the more likely firms are to include experts on their audit committees. Further, when firms are classified according to the strength of their governance, only the better- governed companies exhibit this positive relationship. They offer two possible explanations for this finding. Either there are complementarities between different governance mechanisms and so the appointment of experts is just one aspect of good governance, or firms with poor governance which face high litigation risk simply cannot attract the experts they need.

Raghunandan and Rama (2007) hypothesise that audit committee composition and the risk of litigation will influence the diligence with which audit committees carry out their work. They investigate the relationship between diligence, measured by the frequency of meetings, and a series of governance variables as well as a litigation variable that picks up the impact of the firm being in a litigious industry such as pharmaceuticals, software, electronics or retail rather than other industries that are classified as non-litigious. They find that diligence is positively influenced by the litigation variable and a range of governance measures including the proportion of accounting experts on the committee.

Taking these results together we can see that the composition of the audit committee matters a great deal. Firms have an incentive to include experts when they face the risk of legal action, and to include independent members alongside those experts in order to improve their market valuation. However, before giving the impression that the presence of a well-qualified, independent audit committee guarantees good governance and performance, it is necessary to sound a cautionary note. At the time of its bankruptcy, Enron had an exemplary audit committee. It was made up entirely of outside directors, one of whom met all the qualifications of an accounting expert, and the committee met four times a year, which could have been indicative of effort. There is always a danger in taking at face value the outcomes of empirical work in corporate governance. When we think, at an intuitive level, about the inputs made by board members we think about effort, commitment and skill, yet external researchers cannot measure any of these. Instead they have to rely on proxies like the holding of a particular qualification or the number of meetings held. Such proxies are imperfect and cannot substitute for knowing what happens at meetings of the full board or its committees. This is, sadly impossible, although some researchers have managed to obtain access to committee members in order to gain insight into what happens at meetings.

Despite having a small sample of only three Canadian companies, Gendron *et al.* (2004) provide some interesting insights into how audit committees actually work. They were able to interview all the people who attended audit committee meetings; this included not just the members of the committee itself, but also the chief internal and external auditors, the CEO and CFO of the companies. Meeting attendees in all the companies agreed that the main role of the committee members is to ask questions. In two of the companies the questions emphasised the numbers in the financial statements, especially those calculated according to formulae. In the third the questions also related to the narrative accompanying the figures, with committee members keen to see that readers of the annual report did not encounter ambiguities in the language that might cloud their view of the numbers presented. Audit committees have to be concerned with processes as well as reports, and in these companies processes were managed by discussions of the issues raised during internal audits.

While audit committees have inspired a great deal of research, the same cannot be said about remuneration and nomination committees, despite the fact that they have a major impact on the main board. The remuneration or compensation committee, as it is known in the US, has the task of determining the kind of remuneration packages offered to executive directors and often also to senior management. In order to avoid individual directors being able to decide their own rewards, this committee is usually composed entirely of non-executives. The nomination committee has the important role of finding new directors with the necessary skills to fill board vacancies. Once again non-executives usually sit on this committee to ensure that the board remains independent of the CEO. Like the remuneration committee it may rely on the advice of external consultants. As we will see in chapter 5, while consultants can make life easier for board members, their advice can lead to inflated remuneration. In addition, the market for consultancy services is concentrated, which implies that a few businesses exert a great deal of influence on companies, which can lead to uniformity in practices in key areas like compensation and succession planning.

BOARD EVALUATION

The requirement for boards to regularly evaluate their work is a common feature of corporate governance regulation around the world, as you will see in chapter 7. This is not surprising given that the board is a key component, if not the most important part of the internal governance structure of the company. Evaluations can be performed in a variety of ways, depending on the objective of the exercise and the audience to whom the report will be addressed. Minichelli *et al.* (2007) discuss four types of evaluation process which they call market-to-board, market-to-market, board-to-board and board-to-market.

A market-to-board evaluation is undertaken by an external organisation and addressed to the board. It is likely to include an assessment of membership and culture of the board together with an appraisal of how it performs its key tasks. Such an evaluation will give the board an idea of how it is perceived by the market and should enable it to improve if it is less effective than other boards encountered by the external assessors. Any board which chooses to be assessed in this way implicitly indicates its willingness to change if required. A market-to-market evaluation is performed by an external organisation and addressed to the company's external stakeholders, who include current and potential investors. The type of content usually found in these evaluations relates again to the way in which key tasks are performed but also includes commentary on board structures and leadership. Companies that are willing to be appraised and to share information in this way indicate that they take their responsibilities seriously and are committed to transparency. The Institute of Chartered Secretaries and Administrators (ICSA) publishes an annual report on the way in which companies listed in the UK disclose their board evaluation processes in their annual reports. In looking at the 2009 reports issued by the largest 200 companies (Institute of Chartered Secretaries and Administrators, 2010) they find that in general disclosures on board evaluation are unhelpful. The organisation readily admits that it has a preference for external evaluations and notes that only 32 per cent of the companies they examined had engaged an outside body to evaluate board performance.

A board-to-board evaluation is both undertaken by the board and disclosed only to directors. This is the only type of process in which the contribution of individual directors is discussed. While there are likely to be biases in this type of process, it is nonetheless useful for boards to examine their own structures and cultures regularly in order to identify early signs of problems. A board-to-market evaluation is once again undertaken by the board but communicated to external stakeholders. Rather than discussing the performance of individual members, this type of report is more likely to indicate how the board has collectively performed key tasks, how it is led and the culture it embodies. In the UK the Institute of Directors offers a range of services enabling boards to run their own evaluations, and can also facilitate external processes.

Clearly there is a cost involved in this process. The cynic would say that this is yet another example of regulation creating work for consultants and imposing costs on companies. In discussing the role of the audit committee we saw that it is important to ensure that auditors do not sell other services to companies; in chapter 5 on remuneration a similar issue will be raised in relation to remuneration consultants. Board evaluation by external consultants can raise issues of independence and conflict of interest if those consultants are also active in helping companies to find new board members.

CONCLUSION

The board is a feature shared by companies the world over. It plays a crucial role in the management of the business and in communicating with and safeguarding the interests of shareholders. In many countries, including the US and UK, each company has a single board, with a majority of members recruited from outside the company. In the US the chair of the board will probably also be the CEO, but in many other parts of the world an independent director usually chairs the board. In parts of continental Europe and Asia companies have two boards, a management board that runs the business and a supervisory board that monitors the decisions reached by the management board and is therefore accountable to shareholders and other stakeholders. The majority of supervisory board members are non-executives, but in some countries a proportion of them may be chosen to represent the employees' rather than the shareholders' interests. The prevalence of independent directors on boards together with the separation of the roles of CEO and chair can be seen as a victory for the agency-theoretic approach to corporate governance. This victory comes despite mixed evidence on the performance implications of these two governance mechanisms. The evidence suggests that for the majority of companies operating in a well-regulated environment the presence of independent directors and the avoidance of duality make little difference to firm value.

Boards increasingly delegate specific tasks to subcommittees of the main board. Each board can choose to set up as many committees as it feels necessary, but the most commonly observed are the audit, remuneration and nomination committees. Academic interest has centred on the audit committee, perhaps because accounting scandals have focused attention on the quality of financial reporting and auditing. Here there is evidence that the composition of the committee is important. The inclusion of independent members and of experts adds value to the firm.

KEY POINTS

- The board of directors has two key roles, to give strategic leadership and to supervise the company on behalf of the shareholders.
- In some countries a single board undertakes both roles, in others a management board takes care of strategy while a supervisory board undertakes the stewardship function. There is no empirical evidence to suggest that one form is better than the other.
- The chair takes responsibility for running the board. While it is common to stipulate that the CEO cannot also be the chair, the evidence on duality is mixed so we cannot conclude that corporate value is affected by the practice.
- Independent directors play an increasingly important role in governance. While boards and subcommittees are dominated in numerical terms by independent directors there is no evidence that this improves corporate performance.
- Boards increasingly delegate certain areas of decision-making to subcommittees of (mainly) independent directors. The subcommittees most often used deal with the audit function, the remuneration of executives and the nomination of new board members.

CASE STUDY   He's more than just a CEO, he's Marks and Spencer's Chairman of the Board – Sir Stuart Rose

Marks and Spencer plc is a British retailer with a long history and a reputation as a 'national treasure'. Stuart Rose returned to Marks and Spencer in 2004, having worked for the company during the 1970s and 1980s. In the meantime he had earned a reputation as a shrewd businessman with a talent for turning around ailing retailers. This made him the ideal CEO for Marks and Spencer, whose market share was falling and whose independence was in doubt as it faced a hostile takeover bid from the Arcadia Group, headed by the charismatic Philip Green. Under Rose's leadership the company returned to its core business of women's clothing by acquiring the Per Una brand and selling off its financial services division; with its shareholders' support it fended off the takeover bid. The strategy worked and the company's share price rose steadily until early 2008, when the sector faced problems due to concerns over falling consumer spending.

On 10 March 2008 the company issued a statement in which it explained that the then Chairman, Lord Burns, would step down, and Sir Stuart Rose (as he had become in 2007 when knighted for his services to the retail industry and to corporate social responsibility) would be appointed as executive chair in his place. The UK's Combined Code of Corporate Governance operating at that time required companies to comply with or explain reasons for their non-compliance with the Code, part of which stated that the roles of Chair and CEO should be held by different individuals. Further, the code required companies to discuss a change like this one with major shareholders before implementing it. Instead the company simply made the announcement on 10 March. The company's institutional shareholders reacted angrily. According to a poll in the *Sunday Times*, institutions holding 15 per cent of the firm's equity were opposed to Rose holding the dual role. Richard Buxton, head of UK equities at Schroders, which at the time held 2 per cent of the equity, called on Marks and Spencer to sack Rose if he did not step back from one of the roles. He claimed that he had tried to meet with the company but had been refused. Peter Chambers, the chief executive of Legal and General Investment Management, stated that he wanted to see companies complying with the code, rather than explaining why they didn't comply. The stock market reaction was more muted; the share price fell less than 1 per cent, a smaller fall than on the preceding two days.

Lord Burns wrote to all the shareholders on 3 April. In his letter the outgoing chairman explained that when Stuart Rose had joined the board in 2004, the plan was for him to remain in post until 2009. The downturn in the retail sector, together with the company's change in strategy, had led to a complete board turnover, leaving the company with a succession problem. With no clear successor already in place on the board, its members agreed that Stuart Rose should stay until 2011. Further, they felt it would be desirable for him to take on the role of chair for three reasons. First, this would indicate a change in his responsibilities and encourage the executive directors to focus on their new roles in the company and on the board. Second, it would allow Rose to adjust his role as CEO as the new executive directors developed in their own roles, and third, it would make it easier to handle the transition to a new CEO. In recognition of the fact that the move was at odds with what had become standard corporate governance practice the board also appointed Sir David Michels, the Senior Independent Director, to the role of deputy chair. Finally, the letter explained that Marks and Spencer had not discussed any of this with shareholders beforehand because this change was part of far-reaching board-level changes which it wanted to remain confidential until implemented. The letter finally brought the company some good news. Brandes, a Californian fund manager and the company's largest shareholder, announced that it supported the decision.

Marks and Spencer held its AGM on 9 July, amid press speculation that it would be a bloody affair. In fact, only 5 per cent of the shareholders at the meeting were prepared to go so far as to vote against Rose's re-election, but a substantial 17 per cent abstained. To put this figure in context, there were 13 votes at the meeting, and the next highest abstention rate of 4 per cent was recorded on the vote to approve the remuneration report. The day before the AGM Bloomberg had reported that investors, including the Universities Superannuation Scheme, the Railway Pensions Trustee Co. and Stichting Pensioenfonds ABP, would show their disapproval by voting against the annual report. The prediction of around 1 per cent voting against was accurate as the figure reported was 1.24 per cent. The press took a particular interest in this AGM, but subsequent reports concentrated on the views expressed by individual shareholders who were concerned that the company no longer sold clothes suitable for the middle-aged women who used to make up the majority of its customers. At one point Sir Stuart volunteered to take one angry shareholder shopping at a branch of Marks and Spencer in order to prove that the retailer still catered for this market.

The promise of a shopping spree did not make everyone happy. Institutional investors continued to complain about the situation, and at the 2009 AGM 14 per cent abstained in the vote to re-elect Rose. Interestingly, the shareholders were also given the chance to vote on a resolution to bring forward the appointment of an independent chair to 2010. A total of 36 per cent of shareholders were in favour and 4 per cent abstained, leaving a majority in favour of the original scheme to give Sir Stuart the dual role until 2011.

In November 2009 Marks and Spencer announced that it had finally found a suitable new chief executive. Marc Bolland, the CEO of Morrisons, a supermarket chain, had agreed to take up the post at the end of January 2010. The stock market reacted well from Marks and Spencer's point of view as the price rose by 6 per cent; but on the same day Morrisons' shares fell by 5 per cent. The media agree that while Marks and Spencer is a smaller company than Morrisons the CEO's job is bigger because the company has such an iconic status.

Corporate governance reform began in earnest in the UK when the Cadbury Report was published in 1992. It recommended that the CEO of a company should not chair the board. This principal has become so embedded in UK corporate governance that even a 'star' businessman like Sir Stuart could not go against it without feeling the wrath of the company's institutional investors. Peter Chambers's comment made at the time was interesting. Even though the regulation states that companies should comply with the Code or explain why they do not, he was not interested in the explanation, he just wanted to see compliance. It seems that some investors see corporate governance mechanisms as something that must be imposed on companies rather than chosen by them.

CASE-STUDY QUESTIONS

1 Briefly outline the arguments against allowing the CEO of a company to act as the chair of its board.
2 Do you feel that the reasons for appointing Sir Stuart as chair as outlined in Lord Burns's letter were sufficient to outweigh the arguments you outlined in your answer to question 1?
3 Do you feel that the board in this case acted according to the tenets of steward- ship theory or of agency theory?

REVISION QUESTIONS

1 What are the duties of directors under UK law?
2 If you were designing a board structure from scratch, would it be a unitary or a dual board, and why?
3 Can independent directors make a meaningful contribution to debates on corporate strategy?
4 Why do most governance systems frown on the CEO chairing the board?

5 Should we have regulation that restricts the number of boards on which a director can sit?

6 Why do boards delegate certain topics to specialist subcommittees?

REFERENCES

Adams, R.B. and Ferreira, D. (2007) 'A Theory of Friendly Boards' *Journal of Finance* 62 (1) 217–250

Agrawal, A. and Knoeber, C.R. (1996) 'Firm Performance and Mechanisms to Control Agency Problems Between Managers and Shareholders' *Journal of Financial and Quantitative Analysis* 31 (3) 377–397

Business Roundtable (1990) 'Corporate Governance and American Competitiveness: A Statement of the Business Roundtable' *Business Lawyer* 46, 241–252

Calleja, N. (1999) ''To Delegate or Not to Delegate': Board Committees and Corporate Performance in Australia's Top 100 Companies' *Sydney Law Review* 25 (5) 5–35

Chan, K.C. and Li, J. (2008) 'Audit Committee and Firm Value: Evidence on Outside Top Executives as Expert-Independent Directors' *Corporate Governance: An International Review* 16(1) 16–31

Choi, J. J., Park, S.W. and Yoo, S.S. (2007) 'The Value of Outside Directors: Evidence from Corporate Governance Reform in Korea' *Journal of Financial and Quantitative Analysis* 42 (4) 941–962

Coles, J.W., McWilliams, V.B. and Sen, N. (2001) 'An Examination of the Relationship of Governance Mechanisms to Performance' *Journal of Management* 27 (1) 23–50

Companies Act 2006, London: HMSO

Dahya, J., Dimitrov, O.O. and McConnell, J.J. (2008) 'Dominant Shareholders, Corporate Boards, and Corporate Value: A Cross-Country Analysis' *Journal of Financial Economics* 87 (1) 73–100

Davies, P. (2000) 'Board Structure in the UK and Germany: Convergence or Continuing Divergence?' *International and Comparative Company Law Journal* 2 (4) 435–456

Davis, J. H., Schoorman, F.D. and Donaldson, L. (1997) 'Toward a Stewardship Theory of Management' *Academy of Management Review* 22 (1) 20–47

Demb, A. and Neubauer, F.F. (1992) *The Corporate Board: Confronting the Paradoxes* Oxford University Press

Elsayed, K. (2007) 'Does CEO Duality Really Affect Corporate Performance?' *Corporate Governance: An International Review* 15 (6) 1203–1214

Ferris, S.P. Jagannathan, M. and Pritchard, A.C. (2003) 'Too Busy to Mind the Business? Monitoring by Directors with Multiple Board Appointments' *Journal of Finance* 58 (3) 1087–1111

Fich, E.M. and Shivdasani, A. (2006) 'Are Busy boards Effective Monitors?' *Journal of Finance* 61 (2) 689–724

Financial Reporting Council (2010) 'The UK Corporate Governance Code' FRC

Gendron, Y., Bedard, J. And Gosselin, M. (2004) 'Getting Inside the Black Box: A Field Study of Practices in "Effective" Audit Committees' *Auditing* 23 (1) 153–171

Gevurtz, F.A. (2004) 'The Historical and Political Origins of the Corporate Board of Directors' *Hofstra Law Review* 33 (1) 89–174

Hill, S. (1995) 'The Social Organization of Boards of Directors' *British Journal of Sociology* 46 (2) 245–278

Institute of Chartered Secretaries and Administrators (2010) 'Review of the 2009 Annual Reports of the FTSE 200 Companies' ICSA

Jiraporn, P., Davidson, W.N., DaDalt, P. and Ning, Y. (2009) 'Too Busy to Show Up? An Analysis of Directors' Absences' *Quarterly Review of Economics and Finance* 49 (3) 1159–1171

Kang, E. and Zardkoohi, A. (2005) 'Board Leadership and Firm Performance' *Corporate Governance: An International Review* 13 (6) 785–799

Kessler, R.A. (1959) 'The Statutory Requirement of a Board of Directors: A Corporate Anachronism' *University of Chicago Law Review* 27 (4) 696–736

Kiel, G.C. and Nicholson, G.J. (2003) 'Board Composition and Corporate Performance: How the Australian Experience Informs Contrasting Theories of Corporate Governance' *Corporate Governance: An International Review* 11 (3) 198–205

Klein, A. (1998) 'Firm Performance and Board Committee Structure' *Journal of Law and Economics* 41 (1) 275–303

Krishnan, J. and Li, J.E. (2009) 'Audit Committee Financial Expertise, Litigation Risk and Corporate Governance' *Auditing: A Journal of Practice and Theory* 28 (1) 225–240

Krivogorsky, V. (2006) 'Ownership, Board Structure and Performance in Continental Europe' *International Journal of Accounting* 41 (2) 176–19

Linck, J.S., Netter, J.M. and Yang, T. (2008) 'The Determinants of Board Structure' *Journal of Financial Economics* 87 (2) 308–328

Maassen, G. and Van den Bosch, F. (1999) 'On the Supposed Independence of Two-tier Boards: Formal Structure and Reality in The Netherlands' *Corporate Governance: An International Review* 7 (1) 31–37

Minichelli, A., Gabrielsson, J. and Huse, M. (2007) 'Board Evaluations: Making a Fit Between the Purpose and the System' *Corporate Governance: An International Review* 15 (4) 609–622

O'Donnell, C. (1952) 'Origins of the Corporate Executive' *Bulletin of the Business Historical Society* 26 (2) 55–727

Peng, M.W., Li, Y., Xie, E. and Su, Z. (2010) 'CEO Duality, Organizational Slack, and Firm Performance in China' *Asia Pacific Journal of Management* 27 (4) 611–624

Perry, T. and Peyer, U. (2005) 'Board Seat Accumulation by Executives: A Shareholder's Perspective' *Journal of Finance* 60 (4) 2083–2123

Pettigrew, A. and McNulty, T. (1995) 'Power and Influence in and Around the Boardroom' *Human Relations* 48 (8) 845–873

Raghunandan, K. and Rama, D.V. (2007) 'Determinants of Audit Committee Diligence' *Accounting Horizons* 21 (3)

Roberts, J., McNulty, T. and Stiles, P. (2005) 'Beyond Agency Conceptions of the Work of the Non-Executive Director: Creating Accountability in the Boardroom' *British Journal of Management* 16 (s1) S5–S26

Rosenstein, S. and Wyatt, J.G. (1990) 'Outside Directors, Board Independence, and Shareholder Wealth' *Journal of Financial Economics* 26 (2) 175–191

Sarbanes-Oxley Act of 2002 Pub. L. No. 107–204, 116 Stat. 745 (Codified as amended in scattered sections of 15 U.S.C)

Vafeas, N. and Theodorou, E. (1998) 'The Relationship Between Board Structure and Firm Performance in the UK' *British Accounting Review* 30 (4) 383–407

Xiao, J.Z., Dahya, J. and Lin, Z. (2004) 'A Grounded Theory Exposition of the Role of the Supervisory Board in China' *British Journal of Management* 15 (1) 39–55

SUGGESTIONS FOR FURTHER READING

Hermalin, B.E. and Weisbach, M.S. (2003) 'Boards of Directors as Endogenously Determined Institutions: A Survey of the Economic Literature' *Economic Policy Review* 9 (1) 7–26. This paper starts from the premise that boards exist to mitigate the agency problems that exist between shareholders and management. It goes on to review the empirical literature on board composition and corporate performance and suggests new areas for research.

Institute of Directors (2010) 'Board Evaluations and Board Effectiveness: An Outline of the IoD Services and Approach' IoD available at http://www. iod.com/mainWebSite/Resources/Document/board_evaluation_outline.pdf. This document provides a useful summary of the issues that are raised during an evaluation. It also includes a scale of charges made by the IoD for services in this area. Given that this is a not-for-profit organisation, you can imagine that consultancy companies would charge rather more.

Masulis, R.W. and Mobbs, H.S (2009) 'Are All Inside Directors the Same? Do They Entrench CEOs or Facilitate More Informed Board Decisions?' ECGI Finance Working Paper no 24/2009, forthcoming in the *Journal of Finance*. This research offers new evidence on the influence of executive directors on the performance of their companies by considering their activities on other boards.

http://www.nacdonline.org/ the National Association of Corporate Directors was formed in 1977 to provide resources for the directors of American companies. This site offers access to a variety of materials on corporate governance as seen from the perspective of directors.

STAKEHOLDERS

INTRODUCTION

During the years since corporate governance emerged as a distinct subject area, there has been huge interest in the fundamental question 'in whose interests should companies be run?' Some authors have answered very definitely that companies belong to their shareholders so they should be operated only with profit in mind. Others have answered equally definitely that companies are an important part of our social framework so they should be organised so as to benefit a wider stakeholder group. The shareholder and stakeholder perspectives have vied for supremacy in the contest to become the dominant theoretical approach. The fact that neither has been crowned the victor can be explained in (at least) two ways. The first is that as we saw in chapter 1, corporate governance is not the domain of a single 'breed' of social scientist. Academics from a variety of disciplines have made significant contributions to the field, and they inevitably arrive at the topic from different starting points. The second is that commentators frequently classify national systems of corporate governance in terms of their orientation towards either shareholders or stakeholders. The UK and US are held up as examples of shareholder-centred systems while Germany and Japan are said to represent a stakeholder orientation. For these reasons the two approaches have coexisted, sometimes uneasily, for as long as academics have been interested in governance.

The word 'stakeholder' has been used since the 1960s. At that time it was used to describe groups on which the company relies for its existence; they would include shareholders, lenders, employees, suppliers and customers. In general terms, stakeholders were deemed to be groups that have the power to affect the business. Over time the definition has changed. Today the word includes not just those groups with the power to affect the business, but also those who are affected by it, so it includes the local community and the environment in general. National codes of corporate governance often mention stakeholders. Most discuss the importance of creditors, suppliers and customers, all of whom qualify under both definitions; others provide long lists of stakeholders, some of whom qualify only since the definition has been broadened. The government features as a stakeholder in Brazil, Turkey and India, the community is mentioned in the codes from Indonesia, Lithuania, Malta, New Zealand and Taiwan, local doctors and schools appear in the Czech Republic's code and trade unions and non-governmental organisations are listed as stakeholders in the Turkish code. Clearly regulators disagree on how widely the term 'stakeholder' should be defined.

Before looking at particular stakeholder groups we will present an overview of *stakeholder theory* and *transactions costs economics*, both of which offer useful insights into how and why companies should manage relationships with stakeholders. We will then go on to consider the relationships between companies and their employees, lenders, suppliers and customers, in order to see how, if at all, these groups can play a role in corporate governance. The case study at the end of the chapter looks at the problems faced by Primark, a British retailer criticised for its apparently unethical purchasing policy. The company's response was to publicise its involvement in the governance of the businesses in its supply chain. This provides an illustration of one of the ways in which governance practices are diffused around the world.

THEORETICAL BACKGROUND

Two rather different theoretical perspectives are relevant to the study of the relationships between a firm and its stakeholders. Stakeholder theory is rooted in *Kantian ethics*, which emphasises the duty to treat people as ends, never as means to an end. In this context managers have an ethical duty to consider the needs of all stakeholders, not to treat them simply as *factors of production*. Transactions cost economics, sometimes known as new institutional economics, recognises that production costs are not the only costs to be considered when deciding how to produce output. The costs of transacting across markets are relevant and should be taken into account in decisions on outsourcing and vertical mergers. In this section we will explore the two theories before using them to discuss relationships between the company and particular groups of stakeholders.

Stakeholder theory

Stakeholder theory is often attributed to Freeman, who has written and co-authored many books and papers on the subject. However, as he points out in a recent book (Freeman *et al.*, 2010), it might be better to describe it as an approach rather than a theory, because the term stakeholder is used by writers from many disciplines, writing about various aspects of management and organisation. These writers share common ground in that they start from the idea that firms or their managers have an ethical duty towards stakeholders, but they have not developed a unified theory because they seek to investigate different aspects of business; however, in keeping with most of the literature we will continue here to refer to stakeholder theory.

The theory suffers from the fact that there is no single agreed definition of a stakeholder. Early work in the area took the view that stakeholders are groups that affect the firm, while later definitions included also those groups that are affected by it. The early approach would therefore include employees, suppliers, customers and providers of finance, while the later one would include the local and global environment and society. This later definition clearly broadens the scope of the approach and runs the risk of including so many diverse groups that the stakeholder concept becomes unworkable.

Over time more precise definitions have been offered. Starting from the idea that stakeholders affect the firm, Phillips (2003) distinguishes between *normative* and *derivative stakeholders*. The normative group includes those individuals to whom the firm has a clear moral obligation and therefore in whose interests the firm must be run. This includes suppliers of finance, materials and labour as well as customers and the local community. The derivative group includes organisations that have the power to affect or be affected by the normative stakeholders. This group is relevant to management because of its effect on the normative stakeholders as much as because they directly affect the firm. Phillips (2003) includes activists and the media in this category. This distinction implies that managers should make decisions in order to benefit the normative stakeholders, but that they may be constrained by the activity of derivative stakeholders. In a similar vein Van der Laan *et al.* (2008) distinguish between *primary* and *secondary stakeholders*. Primary stakeholders are defined as groups with which the firm makes frequent exchanges, and therefore on which it relies for survival. If the firm's relationship with a primary stakeholder goes sour, it will be ended. Examples include customers and employees. The firm has more limited exchanges with secondary stakeholders such as the environment and society, but cannot simply cease contact with them. For that reason, rather than seeking to manage a relationship with a particular secondary stakeholder, it will instead try to establish a good reputation which will be of benefit later should an exchange take place. In their empirical work, Van der Laan *et al.* (2008) find that firms can improve their accounting performance by improving their relationships with primary stakeholders, specifically with employees, customers and investors, while actions designed to benefit secondary stakeholders can lead to deterioration in financial performance.

In contrast, Harrison and St. John (1994) classify stakeholders according to the degree of influence they exert on the firm and which they feel from it. Going from low to high influence they distinguish between the broad environment, the operating environment and the organisation. As you would probably guess, the broad environment includes society, the economy and the legal-political system; firms find it difficult to have much impact here. The operating environment includes suppliers of material inputs as well as competitors and the local environment; here the firm has some influence over, and is affected by this group. Finally the organisation includes those individuals and groups with formal links to the firm such as suppliers of finance and labour; in this case there is strong influence in both directions. In discussing how management should deal with stakeholders, Harrison and St. John (1994) revert to the effect of stakeholders on the firm, arguing that management should interact more with those stakeholders having a major influence, and less with those who have little influence. They go on to label high interaction as *bridging*, presumably because management is obliged to 'build bridges' with important stakeholders; and they label low interaction as *buffering*, because here the aim is to buffer or protect the firm from adverse influences.

The concepts of the normative and primary stakeholder and of the organisation are clearly very similar, so here we will concentrate on these groups and consider the implications of bridging activities for the way in which the firm is run. As a starting point we will consider how a stakeholder orientation might lead to different corporate behaviour from that observed in a shareholder-centred company. We saw in chapter 2 that the shareholder view stems from the neoclassical economist's theory of the firm. In this theory the firm has a clear objective – to maximise profit. If we are willing to assume that the capital market is efficient, profit maximisation will lead to the maximum possible value of the firm, which is clearly what shareholders want. In order to achieve this, managers must focus on the implications of increasing output of the firm's product, ensuring that they produce up to the point at which the marginal or incremental costs of production are equal to marginal revenue. This apparently simple formula for making shareholders better off highlights the potential for conflict between shareholders and stakeholders. The most obvious ways of improving profit are to reduce costs or increase revenues. If market conditions allow, the former can be done by reducing production costs which implies making employees, suppliers or both worse off, while the latter can be achieved by increasing price which makes consumers worse off. All these groups qualify as normative or primary stakeholders; which explains why so many authors use the phrase 'shareholder versus stakeholder' in discussing the two approaches to the firm. Of course, in the stakeholder view shareholders are stakeholders, so managers cannot ignore their needs, but equally they cannot place their needs above those of other groups.

According to stakeholder theory, managers must explicitly recognise that they have ethical duties to all stakeholders, so while there may be times when they give precedence to one group over another, their overarching aim is to run the company so as to provide satisfactory financial returns and compensation to suppliers of inputs including labour. In this way all stakeholders will be happy to remain part of the business. The economic results of this balancing act may not be very different from those of unconstrained profit maximisation. For example, if management decides to cut wages or bargain aggressively with suppliers they may find that workers strike or leave the company and suppliers pull out of further deals. These actions impose new costs and reduce profit, making shareholders worse off. Keeping other stakeholders happy, productive and loyal may be the best way to raise profits and thereby achieve the shareholders' objectives. This is the type of reasoning used by Jensen (2001) in his formulation of enlightened value maximisation. He argues that the central aim of any company should be to maximise long-term value. However, management will fail in this aim if they simply state it without creating structures in which stakeholders are valued and can work to improve value. When managers are faced with decisions involving a trade-off between different stakeholders they should always recall their primary aim of value maximisation and make the choice that improves value. While to some people this looks like a neat solution to the shareholder versus stakeholder conflict, to stakeholder theorists it remains unacceptable because it denies the existence of an ethical obligation to the firm's stakeholders. For the outsider looking into a company and observing its management, there may be few observable operational differences between an enlightened value-maximising firm and one with a stakeholder objective. However there could be somewhat different governance mechanisms in operation. The enlightened value maximiser might, for example, encourage employee representation on the board of directors or create stakeholder committees which encourage information sharing. We will discuss the implications of such mechanisms in the next section, which examines specific stakeholders in more detail, after first introducing the second theory which underpins the importance of stakeholders in corporate governance.

Transactions cost economics or new institutional economics

New institutional economics is concerned with why it is that some economic activities are coordinated by markets while others take place within corporate hierarchies. In neoclassical economics profit maximisation is equivalent to cost minimisation, but the only costs that are considered are the costs of producing output. New institutional economics considers transactions costs as well. As the name implies, transactions costs are the costs of trading in markets. They include not just direct costs like fees or taxes applicable in specific markets, but also the costs of searching for the appropriate product or service. When the firm's objective becomes the minimisation of the sum of production and transactions costs it becomes clear that if production costs are high but transactions costs are low it would be sensible to buy in certain goods and services rather than to produce them in-house, but if transactions costs are also high it may be better to bring more activity inside the firm and to pay the high production costs. Production costs are determined by the state of technology, so the key question is 'what determines the level of transactions costs?'

Transactions costs economics explicitly recognises the uncertainty that exists in any transaction. Unless the product in question is a standardised commodity, buyers will always be uncertain about quality and may also worry about delivery, while sellers will be concerned about the possibility of late or no payment. These concerns arise because of two fundamental human characteristics, *bounded rationality* and *opportunism*. Bounded rationality simply means that it is impossible for any individual to fully understand every aspect of each trade they enter. When buying a car, for instance, a person may read specialist magazines and talk to knowledgeable people but the cost of eliminating every uncertainty is so great that if they collect every available scrap of information they will never get around to making the purchase. Their problems with this purchase are made worse by the fact that they fear that the car salesperson will take advantage of their lack of knowledge to sell them something that is not suitable for them, in other words, they may behave opportunistically to ensure a sale. Here is the major contrast between stakeholder theory and transactions costs economics. Stakeholder theory is based on the idea that it is wrong to use people as means to an end, yet this is exactly what transactions costs theory assumes will happen unless mechanisms can be put in place to prevent it.

Every business uses material and labour inputs to produce an output. Management is aware that they, as users of inputs, suffer from bounded rationality because when buying inputs they are unsure of their quality. They are also aware that the input suppliers may behave opportunistically and attempt to supply inferior products. Equally, the input suppliers fear opportunistic behaviour by the management team which may make late payments or attempt to change the nature of the deal struck with the supplier. This problem can be solved in two ways. Either the buyer and seller of the input can agree a contract which defines exactly what each party has to do, or they can create a governance mechanism which monitors both parties and/or encourages them to build up trust which will reduce opportunism and allow for greater information sharing to overcome bounded rationality. Either mechanism can reduce transactions costs; the choice depends on the nature of the input being traded and on the cultural context within which the exchange takes place.

The more complicated the input being supplied, the harder it is to describe completely both parties' responsibilities in a contract. Contracts for commodities like wheat or oil are easy to specify because everyone agrees on the characteristics of the product. A contract for services is harder to write and enforce because the quality of the service provided is not observable at the time the contract is signed. For example, when a business employs a receptionist it cannot be sure that they will be courteous to all visitors on all occasions, in other words, the quality of the service is only observed as it is being provided. In some instances quality is only discernible after the service has been provided, as is the case with some medical procedures. In such cases governance mechanisms are more effective that contracts. Culture plays a part in that some situations naturally lead to trust and others do not. For example, in the aftermath of a strike employers and employees are likely to demand binding agreements from one another rather than suggest a looser monitoring system. In societies built on consensus decision making, governance mechanisms are likely to be preferred to explicit contracts.

KEY STAKEHOLDING GROUPS

In this section we will consider four groups of primary stakeholders: employees, lenders, suppliers and customers. We will think about the nature of the duties owed to them by the company and the ways in which they may become involved in corporate governance.

Employees

In chapter 2 we considered the argument that shareholders have a special place in corporate governance because they bear residual risk. In the event of bankruptcy they can expect to lose the entire value of their capital because the firm will be liquidated in order to repay creditors. Boatright (2004) argues that shareholders are not unique in this respect. Employees are required to build up *firm-specific human capital*, in other words, skills that are required in this particular context but have limited usefulness elsewhere. If the firm goes bankrupt its employees will lose the value of their firm-specific human capital, making them bearers of residual risk and hence entitled to some control rights. Unlike shareholders, employees spend their working lives in the firm and so have greater insight into its day-to-day operations, giving them unique information that can improve the quality of decision-making, provided that a forum exists in which they can pass on that information. In practice, the status of employees and their role in the governance process varies tremendously both between countries and between companies in any given country.

Employees have a guaranteed place in corporate governance in those few countries where codetermination is legally mandated. It is found in various forms in Northern and Eastern European countries but is rare elsewhere. Codetermination is a decision-making process in which management has a duty to involve employees in decision making through board representation. It is usually practised in countries which operate the dual-board system which was described in chapter 3, in which a management board makes decisions which are then scrutinised by a supervisory board onto which employees can elect a fixed proportion of members. That proportion is one-third in Denmark and in Austria, where the proportion also applies to the board's sub-committees. In Norway the one-third rule applies to companies with more than 50 employees, while in Luxembourg it affects companies with at least 1000 employees or with government ownership of at least 25 per cent. German workers elect one-half of the members of the supervisory board in companies with over 2000 employees, and one-third in companies with a workforce of between 500 and 2000. In Sweden, too, employee representation depends on firm size, but is it not specified in terms of a proportion of board members. Instead, in companies with between 25 and 1000 employees the workers can elect two board members and two deputies, while in companies with over 1000 employees the workers elect three members and five deputies. The situation in Finland is more complex. Employees must negotiate with the firm to decide how many board members they can elect. If negotiations fail, the company moves to a default position in which employees nominate representatives to join the board, the supervisory board or a management team that lies outside the scope of company law. It is up to the firm's management to decide which body the representatives will join. In practice this system leads to little board representation of employees.

Codetermination is encouraged in several of the emerging markets of Eastern Europe, but even where it is mandatory the regulations tend to be imprecise. In Slovakia, employees elect one-half of the board in state-owned companies, and one-third in private companies, unless the company itself decides to increase the proportion to one half. The situation in Slovenia is similar; companies with supervisory boards can decide whether to allow employees to elect one-third or one-half of the board's members. The corporate governance codes in the Czech Republic and Turkey encourage board participation by employees but do not prescribe it, while in Serbia, if employees are permitted to sit on the management board they do not necessarily have the right to vote.

Research on employee representation on boards has focused on the extent to which employees are able to affect decision-making by pursuing their own agendas. Rose (2008) interviewed employee representatives on Danish boards to find out how they perceived their role in the decision-making process. Of these, 40 per cent believed they had some influence while 29 per cent felt they had a high degree of influence; only 7 per cent believed they had no influence at all. Not surprisingly, when they compared themselves with other board members they felt their priorities were different. The labour representatives claimed a greater interest in employees, trade unions, the community, environment and society and a lesser concern for owners, dividends and the stock market.

Other authors have suggested that because labour representatives have different priorities from shareholders, they may cause boards to make decisions that are not always in shareholders' best interests. Fitzroy and Kraft (1993) and Gorton and Schmidt (2004) have examined this hypothesis in the context of a comparison between German companies whose employees elect one-third of the board and those that elect one-half. Fitzroy and Kraft (1993) compare a sample of companies in 1975 and 1983, so that they could see the impact of the 1976 Codetermination Act that introduced the requirement for companies with over 2000 employees to allow employees to elect one-half of the board. They find that equal board representation of labour depressed value added, return on equity and total factor productivity. The German economy was experiencing a downturn in both 1975 and 1983, so the authors argue that the results were due to labour hoarding during the recession. Interestingly, Gorton and Schmidt (2004) report a similar finding over the period 1989–93. They find that equal board representation leads to a higher ratio of employees to sales. Taken together these two papers imply that whatever the state of the economy, employment is higher in firms where employees have more board control, indicating that employees influence the objectives of the company, and reduce the surplus available for distribution to shareholders as they protect labour interests.

Fauver and Fuerst (2006) argue that this is only half of the story. They hypothesise an inverted U-shaped relationship between labour representation on the board and corporate performance. Over some levels of representation the company benefits from improved relationships with employees and better information flows from workers to management. As representation grows beyond an optimal level there is increased pressure to hoard labour which increases costs and damages company performance. In their empirical work they find some support for this argument, certainly on the upward-sloping part of the curve, when they look at the interaction between labour representation and corporate complexity. In companies that require specialist skill sets there is a positive relationship between firm value and employee representation, which is entirely consistent with transactions costs theory which posits that special governance arrangements are required to deal with complex situations. Further, they report that higher labour representation leads to higher dividend payments which they interpret as a reduction in agency costs, implying that employee-directors have a valuable monitoring function which is beneficial to all stakeholders.

Outside countries where codetermination is legally required it is rare to find employees sitting on boards. In the UK and US the phrase 'management's right to manage' summarises the view that decision making is the responsibility of a few carefully chosen people and that information normally flows down the corporate hierarchy to the workforce rather than upwards from it. This approach, however, is not without its critics even in the US, where some legal scholars argue in favour of greater employee participation in decision making. Bodie (2007) argues that employees should be able to take part in non-binding votes on corporate restructuring. The outcome of the vote would then form part of the information given to shareholders before their vote on the matter, giving them a new perspective on the proposed deal. Craver (1997) goes further, suggesting that codetermination should be introduced in the US. He recognises that this could lead to conflicts on the board, as shareholders and employee representatives pursue their separate agendas. To combat this he argues that all directors would have a dual fiduciary duty to both shareholders and employees. We will return to the controversial notion of multi-fiduciary duties later in this chapter.

Lenders

Lenders occupy an interesting and at times controversial place in corporate governance. They have been characterised as part of the agency problem by Jensen and Meckling (1976), who argue that there is an inevitable tension between shareholders and bondholders because of their differential rights in the event of bankruptcy. When a firm goes into liquidation the creditors take control of the firm, making them important actors in the corporate governance process. However they may be important even before bankruptcy, because in order to protect themselves they impose restrictive *covenants* as part of their loan agreements, allowing them to become involved in governance before liquidation occurs. Some legal scholars have argued that creditors should not be left in the position of having to protect themselves; instead they should be able to benefit from the same type of fiduciary duty enjoyed by shareholders. Here we will consider why there may be a conflict between lenders and shareholders, how lenders use covenants to protect their interests and how this leads to their involvement in corporate governance. We will then go on to discuss the controversy surrounding the idea that managers owe a fiduciary duty to all suppliers of funds and indeed to other groups, not just to shareholders.

We began our discussion of employees by suggesting that they, like shareholders, bear residual risk because they lose all their firm-specific capital in the event of bankruptcy. Lenders are in a very different situation, which may lead to conflicts between them and other stakeholders. Lenders enter an agreement to receive a particular rate of interest during the lifetime of the loan, and to have the principal repaid when the loan matures. Their position is certain as long as the company has sufficient cash to make the agreed payments. If the company does not have enough cash, the lenders can force it into liquidation and will be at the head of the queue of people waiting to get (at least some of) their money back. In the event of liquidation the shareholders are at the back of the queue and are unlikely to recover anything. The legal precedence of lenders over shareholders in the case of bankruptcy is reflected in the accounting treatment of routine payments to the two groups. Interest payments are a cost to the firm, so are paid before profit is declared and taxed. Dividend payments are a distribution of after-tax profit, so the higher the payments made to lenders, the smaller is the residual available for the shareholders. Here then are the foundations of a potential conflict between the two groups.

The conflict may become real when the company comes to choose new projects. Suppose the company has borrowed money and has a commitment to pay interest of £10,000 this year. It faces a choice of two projects; each has an expected payoff this year of £50,000, but this masks the fact that A may produce either £0 or £100,000 with equal probability, while B may produce £10,000 or £90,000, again with equal probability. From the lenders' point of view, B is clearly superior because it guarantees sufficient cash flow for the firm to be able to meet its obligation to pay interest. However, the shareholders may well prefer A. In both cases, if things go wrong there is nothing left for them, but if things go well A has a residual value of £90,000 while B's residual value is only £80,000.

You may argue that this example is flawed because it assumes that the shareholders take a very short-term view of the firm. Indeed it does, because if A is chosen and things go badly the lenders will force the firm into liquidation so as to get some money back, and the shareholders' equity will have zero value. However, before you dismiss the idea that shareholders have an incentive to make the lenders' position more risky, consider a situation in which this would be rational. Suppose the firm is already in *financial distress*. That is, the firm cannot generate enough cash to meet all its obligations simultaneously. This means that by making interest payments when they are due, the company cannot afford to pay other bills. As far as the shareholders are concerned, this company looks as if it is going to go bankrupt. If it does they will lose their stake, so why not take a risk and try to get something out of it? After all, if it fails all that happens is that the end comes slightly quicker than it otherwise would, and part of their portfolio is wiped out. If it works, they get a return. In this situation it is rational for self-interested shareholders to encourage managers to accept the risky project. The managers may agree, seeing this as a last-ditch attempt to save the company and their jobs. The managers and shareholders are even more likely to go ahead and take the risk if the company is located in a part of the world where legislation shields the firm from lenders' attempts to force liquidation. The best-known example of such a situation is Chapter 11 of the US bankruptcy law. By using the protection this offers, a company is temporarily relieved of the obligation to make interest payments, while it is reorganised.

This is not the only way in which shareholders or indeed managers can change the risk faced by lenders during financial distress. Rather than investing in very risky projects, they may go to the other extreme and refuse to invest in order to avoid further risk. In the longer run this is just as damaging because it restricts future cash flows and hence the firm's ability to make payments to any stakeholders.

While this strategy leaves unused funds in the business, another damaging course of action in the face of financial distress is to use cash to pay dividends to the shareholders. Shareholders who vote in favour of dividend payments in this situation jeopardise lenders just as much as they would by choosing risky projects or refusing to invest at all.

Empirical evidence on the relationship between bond spreads and corporate governance variables supports the existence of an agency problem between bondholders and either managers or shareholders, and indicates that better governed firms enjoy a lower cost of borrowing because the firm appears less risky. Cremers *et al.* (2007) show that higher bond yields are associated with the presence of a single blockholder, indicating that bondholders believe a controlling shareholder will attempt to transfer risk to lenders. However, when a firm with a single blockholder adopts anti-takeover devices, the relationship becomes negative, as it is in the case of companies with multiple blockholders. This shows that when lenders have further protection in the form of anti-takeover devices or the presence of other large shareholders their situation is less risky. Not all researchers agree that multiple blockholders benefit bondholders. Bhojraj and Sengupta (2003) find that the larger the proportion of equity held by blockholders, the higher are bond yields and the lower are credit ratings. However they also find that other indicators of good governance do lead to higher ratings and lower yields. The higher the percentage of outside directors on the board, and the higher the proportion of equity owned by institutions that are not blockholders, the lower is the cost of borrowing and the higher is the credit rating. While the measures used in these papers differ, the results indicate that an agency problem exists between lenders and managers and/or shareholders, and the problem can be eased by good governance.

Rational lenders will not simply wait for companies to adopt sound governance. They will take steps to protect themselves by imposing covenants on the loan. Debt covenants form part of the terms and conditions of the loan. They specify a set of circumstances under which the lender can demand immediate repayment of the loan. The circumstances may relate to the liquidity or profit levels of the company or to levels of spending on investment or dividends. In other words, they point to behaviour which could lead to default and allow the lender to step in and demand repayment while there is still a good chance of getting some money from the firm. This direct disciplinary nature of debt explains why it is suggested as a bonding device for managers to use to show shareholders that they are trustworthy. When managers choose to issue debt rather than equity they voluntarily submit to debt covenants that reduce their decision-making autonomy and thereby indicate that they will not use the company's cash flows for their own benefit. They also draw lenders into the firm's corporate governance system.

While covenants give lenders the benefit of protection against opportunistic behaviour by managers and shareholders, they also impose a cost on them. Having specified that the company must, for example, maintain a particular level of liquidity, it is then up to the lender to monitor the firm's liquidity levels to ensure that the covenant is not breached. If the company fails to maintain adequate liquidity this quarter and the lender lets it pass, it may then be impossible to call in the loan in the future if liquidity levels fall again. This is because the court may apply the so-called 'doctrine of waiver', which states that once you have waived a right to act today, you effectively give up that right in the future too. In a country like the US whose legal system includes the doctrine of waiver, debt covenants therefore give lenders a continuous monitoring function, making them an important part of the governance process. In an interesting study of the collapse of L.A. Gear, De Angelo *et al.* (2002) show that the covenants imposed by the Bank of America restricted the company's discretion far more than the simple need to keep making interest payments, which was highlighted by Jensen and Meckling (1976) in their discussions of bonding. The bank imposed restrictions on the company's net worth and quarterly earnings figures which effectively imposed minimum operating standards. L.A. Gear was forced to highlight situations where it was close to a breach of the covenants in order to avoid immediate liquidation. This enabled the bank to continually renegotiate its lending and reduce the risks associated with this particular lender.

Nini *et al.* (2009) support the view that creditors have an important governance role to play. They examine a large sample of American firms that breached loan covenants during the period 1996–2007. Very few lenders exercised their right to demand immediate repayment; instead they worked with firms to strengthen governance through strategies such as changing the CEO, restructuring and reduced capital spending. The interventions led to improved operating performance and market value, and even prompted the authors to suggest that the weak evidence of a link between shareholder-based governance and corporate performance can be explained by the fact that lenders bear the brunt of the monitoring process.

Box 4.1 *Crédit Lyonnais Bank Nederland v. Pathé Communications Corp.*

At the time of this case Pathé Communications (PCC) owned 98 per cent of the equity in MGM, which had just defaulted on loans provided by Crédit Lyonnais. The bank obtained agreement to set up an executive committee which would take on most of the powers of the MGM board until such time as PCC could reduce the company's debt to an acceptable level by selling assets. Crucially the executive committee retained the right to approve all asset sales suggested by PCC.

When it rejected the company's plan on the grounds that it would impair the company's ability to continue in business, PCC claimed that there had been a breach of the fiduciary duty owed to it as the major shareholder in MGM. The judge held that no such breach had occurred because when a company is in the 'zone of insolvency' the board owes a duty to the company rather than to its shareholders.

There is little doubt that lenders and shareholders find themselves in conflict with shareholders, and that lenders play an important governance role. Does this mean that they, like shareholders, should benefit from a fiduciary duty owed by corporate management? It has become common to argue that the concept of fiduciary duty is being extended to include stakeholders in both the UK and the US. Keay (2010) argues that s.172 of the UK Companies Act 2006, in which directors are told to take account of stakeholders' interests, is leading British governance down a stakeholder path. To put this section in context, directors are required to consider stakeholders when running the company for the benefit of its members. In other words, it implies enlightened value-maximisation. Tung (2007) suggests that the ruling in the 1991 case of *Crédit Lyonnais Bank Nederland v. Pathé Communications Corp.* (the facts of which are given in box 4.1) set American law on a path towards a set of multi-fiduciary duties. The judge in this case ruled that when a company is in the 'vicinity' of bankruptcy its management has a fiduciary duty to its creditors as well as to its shareholders; and in this instance the judgement went against the majority shareholder and in favour of the creditors. A more recent judgement from 2007 (see box 4.2) has apparently overturned this view, but it is unlikely that the debate will simply go away.

Box 4.2 *North American Catholic Educational Programming Foundation, Inc. v. Gheewalla*

In this case the North American Catholic Educational Programming Foundation (NACEPF) was a creditor of Clearwire Holdings, Inc. The NACEPF claimed that while Clearwater was in the zone of insolvency it had failed to preserve its assets for the benefit of its creditors and had thereby breached its fiduciary duty to them. In this case the judge ruled against the Pathé decision by stating that no such fiduciary duty existed because creditors have other forms of legal protection available to them.

Tung (2007) is very critical of the concept of multi-fiduciary duties. He argues that while shareholders have common rights, lenders are not a cohesive group because they hold different types of debt, some secured, some not; some long-term, some short-term; and so on, such that their different contracts have already taken account of their individual situations. This argument could also be applied to employees when some have indefinite employment and others have short-term contracts. Further, Tung (2007) is concerned that if fiduciary duties are extended to other groups this will lead to inefficiencies in bargaining and increased costs of litigation with stakeholders. It will be interesting to see how both case law and governance practices evolve in response to this controversy.

Suppliers

Most companies, unless they choose a strategy of vertical integration, are part of a supply chain. A supply chain is a group of companies each of which plays a different part in the variety of production processes that transforms raw materials into finished products. A consumer buying a car may think of it as a Ford or a Fiat, but in fact those companies have assembled a number of parts from different suppliers without whom the company would cease to exist, at least in its current form, making those suppliers stakeholders in Ford and Fiat. In this example the motor manufacturer is the dominant company in the supply chain. It can dictate the nature of the relationship between itself and an individual supplier, but it will choose different types of relationship based on the type of input traded. Broadly speaking, companies within supply chains can choose between agreements which are self-enforcing or enforced by a third party (Dyer and Singh, 1998). Third-party enforcement is costly unless the relationship between the companies is easily specified in a contract, as is the case when a standardised product is traded. When the end product and its component parts change frequently, for example because they are fashion items, a self-enforcing agreement is more cost effective. This type of agreement may be formal or informal.

In a formal agreement the supplying company either invests in assets which are used solely for the supply of products to a particular purchaser, or uses a production process specified by the purchaser. Williamson (1979) argues from a transactions costs approach that this is efficient for both parties. While it may appear that the supplier has a lot to lose from the arrangement, in fact the purchaser clearly needs a specialist input and cannot easily switch to another supplier, so this type of arrangement in which both sides are 'locked in' is beneficial for both. However, not everyone agrees that this type of arrangement has benefits for both parties. British supermarkets have been criticised for the way they manage relationships with the suppliers of fresh vegetables. Most of the fresh vegetables available in British supermarkets come from Africa. The African growers are required to standardise the product as much as possible and to wash, package and keep the vegetables in cold storage prior to shipping. Supermarkets dictate what processes are to be used, and require the growers to invest in the necessary equipment. This type of activity has been criticised by the British media, which views this as an unequal relationship in which the supermarkets exploit their suppliers. Dolan and Humphrey (2000) explain that African horticulture has been fundamentally changed by its relationship with British supermarkets. Companies that previously exported fresh produce have bought small horticultural businesses to create large suppliers, which although they cannot match large supermarket chains in terms of market power, are less vulnerable than smaller suppliers would be. Even when suppliers are required to purchase specific assets, this does not eliminate opportunism. Production arrangements must be verified, for example Tesco has teams of people, 'hit squads', whose job is to make unannounced spot-checks on the growers to make sure that the vegetables are being correctly harvested, washed and packaged. Clearly this is expensive, so some visits are contracted out to external auditors.

Informal agreements are based on trust and information sharing between the supplying and purchasing companies. A good example of this approach is Toyota (Dyer and Singh, 1998), which has an operations management consulting division which sends consultants to spend time in its supplier's plants, explaining Toyota's needs and sharing knowledge with a group of companies with which it has established long-term relationships. In contrast, at that time General Motors had short-term contracts with its suppliers and retained proprietary knowledge. When Dyer and Singh wrote their paper, General Motors' procurement costs were six times those of Toyota. This example illustrates the benefits that can arise from the type of inter-firm agreements that are possible within a keiretsu. They go on to report that companies like Hewlett-Packard, Xerox and Microsoft are increasingly recognising the need for good relationships within their supply chain, and are appointing directors of strategic alliances. This type of initiative is valuable because it protects the company from the risk of buying shoddy inputs, but it also helps it to protect its reputation which can be affected if it is seen to be buying inputs from companies with poor ethical track records. The Primark case at the end of this chapter looks at this aspect of supply-chain management.

Customers

No company can survive without customers, yet the corporate governance litera-ture says very little about this vital group of stakeholders. It is true that they are always mentioned as primary stakeholders, but one has to read literature on marketing to gain an understanding of the ways in which customers affect the companies whose products and services they buy. Clearly if customers are happy with the products they buy they will make repeat purchases and may even tell their friends about them, leading to an increase in market share and profitability and ultimately in share price for the company that can create happy customers. A number of papers have used the American Customer Satisfaction Index (ASCI) to study the influence of customer satisfaction on corporate performance. The ASCI was developed at the Ross School of Business at the University of Michigan. It uses interviews with customers to derive an index of satisfaction ranging from 0 to 100, with higher index values indicating more satisfaction.

Researchers have used a variety of methodologies to illustrate the relationship between corporate performance and customer satisfaction. Anderson *et al.* (2004) and Fornell *et al.* (2006) use simple regression models in which a performance measure is regressed on company ASCI scores together with a variety of control variables. They find that both the market value of equity (Fornell *et al.*, 2006) and Tobin's q (Anderson *et al.*, 2004) are positively and significantly related to customer satisfaction. Fornell *et al.* (2006) go on to create a portfolio comprising the compa-nies in the top 20 per cent of ASCI scores. They find that this portfolio outper-forms the Dow Jones Industrial Average. In a similar vein, Aksoy *et al.* (2008) create portfolios with high and low ASCI scores and find that the companies with high (low) scores outperform (underperform) the Standard and Poor's 500 index. They also calculate risk-adjusted returns for the companies with high ASCI scores and find that this group produces positive abnormal returns, confirming the link between customer satisfaction and corporate performance.

Recently there has been a lot of interest in the so-called 'ethical consumer', an individual whose buying decisions are based on personal ethics, and who therefore takes an interest not just in what companies make but how they produce it. An ethical consumer might seek out products that are made with organic ingredients or are fairly traded, and would not buy products made using child or forced labour or that have been tested on animals. If the ethical consumer is an important phenomenon, then companies should be aware of this, and consider whether or not they need to change their production methods and supply-chain management or even to become more involved in activities related to corporate social respon-sibility. Carrigan and Atalla (2001) note that while many consumers are aware of well-publicised cases of unethical behaviour, such as Nestlé's marketing of breast milk substitutes and Exxon's behaviour with respect to environmental damage, they are not generally aware of ethical issues. They also discuss the evidence that even where consumers are aware of ethical issues and say they are important, this awareness does not lead them to change their buying behaviour. In their own empirical work they interview groups of people aged 18 to 25 and find that while they are aware of low pay and conditions for workers in developing countries employed by large multinational companies, they are not concerned. Instead they believe that multinational companies treat their employees better than local businesses do, and so they would not change their buying behaviour in the light of scandals over working conditions. Interestingly, while these groups are apparently unconcerned about human rights, they are prepared to boycott brands whose production violates animal rights. The authors acknowledge that consumers in other age categories might have different attitudes, but their findings support the view that while consumers often say they are concerned about ethics, they are not always so concerned that it affects their behaviour.

Despite this, Luo and Bhattacharya (2006) comment on the growing use of 'cause' advertising in which companies discuss their concerns over social issues rather than their products. Recent examples seen in the UK include the Pampers nappies advertisements in which consumers are encouraged to buy the product because Procter and Gamble is supporting a tetanus vaccination campaign run by UNICEF, and the Triple Velvet toilet tissue advertisement that features the tree-planting scheme run by Svenska Cellulosa Aktiebolaget (SCA). They suggest that companies advertise in this way to promote their social responsibility, which contributes to customer satisfaction, which then leads to higher corporate value. They find empirical support for this hypothesis in that customer satisfaction, again measured by ASCI scores, is affected by corporate social responsibility rankings from the *Fortune* America's Most Admired Companies database. In turn customer satisfaction has a positive effect on both Tobin's q and stock market returns.

In some cases satisfied customers become an important element of a company's marketing strategy, with or without explicit intervention by the company concerned. This can happen when customers form 'brand communities', groups of customers who share a passion for a particular brand, meet together in either a physical or a virtual sense to talk about or experience the brand, and may then try to persuade others to join them. Possibly the best-known brand community is the network of Harley-Davidson Owners' Groups (HOGs). The company encourages new owners to join HOGs which receive some funding from Harley-Davidson. The HOGs themselves organise local chapters with their own events, as well as national events bringing together bike riders from all over a particular country. Apple customers are an equally loyal group of people who will happily extol the virtues of Apple products to anyone who will listen, and also form their own user groups which are completely independent of the company. In fact, when Apple discontinued production of the Newton, an early personal digital assistant, Apple user groups continued to provide support for the device (Algesheimer *et al.*, 2005). This is an example of the loyalty and enthusiasm customers feel for a particular product, but it also shows how customers can subvert corporate strategy by increasing the lifetime of a product that the company would like to replace. Most brand communities from around luxury or niche products, but in rarer cases manufacturers can create a similar excitement around products with a mass appeal. Cova and Pace (2006) describe how Ferrero created a website devoted to Nutella. Consumers use the site to share photographs, recipes and simply their reasons for loving the product. Websites like this become part of a strategy of *relationship marketing*.

Early marketing literature concentrated on how to attract new customers, while relationship marketing considers how companies can retain loyal customers. Berry

(1995) describes three levels of relationship marketing activities. Level one uses competitive pricing to inspire brand loyalty, level two uses social interaction or regular communication to retain customers, while level three involves tailor-making solutions to individual customer's problems. This type of relationship marketing is relevant in areas such as software supply to major businesses, or dress-making services for wealthy clients, but it is hard to see how it can be applied in a mass market. The proliferation of loyalty cards issued by supermarkets and coffee shops can be seen as an element of level two relationship marketing. In addition to providing a reason for regular direct mailings to members, these cards also allow companies to collect a lot of information about their customers and their buying habits, which can be helpful in determining future strategy. However, they have become so widespread that they may no longer serve a social function.

Clearly customers are a vital stakeholding group, but unlike the other stake-holders considered here, they may be a rather less coherent and more fluid group. Most companies rely on a stable group of employees and suppliers, and if they need to borrow would go to a bank or other lender with whom they have an estab-lished relationship. Customers in some industries would seek out a particular supplier, but in some cases will show little brand loyalty. This author carries many loyalty cards in her purse, indicating that in fact she is disloyal in her choice of supermarket and café. In cases like this neither companies nor customers have the incentive to work together over governance issues. Cooperation is more likely in the case of products with longer lifetimes such as motorcycles and cars, where both parties can gain from long-term relationships and information sharing.

CONCLUSION

Every company has multiple stakeholders including employees, lenders and suppliers as well as shareholders. The literature on stakeholders treats them as discrete groups, but of course in many cases they will overlap. It is easy to see that an employee might also consume their employer's products and own some equity thanks to a share-ownership scheme. All academic authors agree that company managers must be concerned about their stakeholders because without them the company could not exist. Where they disagree is over whether that concern extends to an ethical or fiduciary duty of the kind usually associated with share-holders. Stakeholder theorists say that it does and therefore that stakeholders should take part in corporate governance mechanisms. The extent to which stake-holders take part in governance varies around the world. Many European countries have legislation on codetermination allowing the employees of large companies to elect supervisory board members. This does not happen in the UK and US, but some scholars argue that subtle changes in the law in both countries are leading to a situation in which directors owe a fiduciary duty to stakeholders as well as to shareholders. There is certainly evidence that creditors play an important role in the governance of the firm to which they lend and that dominant companies in supply chains affect the policies of other companies in the chain.

These observations serve to reinforce the idea that there is no single set of prac-tices that can be labelled 'good corporate governance'. Companies within a single country will differ in governance terms depending on their size, leverage and place in their supply chain. Inter-country differences will be greater because of the influence of local law and culture.

KEY POINTS

- Stakeholders can be narrowly defined as groups with the power to influence the company, or more broadly defined to include groups that are influenced by it. Corporate governance usually focuses on the former definition, while the latter would be used in discussions of corporate social responsibility.
- A stakeholder approach to management starts from the point of view that managers have an ethical duty towards stakeholders, and that they should not consistently subordinate the needs of one group to another. It recognises that each stakeholder has access to a unique information set and can therefore contribute something distinct to the governance process.
- The shareholder approach to corporate governance can accommodate the needs of stakeholders through the concept of enlightened value-maximisation. Stakeholder theorists would not endorse this approach because it uses value creation as the criterion for making trade-offs between stakeholders.
- Transactions costs economics provides a framework in which one can analyse why some stakeholders have formal contracts with companies while others have relationships based on trust. Generally, the more complex the product that is traded, the harder it is to write a contract so trust becomes a cost-effective way of maintaining the relationship.
- Lenders and dominant companies within supply chains perform governance activities in most countries, but employees are involved only in countries where codetermination is practised.
- The literature on corporate governance includes customers as an important stakeholding group but offers little guidance on how they can become involved in governance. The marketing literature shows how for some product types customers can become a valuable part of companies' marketing strategies.

CASE STUDY Supply-chain management and the real cost of fashion at Primark

Primark has become a force to be reckoned with on the British high street. It is the UK's leading supplier of value fashion and was loved by budget-conscious teenagers before the credit crunch prompted their parents to start shopping there. It has managed to increase like-for-like sales while other retailers have struggled through the recession. Primark is owned by Associated British Foods plc, a company founded in 1935 as the parent of seven bakery subsidiaries. Looking at the businesses that make up Associated British Foods, Primark stands out as the cuckoo in the nest alongside brands like Allinson's bread, Billington's sugar and Twinings tea. However, this cuckoo was responsible for generating 33 per cent of the group's profit in 2009.

Primark is popular because it is cheap. Some people have questioned how the company is able to sell products as cheaply as it does. The answer given on the Primark website is that the company is able to buy in bulk, uses the best available logistics systems and doesn't incur advertising costs. In 2008 the British charity War on Want added another reason – buying from sweatshops. The charity published a report in which it named Primark, along with ASDA and Tesco, as a purchaser of clothing made in Bangladeshi factories where people work for up to 90 hours a week earning less than the estimated living wage. *Panorama*, a TV documentary programme, then went on to report that it also sourced garments from Indian factories that subcontract work to home workers using child labour and from British suppliers employing illegal immigrants. The company was quick to respond by changing suppliers and publishing details of its ethical policy.

Primark has a code of conduct for its suppliers. The code is based on the declaration issued by the International Labor Organization in 1998. It states that no bonded or child labour should be used, workers should be able to associate freely and engage in collective bargaining, working conditions should be safe and hygienic, wages should meet the local standard of a living wage, hours of work should not be excessive, employment should be regular and there should be no discrimination. Before agreeing to buy from a supplier, Primark uses a third party to check that it meets the standards laid down. Existing suppliers are audited to ensure that they continue to comply. Primark reports that in 2008 it organised checks at 162 suppliers and 340 production facilities. Of these audits, 70 per cent were carried out by third-party professionals and the remaining 30 per cent by a team from Primark itself. The company gives a detailed description of the most commonly observed breaches of their code, and goes on to explain how they use remediation to change practices. In the remediation process, Primark works with its suppliers to encourage them to improve working conditions and management systems. Finally the company offers training to its suppliers to enable them to meet the code of conduct.

Clearly a case like this can be considered from many different viewpoints. Readers will have a view on the ethics of the situation, but here the focus is on corporate governance. This case highlights the fact that companies are judged not just on their own performance, but on their choice of suppliers and the way they monitor their supply chains. Ethical consumers and charities expect companies to adhere to certain principles even when operating abroad in countries where the principles are not the norm. A statement on the Primark website says that the Indian companies that sub-contracted work to child labourers denied the practice even in the face of evidence supplied by the BBC. This illustrates the fact that it is very difficult to monitor complex global supply chains. The way in which Primark and others audit their suppliers also shows that one company can exert control over the decisions of another without any ownership rights. The corporate governance literature has traditionally concentrated on the way in which management has taken over control from owners. Here we have an example of control being taken by the management of other companies.

CASE-STUDY QUESTIONS

1 Why does Primark have an incentive to monitor its supply chain closely?
2 Given your knowledge of transactions costs economics, is Primark's supply chain management efficient?
3 Should Primark treat as stakeholders the people who are employed by its suppliers?

REVISION QUESTIONS

1 What kinds of stakeholders have the greatest incentive to get involved with corporate governance?
2 Do managers have fiduciary duties to stakeholders?
3 What is codetermination, and in what ways might it benefit companies?
4 What are debt covenants, and how might they be useful in corporate governance terms?
5 Why do some supply chains rely on contracts while others use trust to govern relationships?
6 How would a stakeholder-oriented company differ from one with a shareholder focus?

REFERENCES

Aksoy, L., Cooil, B., Groening, C. Keiningham, T.L. and Yalçin, A. (2008) 'The Long Term Stock Valuation of Customer Satisfaction' *Journal of Marketing* 72 (4) 105–122

Algesheimer, R., Dholakia, U.M. and Herrmann, A. (2005) 'The Social Influence of Brand Community: Evidence from European Car Clubs' *Journal of Marketing* 69 (3) 19–34

Anderson, E.W., Fornell, C. and Mazvancheryl, S.K. (2004) 'Customer Satisfaction and Shareholder Value' *Journal of Marketing* 68 (4) 172–185

Berry, L.L. (1995) 'Relationship Marketing of Services – Growing Interest, Emerging Perspectives' *Journal of the Academy of Marketing Science* 23 (4) 236–245

Bhojraj, S. and Sengupta, P. (2003) 'Effects of Corporate Governance on Bond Ratings and Yields: The Role of Institutional Investors and Outside Directors' *Journal of Business* 76 (3) 455–475

Boatright, J.R. (2004) 'Employee Governance and the Ownership of the Firm' *Business Ethics Quarterly* 14 (1) 1–21

Bodie, M.T. (2007) 'The Case For Employee Referenda on Transformative Transactions as Shareholder Proposals' *Washington University Law Review* 87, 897–905

Carrigan, M. and Atalla, A. (2001) 'The Myth of the Ethical Consumer – Do Ethics Matter in Purchase Behaviour?' *Journal of Consumer Marketing* 18 (7) 560–577

Companies Act 2006, London: HMSO

Cova, B. and Pace, S. (2006) 'Brand Community of Convenience Products: New Forms of Customer Empowerment – The Case of "My Nutella the Community"' *European Journal of Marketing* 40 (9/10) 1087–1105

Craver, C.B. (1997) 'Mandatory Worker Participation is Required in a Declining Union Environment to Provide Employees with Meaningful Industrial Democracy' *George Washington Law Review* 66 (1) 135–171

Cremers, K. J. M., Nair, V.B. and Wei, C. (2007) 'Governance Mechanisms and Bond Prices' *Review of Financial Studies* 20 (3) 1359–1388

De Angelo, H., DeAngelo, L. and Wruck, K.H. (2002) 'Asset Liquidity, Debt Covenants, and Managerial Discretion in Financial Distress: The Collapse of L.A. Gear' *Journal of Financial Economics* 64 (1) 3–34

Dolan, C. and Humphrey, J. (2000) 'Governance and Trade in Fresh Vegetables: The Impact of UK Supermarkets on the African Horticultural Industry' *Journal of Development Studies* 37 (2) 147–175

Dyer, J.H. and Singh, H. (1998) 'The Relational View: Cooperative Strategy and Sources of Interorganizational Competitive Advantage' *Academy of Management Review* 23 (4) 660–679

Fauver, L. and Fuerst, M.E. (2006) 'Does Good Corporate Governance Include Employee Representation? Evidence From German Corporate Boards' *Journal of Financial Economics* 82 (3) 673–710

Fitzroy, F.R. and Kraft, K. (1993) 'Economic Effects of Codetermination' *Scandinavian Journal of Economics* 95 (3) 365–375

Fornell, C. Mithas, S., Morgenson, F.V. and Krishnan, M.S. (2006) 'Customer Satisfaction and Stock Prices: High Returns, Low Risk' *Journal of Marketing* 70 (1) 3–14

Freeman, R.E., Harrison, J.S., Wicks, A.C., Parmar, B.L and De Colle, S. (2010) *Stakeholder Theory: The State of the Art* Cambridge University Press

Gorton, G. and Schmidt, F.A. (2004) 'Capital, Labor, and The Firm: A Study of German Codetermination' *Journal of the European Economic Association* 2 (5) 863–905

Harrison, J.S. and St. John, C.H. (1994) *Strategic Management of Organizations and Stakeholders: Concepts and Cases* West Publishing

Jensen, M.C. (2001) 'Value Maximisation, Stakeholder Theory, and The Corporate Objective Function' *European Financial Management* 7 (3) 297–317

Jensen, M.C. and Meckling, W. (1976) 'Theory of the Firm: Managerial Behavior, Agency Costs and Ownership Structure' *Journal of Financial Economics* 3 (4) 305–360

Keay, A. (2010) 'Shareholder Primacy in Corporate Law: Can It Survive? Should It Survive?' *European Company and Financial Law Review* 7 (3) 369–413

Luo, X. and Bhattacharya, C.B. (2006) 'Corporate Social Responsibility, Customer Satisfaction, and Market Value' *Journal of Marketing* 70 (4) 1–18

Nini, G., Sufi, A. and Smith, D.C. (2009) 'Creditor Control Rights, Corporate Governance, and Firm Value' EFA 2009 Bergen Meeting Paper, available at http://ssrn.com/abstract=1344302

Phillips, R. (2003) 'Stakeholder Legitimacy' *Business Ethics Quarterly* 13 (1) 25–41

Rose, C. (2008) 'The Challenge of Employee-Appointed Board Members for Corporate Governance: The Danish Evidence' *European Business Organization Law Review* 9 (2) 215–235

Tung, F. (2007) 'The New Death of Contract: Creeping Corporate Fiduciary Duties For Creditors' Emory University School of Law and Economics Research Paper Series, Research Paper No 07-24

Van der Laan, G., Van Ees, H. and Van Witteloostuijn, A. (2008) 'Corporate Social and Financial Performance: An Extended Stakeholder Theory and Empirical Test With Accounting Measures' *Journal of Business Ethics* 79 (3) 299–310

Williamson, O.E. (1979) 'Transaction-Cost Economics: The Governance of Contractual Relationships' *Journal of Law and Economics* 22 (2) 233–261

SUGGESTIONS FOR FURTHER READING

Cowe, R. (2001) 'Corporate Governance: The Stakeholder Challenge' Certified Accountants Educational Trust, available at http://www.accaglobal.com/pubs/members/publications/sector_booklets/public_sector/90640.pdf. This booklet examines recent changes to company law in the UK from a stakeholder viewpoint. It also provides a brief overview of the development of corporate governance regulation in the UK.

Deakin, S. (2005) 'The Coming Transformation of Shareholder Value' *Corporate Governance: An International Review* 13 (1) 11–18. This paper argues that contrary to popular belief, shareholder primacy is based on the cultural norms surrounding the hostile takeover movement, rather than on company law. It goes on to suggest that shareholders should use their power as agents of society.

Triantis, G.G. and Daniels, R.J. (1995) 'The Role of Debt in Interactive Corporate Governance' *California Law Review* 83 (4) 1073–1114. The authors argue that each stakeholder has a unique perspective on the firm and that in reacting to one another's actions stakeholders can collectively contribute to corporate governance.

5 REMUNERATION

⟫ **LEARNING OBJECTIVES**

- To appreciate the implications for directors' remuneration of Maslow's hierarchy of needs, equity theory and agency theory
- To understand the roles of remuneration committees and consultants in constructing the compensation packages given to directors, and to appreciate potential conflicts of interest between committees and consultants
- To comprehend how payments in the form of equity and share options can align the interests of board members and shareholders
- To gain an appreciation of the empirical evidence on the relationship between CEO remuneration and company performance
- To appreciate the relevance of shareholder votes on directors' compensation

INTRODUCTION

Directors' remuneration is one of those topics that from time to time grips the public's imagination, only to be replaced by some other concern as the media changes the news agenda. During the 1990s there was outrage in the UK over the high salaries paid to the chief executives of newly privatised companies. The recent banking crisis has brought remuneration back into the spotlight. Our newspapers have been full of headlines about greedy bankers and their bonuses. Commentators blame compensation devices such as stock options for promoting risk-seeking behaviour and dubious lending practices that have led to the collapse of some banks and the state rescue of others. Following government intervention to save banks in the US and UK, there is now a call to modify the way bankers are paid. In the US some non-financial firms were given state aid along with the banks under the Troubled Asset Relief Program (TARP). One of the conditions of TARP was that these companies should show restraint in setting the pay of their CEOs. One of the casualties of this policy was the temporary CEO of General Motors whose salary was cut by 25 per cent (*New York Times*, 3 December 2009). The company expressed concern that the government's actions on pay would make it hard to recruit a replacement. For the UK the Walker Committee has made recommendations concerning the overview of payments to highly paid employees who are not board members. There are signs that the recession has made British shareholders more critical of remuneration practices; in 2008 only 3 per cent of FTSE100 companies received substantial (20 or more per cent) votes against their remuneration reports; the proportion rose to 20 per cent in 2009 (*Daily Telegraph*, 21 January 2010). There is clearly concern over remuneration on both sides of the Atlantic.

The remuneration packages awarded to company directors are supposed to attract good candidates to take board positions, to enable the company to retain them and to motivate the directors to work to enhance shareholder wealth. The rewards received by company directors seem so large to the person in the street, and certainly to the average student reading this book, that it is hard to imagine how anyone could need that much money. That certainly makes the packages attractive, but are they motivating, or have directors reached the point where they are so wealthy that promises of more money are meaningless? In the next section we will review some of the theories underlying the relationship between remuneration and motivation. While Maslow's hierarchy of needs suggests that company directors should not be motivated by money, equity theory implies that they are motivated by the prospect of earning more than their peers. However, the debate has been dominated by agency theory, which implies that monetary rewards based on corporate performance are the key to aligning the interests of the board with those of the shareholders. We will concentrate on the types of remuneration packages offered to directors of companies in the US and UK. This choice simply reflects the fact that it is much easier to get information on executive compensation in these countries than in continental Europe and Asia. While the institutional arrangements for deciding how to pay directors are similar in both countries, American directors are usually paid much more than their British counterparts, but the fixed component of their packages is smaller. We will briefly describe the available evidence on the sometimes weak relationship between corporate performance and board remuneration before discussing non-executive directors as a special case. In the UK non-executives are paid a fixed fee in order to promote independence. This is in contrast with American practices. The evidence from the US suggests that variable remuneration for non-executives can be of benefit to the company. Finally we will discuss the importance of shareholder votes on executive remuneration, a theme which is taken up in the case study on Telstra, the Australian telecommunications company that faced a media and shareholder backlash over its remuneration policies in 2006.

THEORETICAL APPROACHES TO MOTIVATION AND REMUNERATION

Most regulators and writers agree with the UK's Code of Corporate Governance that the aim of the remuneration system is to attract, retain and motivate directors. This view of the world implies that decision makers are best motivated by extrinsic rewards, in other words by (usually) monetary payments which can be used to indirectly satisfy an underlying need. This understanding so dominates both economics and finance, that readers who come from these academic backgrounds might be surprised to discover that there is an alternative view. However, psychologists argue that intrinsic motivation is at least as important. In this case an activity is valued in its own right and people will therefore work hard at it either because it is in itself enjoyable or because it has a social function which makes them feel obliged to expend significant effort. We saw in chapter 3 that according to stewardship theory, chief executives are motivated in this way. In the following subsections we will discuss three competing theoretical approaches to motivation and reward.

Maslow's hierarchy of needs

Maslow's hierarchy of needs (Maslow, 1943) is a psychological construct that has been used by social scientists to describe how people are motivated in a variety of situations. The hierarchy suggests that every human being has five types of need, but that low-level needs must be met before the person can strive to achieve higher-level goals. The needs, which are illustrated in figure 5.1, are physiological, safety, social, esteem and self-actualisation.

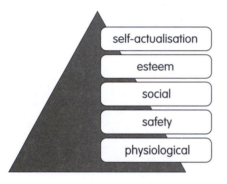

Physiological needs are the most basic survival needs shared by human beings and animals, the need for things like food and sleep. If these needs are not adequately met the individual is barely living and so cannot aspire to achieve anything. At the simplest level, safety needs include shelter and a continuing food supply, but in addition to physical security could include emotional well-being. Once this is assured it is possible to try to meet the social need to be part of a wider group like the family, village or organisation. When an individual is happy within various social groups they will look for recognition from peers and others – the need for esteem. Finally they may reach

Figure 5.1   Maslow's hierarchy of needs

self-actualisation, the stage at which their full potential is realised through being in some way responsible for their own destiny.

The hierarchy can be used within the work context to illustrate what the organisation can do to motivate its employees. Entry-level employees are probably already meeting their physiological needs; if they are still seeking safety they can be motivated very easily by simply giving them a job and a wage. Some types of work may automatically fulfil social needs, but when people have to work alone the organisation may need to encourage them to take a proper lunch break in a staff canteen or to join a social club in order to make them feel that they are part of the business and hence achieve the social goal. As the employee moves up the organisational hierarchy, perks can be offered as visible rewards that confer esteem. The promise of a company car or a bigger workspace will motivate the employee to do a good job and move up the organisational ladder. At some stage this will no longer have any effect; the only way to make the employee work harder is to give them more control over their work or environment, allowing them to use their creativity to achieve self-actualisation. Clearly this is the situation we are interested in here. Anyone who is appointed to a board of directors has achieved their needs for safety, social interaction and esteem. At this point in their career they have the chance to really affect change through the decisions made by the board; this opportunity alone brings self-actualisation. This implies that there is no need to make a big fuss over how company directors are paid, because they receive high intrinsic benefits from their jobs.

This idea is clearly at odds with the way in which remuneration is discussed in most of the corporate governance literature. However, there is a wealth of research on the interplay of intrinsic and extrinsic motivation which can shed light on the media debate on why sophisticated remuneration systems have failed to promote decision making that satisfies investors' needs for profit or society's need for ethical behaviour. Bénabou and Tirole (2003) and Osterloh and Frey (2004) discuss a variety of laboratory and field research that investigates how people approach tasks both when they are paid and when they are unpaid. It seems that when undertaking challenging or interesting tasks effort is often reduced once payment is introduced. This is known as *crowding-out*. This type of effect has also been observed in relation to decisions with a social dimension, for example to give blood or to allow toxic waste to be stored in a particular neighbourhood. Once a payment is offered people become less likely to agree to socially important services.

Bénabou and Tirole (2003) investigate the conditions under which crowding out occurs in the workplace. Their theoretical model implies that it is most likely to occur when the agent is less knowledgeable about the task or their own ability to achieve it than the principal. This is highly unlikely in the case of the board of a company with dispersed share ownership; in this situation the board members have both expertise and information that is denied to the shareholders so we might instead expect to see a *crowding-in* effect in which the payment of monetary rewards reinforces the intrinsic motivation to work hard. However, when equity ownership is concentrated in the hands of a blockholder like a family, information asymmetries may be a less important issue and so crowding-in might not occur. Osterloh and Frey (2004) argue within a conventional corporate governance framework that high salaries have crowded out honest behaviour by top management and have had an adverse trickle-down effect in which lower levels of management realise that there are no benefits from behaving ethically, so they too become greedy. They recognise that far less research has been undertaken on crowding-in effects, but that these can occur when an increase in monetary reward is accompanied by supportive feedback on performance.

Equity theory

Equity theory stems from observations on social needs related to fairness. According to equity theory (Adams, 1963), people are less interested in their absolute position in life than in their situation relative to other people. An individual might happily live in a house with three bedrooms that perfectly meets the needs of their family, but if a friend buys a bigger house they may feel inferior and move house in order to improve their status. This is the well-known phenomenon of needing to 'keep up with the Joneses'. In the work environment people consider the ratio of the effort they expend to the payment they receive. At work, someone might be content with their salary until they discover that someone else with a similar role who works as hard as they do earns more money. They will then lose motivation because it appears that their colleague is viewed as more valuable than they are. On the other hand, if they are paid more than their colleague they will view this as unfair and adjust their work input, making more effort so that the two ratios of effort to pay are brought back into line. This psychological trait seems to exist at all levels in society and at all levels within organisational hierarchies. This is borne out by a survey of human resources professionals, consultants and directors undertaken by Bender (2004). All the respondents agreed that they were not personally motivated by money, but that knowing how much they were paid relative to others was a symbol of their worth and therefore important to them. While Maslow's approach implies that being a director is its own reward, equity theory suggests otherwise. Directors will only be motivated to work harder if they are paid more than their peers. This is relevant to the discussion of the use of peer groups in determining remuneration, which will be discussed in a later section.

Agency theory

We looked at agency theory in some detail in chapter 2, so here we will briefly describe two alternative views of the relationship between the agency problem and remuneration. The type I agency problem exists when corporate managers have different objectives from those held by a group of dispersed shareholders. One way of aligning managerial with ownership objectives is through the remuneration system. This is sometimes known as the *optimal contracting* approach. This implies that directors should be rewarded for creating shareholder value, hence the widespread discussion of the importance of remuneration that is 'at risk', in other words, is linked to corporate performance rather than guaranteed, as is the case with fixed salaries, and of the use of shares and options as the means of payment in performance-related bonuses. After all, if the aim of the remuneration package is to make directors behave as if they were owners, surely the best method is to ensure that they are owners. This is consistent with our earlier discussion of crowding-in.

The *managerial power* approach takes a very different view. According to this perspective remuneration systems are part of the type I agency problem rather than the answer to it. This is the case when managers negotiate contracts that look as if they work in favour of shareholders, but in fact allow managers to get rewards they do not deserve. This could be achieved by setting undemanding performance targets, by defining performance in terms of measures which are under managerial control or by justifying high fixed-salary components because they were recommended by external consultants. This is consistent with arguments about crowding-out and will be discussed in the next section, where we consider the design of remuneration packages.

Regulators have been seduced by the optimal contracting view which has encouraged remuneration committees to find ever-more sophisticated ways of tying compensation to corporate performance. Media commentators, on the other hand, are much more sceptical about the ability of these schemes to improve performance and are more likely to echo the managerial power hypothesis in viewing them as part of the problem.

REMUNERATION IN PRACTICE

In this section we consider several different aspects of remuneration policy. For reasons which will be given in the next subsection, most of what we know about remuneration packages is based on data from the US and UK. We will discuss the importance of remuneration committees and consultants before looking at how packages are constructed and at their relationship with corporate performance. We then turn to a consideration of non-executive directors in the UK as a special case before ending the section with a review of the effects of shareholder votes on remuneration.

Disclosure of remuneration practices

Internationally, our knowledge of directors' remuneration packages varies tremendously. We have a lot of information on American compensation, because the details are filed in proxy statements. In the UK listed companies are required to include a remuneration report as part of their annual report. In both countries the information is available for each director, so anyone who is interested in a particular firm or director can find information on their pay as long as they know where to look. The media and activists in both countries take an active interest in the subject. In the US the American Federation of Labor and Congress of Industrial Organizations operate a website in which it is possible to compare your salary with the salary of your company's CEO. Forbes publishes an annual list of not just the highest-paid CEOs, but also those who are overpaid relative to the value they have created for investors. In the UK the *Guardian* publishes an annual list of the best-paid CEOs according to size of company and also points out gender and other differences in pay levels.

This level of transparency is rare. Many Asian companies do not publish any information on how their directors are paid because while their corporate governance codes require disclosure, the codes themselves do not form part of the local stock exchange listing requirements. Disclosure in Japan has just been improved thanks to a new regulation imposed by the Financial Services Agency in 2010. Listed companies are now obliged to disclose the names and total remuneration of both directors and statutory auditors who receive payments of at least ¥100 million, and to explain how the policy is formulated. At the time of writing only a few companies had begun making these disclosures. Interestingly the highest earners in 2009–10 appear to be the few foreign CEOs of Japanese companies. The *Financial Times* (24 June 2010) reported that the highest-paid CEO was Carlos Ghosn of Nissan, who received ¥890 million (around £6.7 million), while the highest-paid Japanese CEO was Susumo Kato of Sumitomo, who received ¥186 million (around £1.4 million). This may indicate that the only way to attract foreign chief executives is to increase rewards above the level that is traditionally acceptable in Japan.

In Belgium companies must disclose details of the package received by the CEO, but can give a total for the other executives. According to corporate governance regulation German companies should disclose information for all directors unless three-quarters of the general meeting votes against the practice, but the law demands disclosure in the notes to the financial statements. French companies must disclose figures on fixed and variable compensation in their annual reports, together with the criteria used to determine the variable portion, but they do not have to indicate how the variable part is paid. In practice, even where full disclosure is required by regulation, 25 per cent of European companies do not disclose the information (Ferrarini *et al.*, 2009). This is why the rest of this section is based on the experience and practices of American and British companies.

Remuneration committees and consultants

The institutional arrangements for determining remuneration have changed a lot over the last 20 years. Prior to the wave of corporate governance reforms that took place around the world during the 1990s, executive board members had a lot of discretion over their level of pay. Today, boards operate remuneration or compensation committees made up of independent or non-executive directors who decide how the executive directors should be rewarded. In law, both types of director share responsibility for decision making. In some countries, like the US, the legal responsibility is reflected in the way they are rewarded. Both directors who work for the company and those brought in from outside are paid in the same way, based on the company's performance. In others, for instance the UK, independent directors are paid differently from executives in an attempt to maintain their independence. In the UK non-executives receive flat fees for sitting on the board; they are not paid according to the performance of the firm, even though in law they are just as responsible as the executives.

The typical remuneration committee is made up of, or numerically dominated by non-executives or independent directors, but they may be influenced by other board members. For example, at Microsoft the committee sometimes holds meetings attended by the executives; at Ford any director can attend, but only committee members can vote. This implies that executive directors could, if they chose, exert subtle pressure on the committee members to improve the packages under consideration. Remuneration committees are also influenced by compensation consultants. Consultants can be valuable in setting board remuneration packages because they have specialist knowledge of the relevant law and how it relates to particular cases such as corporate restructuring; they also have access to information on how other boards are paid. Equity theory tells us that people care about how they rank relative to others. Consultants can ensure that packages are broadly comparable across companies, so that directors feel they are being treated fairly. The compensation consultancy industry is highly concentrated, dominated by a few major players. In their sample of 400 firms featuring in the S&P500 in 2006, Conyon *et al.* (2009) find that 81 per cent were advised by just four consultancy companies. This concentration certainly means that consultants have extensive knowledge of market compensation levels, but there is a fear that the methods used by consultants are likely to bid up directors' pay. The argument is often stated in terms of CEO rewards, but if it is true there is likely to be a trickle-down effect on other directors. Compensation consultants tend to report information on remuneration in relation to a distribution. Rewards that are less than the median are often described as uncompetitive; companies themselves may feel that it looks bad if their CEO is paid less than average, so they increase the level of pay. If the increase gives this CEO a package that is larger than the median, the median itself shifts so that in the next round of pay renegotiations another CEO is rewarded in an uncompetitive way, gets a pay rise, and so the cycle continues.

Conyon *et al.* (2009) examine the influence of compensation consultants on CEO pay in the US and UK. They find a positive relationship between the total compensation levels of CEOs and the use of consultants in the US, but not in the UK. Taken alone this would support the existence of a ratchet effect in the US. However, they also look at the mix of incentives used and find that where consultants are involved in the process, equity plays a bigger role in compensation, indicating that consultants do seek to align managerial and shareholder incentives as agency theory says they should. Voulgaris *et al.* (2010) make the same observation for British firms. It should also be noted that companies may choose to employ consultants when they operate in complex environments and face competition in the managerial labour market. Such firms would be expected to pay higher remuneration to CEOs, so causation would run from remuneration levels to the use of consultants rather than the other way round.

In some companies the compensation consultants who advise the remuneration committee provide additional services which might include devising pay packages for all or some employees and advising on pension plans. Where this happens there is a danger that the consultancy company will become dependent on certain clients for a large proportion of their revenue stream. In such a case the consultancy company has an incentive to take the view that it is engaged by the company rather than by its shareholders, and in order to keep the client happy will suggest higher rewards for the CEO. This potential problem is similar to the one that is created when auditors provide non-audit services to corporate clients, as occurred famously at the Houston office of Arthur Andersen which relied too heavily on Enron. In that type of situation shareholders are placed at a disadvantage because the auditor is afraid to be critical of the board; in the case of compensation consultants they may make shareholders worse off by creating remuneration packages that lead to crowding-out, as discussed in a previous section. This is a relatively new line of research, and as yet there is no agreement on whether or not conflicts of interest faced by compensation consultants lead to excessive CEO pay. Cadman and Carter (2010) find no evidence of this for American companies, while Murphy and Sandino (2010) use a different measure of the provision of additional services and conclude that it does lead to higher CEO remuneration in both the US and Canada.

These concerns are also discussed by the Walker Committee (HM Treasury 2009) in the context of the banking industry. The committee welcomes a draft code of best practice for remuneration consultants, in which consultants pledge to work to high standards of transparency, integrity, objectivity, competence and confidentiality. Under these headings there is specific consideration of the need for openness in describing the range of services offered by the consultant and the method for selecting comparator companies to be used in the determination of remuneration. It appears that this code will be subject to regular updating and may come to form an important part of standard setting in the UK's corporate governance regime.

Remuneration packages

Directors' remuneration packages are made up of a number of elements, but the media's attention is usually drawn to the total remuneration received by a single person – the CEO. Table 5.1 summarises the information on the ten highest paid CEOs in the UK and US provided by Forbes and the *Guardian*, respectively, in their 2009 surveys. Two things leap out at the reader; the first is that the numbers are huge. The total package received by Bart Becht, the highest-paid CEO in the UK, gives him a payout which is 1374 times higher than the average wage paid by Reckitt Benckiser. The second is that the payments made to the CEOs of American companies are much larger than those paid to their counterparts in Britain. The highest-paid CEO in the US is paid ten times more than the highest-paid CEO in the UK, who is paid less than the tenth-ranked American chief executive. This is consistent with empirical studies of international differences in the compensation of CEOs. Bruce *et al.* (2005) show that American CEOs are more highly paid relative to the average worker than are CEOs in other countries. This is borne out by Anderson *et al.* (2007), who present survey results which show that in 2006 the 20 most highly paid European executives received an average reward of $12.5 million, amounting to one-third of the reward received by the average top 20 executives in the American pay league. The CFA (2008) reports similar findings for Japanese CEOs. Randøy and Nielson (2002) discuss CEO remuneration in Sweden and Norway. They provide the very telling example of the CEO of Ericsson, who was paid $1.1 million in 1999, while the CEO of Motorola was paid $58.9 million. They go on to explain that such a level of pay would be socially unacceptable in the Nordic countries where the egalitarian society, reflected in labour representation on the supervisory board, and the tax system that penalises high earners, keep CEO pay relatively low in international terms. Similar cultural factors are at work in Japan where it would be unacceptable for directors to be paid large multiples of the average worker's salary (CFA, 2008). This is interesting given that often, when a British CEO gets a large pay increase, the company justifies it by saying that the market for top managers is international, and talented leaders will leave if they are not paid enough. This does not seem to be a problem in other parts of the world.

In reading table 5.1 it is vital to remember that these remuneration figures are the total from all types of payment, so they include annual bonuses as well as payments made under long-term incentive plans. The fixed elements are often relatively small; returning to Bart Becht, his salary accounted for just 20 per cent of the total package in 2008. This is in contrast to Lawrence Ellison's fixed salary, which was just 2 per cent of his total. Evidence from Bruce *et al.* (2005) indicates that this difference is not unusual; while American CEOs get very high rewards, the fixed component is very small. Given the importance of the performance-related aspect of CEO rewards, we might expect to see particular industries dominating the 'top-ten' lists in specific years. For 2008, five of the American (Irani, Hess, Watford, Papa and Evanson) and three of the British top-ten earners (Aiden Heavey, Charles Goodyear and Frank Chapman) are chief executives in energy companies.

Table 5.1 The ten highest-paid CEOs in the UK and the US, 2008

UK		US	
name	Total remuneration (£m)	name	Total remuneration (£m)[1]
Bart Becht (Reckitt Benckiser)	36.76	Lawrence Ellison (Oracle)	382.07
Aiden Heavey (Tullow Oil)	28.83	Ray Irani (Occidental Petroleum)	152.72
Charles Goodyear (BHP Billiton)	23.82	John Hess (Hess)	106.04
Sir Martin Sorrell (WPP)	19.71	Michael Watford (Ultra Petroleum)	80.21
Arun Sarin (Vodafone)	13.74	Mark Papa (EOG Resources)	62.06
John Pluthero (Cable and Wireless)	10.63	William Berkley (WR Berkley)	60.01
Jean-Pierre Garnier (GSK)	10.33	Matthew Rose (Burlington Santa Fe)	47.07
Frank Chapman (BG Group)	10.01	Paul Evanson (Allegheny Energy)	46.14
Paul Pinder (Capita)	9.86	Hugh Grant (Monsanto)	44.31
Sir Terry Leahy (Tesco)	9.11	Robert Lane (Deere & Co)	42.05

Note: [1] The dollar amounts are converted to pounds sterling using the exchange rate applicable on 31 December 2008, obtained from the IMF website
Source: UK data from the *Guardian* Executive Pay Survey 2009; US data from the Forbes Survey 2009

A typical director's remuneration package includes a variety of components: a fixed salary, benefits in kind, a bonus based on short-term performance and an equity-based component based on long-term performance. The existence of the fixed salary and benefits in kind lends credence to equity theory. Individual directors can observe these and see how they rank relative to their peers, while remuneration committees can use them to ensure that they can attract and retain suitable executives. Of course, the system of basing the fixed element of compensation on a group of comparator companies can lead to distortions or abuse. For example many authors (Conyon and Murphy, 2000; Gregg *et al.*, 1993; Zhou, 2000) have remarked that compensation is higher in larger companies, regardless of their relative profitability. By including large companies in the group of peers, a firm can improve the basic salaries of its executives while apparently operating within accepted conventions. Faulkender and Yang (2008) point the finger of blame at compensation consultants once again, suggesting that they make judicious choices regarding peer groups so as to argue for an increase in salary levels and thereby keep directors happy.

Table 5.2 reports median salaries for chief executives, finance directors and other executive directors in British companies from both the FTSE100 and FTSE250 stock market indices. It also explains how other elements of the remuneration package are related to the base salary. As the table shows, other board members earn significantly less than the chief executive. Annual bonuses are related to the fixed salary and again, the chief executive of the typical FTSE100 company tends to be favoured in that the maximum possible bonus payable constitutes a larger proportion of the total salary than is the case for the finance director (137 per cent as opposed to 132 per cent), who in turn can get a higher proportion than other executives (125 per cent). Notice also that this table bears out remarks made in the previous paragraph. Board members in FTSE100 companies earn larger salaries than those in FTSE250 companies (the median FTSE100 director receiving 1.7 times the salary of a FTSE250 director) whose bonuses are restricted relative to those available in companies with a larger market cap. Most bonuses are based on profitability during the previous year. The only exception is in the case of the typical chief executive of a FTSE250 company whose bonus is based on a measure of personal performance.

The information in table 5.2 masks some potentially important differences in the profit measures used by different companies. AstraZeneca, Next and Tesco use earnings per share (EPS) which is based on bottom-line profitability, that is, profit after all allowable deductions have been made; while others use accounting measures that are closer to cash flow than profit and hence less easy to manipulate, such as growth in, or absolute earnings before interest taxes depreciation and amortisation (EBITDA) used, for example, by BP and Inmarsat. Some companies use a scorecard system in which several key performance indicators are used, for example Vodafone uses standard performance measures like operating profit and free cash flow alongside specific revenue indicators and a measure of 'customer delight'. Royal Dutch Shell includes a market measure alongside operating cash flow and measures of operational excellence and sustainable development. Some energy companies like BP and Inmarsat include capital spending as a performance indicator, while Shire uses revenue-based measures as short-term performance indicators. However performance is measured, the bonus itself may be paid in cash, shares or a combination of the two.

Companies are increasingly making use of deferred bonuses. By deferring payment of the bonus, which is often in the form of shares, directors are given an incentive to continue to perform well, and also to remain with the company, because if they do not they will lose their entitlement to the payment. As table 5.2 indicates, the most common performance measure used to determine the size of the deferred bonus is growth in EPS. The danger with any accounting measure of performance is that it can be manipulated. One of the features of the Enron scandal was the way in which earnings were manipulated so that the company was able to report positive 'earnings surprises' to the stock market so as to bolster the share price and thereby boost the performance element of directors' earnings. Cash-flow measures are less easy to manipulate than bottom-line profits, which can be changed by fairly simple and perfectly legal changes to accounting methods. Of course changes to inventory accounting and depreciation charging must be highlighted in the annual report, so they should not feed into the stock market's assessment of the company, but they would still influence earnings and therefore the annual bonus.

While the annual bonus and deferred bonus reward good short-term performance, long-term performance, usually defined over the previous three years, is also

Table 5.2 Composition of remuneration of UK board members

	Chief Executive		Finance director		Other executive	
FTSE index	100	250	100	250	100	250
Base salary (£000)	820	456	489	288	459	265
Bonus						
Maximum percentage of salary	137	100	132	100	125	100
Most common performance measure	Profit	Personal	Profit	Profit	Profit	Profit
Deferred bonus						
Maximum percentage of annual bonus	100	100	100	100	100	100
Deferral period	3 years	3 years	3 years	3 years	3 years	3 years
Most common performance measure	EPS growth	EPS growth	EPS growth	EPS growth	EPS growth	EPS growth
Performance share plans						
Maximum percentage of salary	200	125	200	124	217	125
Most common performance measure	Relative TSR	Relative TSR	Relative TSR	Relative TSR	Relative TSR	Relative TSR
Share option plan						
Maximum percentage of salary	279	200	200	138	279	113
Most common performance measure	EPS growth	EPS growth	EPS growth	EPS growth	EPS growth	EPS growth

Notes:
EPS = earnings per share
TSR = total shareholder return
Source: KPMG (2009) 'KPMG's Survey of Directors' Compensation 2009' KPMG LLP (UK)

rewarded through share and option plans of the type outlined in table 5.2. Notice that these plans give board members the chance to significantly boost their remuneration packages. The typical FTSE100 director can get at least 200 per cent of their annual salary in the form of shares and at least that in options provided the company meets its performance targets. In deciding the size of share award, remuneration committees measure performance as TSR relative to a comparator group. TSR is calculated as the dividend paid plus the capital gain available over a specific time period, shown as a percentage of the share value at the start of the period. It is popular because it measures performance from the point of view of the shareholder, so if the board implements policies that improve shareholder value, they are rewarded for it. To avoid rewarding directors for share price appreciation due to a buoyant stock market or sudden increase in dividend payout, TSR is measured relative to a group of comparator companies. Usually the company must record TSR at least equal to the median TSR of the comparator group in order for the directors to get their share award. Once an award has been made, the company may require its directors to hold the shares over a fixed period so that they have further incentives to create shareholder value in the future.

Share options give the holder the right to buy shares at a later date at a price specified in the option contract. The price specified in the contract is known as the exercise or strike price. Clearly if it is lower than the market price on the maturity date it is possible to make a profit by exercising the option to buy the share them immediately selling the share in the market. This makes options a useful part of the remuneration package, because rather than rewarding any increase in the share price, these pay off only when the share price rises above the exercise price. This means that the choice of exercise price is crucial in determining how difficult it is to make a profit and therefore how hard the board member will work. In the past share-option schemes have been criticised for using low or variable strike prices and therefore not giving directors sufficient incentives to improve shareholder value. A second important feature of options is that their value rises with the volatility of the underlying share price. This means that directors are encouraged to take risks so as to make the share price more volatile. In the light of recent events you would be right to question the desirability of this feature. It is often argued that corporate managers are more risk-averse that shareholders. This is because finance theory assumes that shareholders hold diversified portfolios, so are not too worried about the risk of any individual security. Managers, on the other hand, are more worried about the risk of their business, because if it fails they will find it hard to get other employment. For this reason it can be argued that managers' risk attitudes can be brought into line with those of the shareholders by rewarding managers using options. This feature of options makes the choice of exercise price all the more important. If the exercise price is very high in comparison with today's share price, directors may take too many risks in order to make a profit on the options and instead cause the firm's market value to fall.

Table 5.2 does not include any information about the payments in kind, or perks that are routinely offered to executive directors. Annual reports in the UK and proxy statements in the US list the kind of perks offered, which in many cases are of the same type that would be given further down the organisational hierarchy, such as a company car, health insurance and in the case of the retail sector, staff discounts. In some cases, however, these benefits are large, either in an absolute sense or relative to the total package. The Ford Motor Company feels that, for security reasons, its CEO should not travel on a scheduled aircraft, so he and his family were given use of the corporate jet until this was sold, at which point he was allowed instead to charter an aircraft. According to the 2009 proxy statement this benefit was worth $344,109, which may sound a lot but was only 2.5 per cent of his total package. In the UK the CEOs of GlaxoSmithKline, Vodafone and AstraZeneca, for instance, all received benefits of more than £100,000 in 2008; in the case of David Brennan of AstraZeneca the figure was over £200,000. While these numbers are small in relation to the total package they are large in absolute size, particularly when you realise that in the 2008/9 financial year the median wage in the UK was £25,428 (Office for National Statistics). In terms of the aims of the package, these benefits may help to attract and retain executives, but they cannot motivate them to produce shareholder returns – in fact this is exactly the type of wasteful spending highlighted by Jensen and Meckling (1976) in their formulation of agency theory.

Pay and performance

If remuneration committees are doing their job well, board remuneration should be sensitive to corporate performance. Most empirical work on this issue has focused on payments to chief executives rather than to all executive directors. Jensen and Murphy (1990) provide the earliest evidence on the relationship between the creation of shareholder wealth and CEO remuneration in the US. Using data from 1974–86 they found that for every additional $1000 of shareholder wealth created, chief executives receive an additional $3.25 spread across salary, bonuses, shareholdings and options. Schaefer (1998) found that the sensitivity had increased to a $12.50 increase in total remuneration for every additional $1000 of shareholder wealth over the period 1991–5, but that the figure is not statistically significant. For Canada, Zhou (2000) reports that CEO pay rises by a significant $5.62 for every additional $1000 in shareholder wealth. In other words, CEO remuneration in North America is linked to corporate performance but the relationship is not so strong that it is likely to be a major motivating factor.

For the UK, Main *et al.* (1996) find a positive relationship between CEO pay and shareholder returns, which is confirmed by Conyon and Peck (1998) for the highest-paid director (usually the CEO). Conyon and Peck (1998) also showed that the pay–performance relationship is stronger in companies where non-executives make up at least 40 per cent of the board. This research was conducted before UK companies were supposed to have boards where the majority of members are independent, and so it provides a rationale for the practice. Buck *et al.* (2003) suggest that there is a danger in designing ever-more complex remuneration packages. They investigate the sensitivity of executive directors' remuneration to their companies' TSR. They find that while remuneration is sensitive to performance, the sensitivity is reduced by long-term incentive plans. This is because the plans are often complicated and define performance in relative rather than absolute terms. In an earlier section we suggested this was a good thing because it avoids the problem of rewarding directors for being lucky, in that they are in post when share prices happen to be rising. On the other hand, shareholders are made better off by absolute increases in share price, not by an increase relative to a group of comparator companies.

Outside North America and the UK there is evidence that CEO remuneration in both Australian and Japanese firms is related to stock market performance (Merhebi *et al.*, 2006 and Kata and Kubo, 2006, respectively). However, Randøy and Nielson (2002) find no such relationship in Norway and Sweden, where there is instead a relationship with accounting performance. Most of these results are encouraging in that they suggest that around the world, companies are rewarding their major decision makers for creating shareholder wealth. This is entirely positive as long as boards are not attempting to manipulate the markets' view of corporate performance. Earlier in this chapter we mentioned the way in which Enron consistently reported good earnings figures so as to boost the firm's share price. Burns and Kedia (2006) examine this phenomenon by looking at the relationship between the misreporting of earnings, measured by subsequent accounting restatements, and the sensitivity of parts of the CEO's remuneration package to the share price. They find that the only share-price sensitivity that is related to misreporting is the sensitivity of the option component of the package. This indicates that options have to be handled with care because, as was hinted earlier, they can encourage excessive risk-taking, in this case in the form of providing an incentive to misstate earnings.

Remuneration of non-executives

While practices regarding the payments made to executive directors are similar the world over, the situation is very different with respect to the payments made to non-executives. In the UK, where independence is prized, this is reflected in the payment of flat fees that compensate for the time commitment made by non-executives. Thus most companies pay the Chair far more than other non-executives and may offer additional fees to directors who chair audit and remuneration committees, although interestingly, not nomination committees. Table 5.3 shows the median fees paid to non-executives in British companies in 2008. It bears out the comments just made, and once again confirms that larger companies make higher payments. In this case the chair of a FTSE100 company can expect to be paid more than twice the fee level paid to the chair of a FTSE250 company. The differentials are much lower for other directors. The idea is that by divorcing compensation from performance, the independence of non-executives remains intact. This is interesting, given that the board as a whole is responsible for directing the company and ensuring that it makes the best possible return for its shareholders. It has become accepted that the only way to get executives to act this way is by linking their rewards to company performance, yet for some reason non-executives do not need this incentive. Given that the non-executives on one board are executives on another, this implies that the same people are motivated in different ways depending on their job description.

This could be consistent with Maslow's hierarchy of needs, if one takes the view that being appointed as an independent rather than as an executive director leads to self-actualisation. Certainly being asked to join another board is a sign of having 'made it' and having achieved a reputation as a good businessperson. Osterloh and Frey (2004) argue that fixed payments for independent directors reduce the incentive to make decisions in their own interests, and so improve corporate governance. Indeed they go further and argue that fixed payments should be more important in the remuneration of all board members, not just non-executives. In addition they point out that public servants like politicians and judges are trusted precisely because they get no monetary benefit from the regulations they introduce. Perhaps if they had been writing more recently they would have use their own framework to suggest that politicians should not be allowed to formulate their own rules on the payment of expenses claims.

Table 5.3 Fees paid to non-executive directors serving on the boards of firms in the UK, 2008 (£000)

	Chair	Senior independent director	Other non-executive
FTSE100	298	85	67
FTSE250	140	50	42

Source: KPMG (2009) 'KPMG's Survey of Directors' Compensation 2009' KPMG LLP (UK)

The situation in other countries is rather different. Non-executives in the US, Austria and Germany are eligible for performance-related rewards. In Denmark and Hungary the rewards can be in the form of shares but not options, and in Spain non-executives can be given shares as long they hold them during their tenure on the board. There is nothing to prevent the non-executive directors in UK companies from owning shares in the companies on whose boards they sit, as long as they are granted without reference to company performance. GlaxoSmithKline PLC is unusual in insisting that 25 per cent of the fees paid to non-executives should be in the form of shares which must be held until they leave the board. The company states that this is necessary to improve the link between shareholders and directors. This contradicts the view that is implicit in British regulation. Few researchers have looked specifically at the pay–performance relationship for non-executives. Yermack (2004) shows that non-executive directors in Fortune 500 companies receive an additional 11 cents for every $1000 extra shareholder value created by their companies. This seems like a trivial amount but other evidence suggests that such incentives are useful. Fich and Shivdasani (2005) find that the value of Fortune 1000 companies is improved when companies introduce stock-option plans for non-executives.

Shareholders and remuneration: 'say on pay'

Given that the aim of remuneration packages is to encourage directors to create wealth for shareholders, it seems only fair that shareholders should have the chance to comment on the way packages are structured. In some countries this is achieved through a shareholder vote on the remuneration report, the so-called 'say on pay'. Shareholders in the UK, the US, the Netherlands, Sweden, Norway and Australia already have the right to vote. Some Canadian companies have voluntarily introduced a shareholder vote but as yet they are not required to do so. The vote is binding in the Netherlands, Sweden and Norway, but in other countries shareholders can only register a protest vote. However, this can be valuable because the media picks up on these votes and draws public attention to offending companies, forcing them to think again when they next determine how to pay their directors. This was exactly what happened at the British company GalxoSmithKline when its shareholders rejected the remuneration report in 2003. The company reacted by reducing severance payments and increasing the performance requirements of its options scheme. The following year it replaced all the members of its remuneration committee (Cai and Walkling, 2009).

'Say on pay' regulation and legislation is relatively recent, so little academic research has been done. However, some unpublished work is available for the UK, which took the lead in introducing a non-binding vote in 2002. Ferri and Maber (2009) compare CEO pay before and after the introduction of the vote. They find that it did not lead to any change in the level or rate of growth of remuneration, but that CEO pay did become more sensitive to poor performance after the vote was introduced. This result fits in with a rather different piece of research undertaken by Carter and Zamora (2009), who look at the determinants of votes against remuneration reports. They find that the proportion of 'no' votes rises with the size of the CEO's salary and as the package is less sensitive to corporate performance. Clearly shareholders are rightly concerned when CEOs are rewarded for failing to increase shareholder wealth.

CONCLUSION

As in so many other areas of corporate governance, agency theory dominates our ideas on how board members should be rewarded. While other theories stress the importance of intrinsic motivation, agency theory tells us that extrinsic rewards are needed to align the interests of directors and shareholders. To this end, remuneration committees, advised by consultants, devise often complicated remuneration packages, including fixed and variable elements, with bonuses paid in response to target short- and long-run corporate performance. While there is evidence that CEOs in particular are made better off when their companies perform well, it is still not certain that the sums involved are actually the key motivating factor for board members. Interestingly, while regulation in the UK encourages the use of performance-related rewards for executive directors, it stipulates that non-executives should be paid fixed fees in order to promote independence. Given that independent thinking is required of all directors whether or not they are employed within a particular business, we find it hard to understand why the two groups are treated in such different ways, given that both are equally responsible in law for the performance of the companies on whose boards they sit.

The recent crisis in the banking industry and subsequent recession have led to a greater awareness among both shareholders and the general public over how directors are paid. Awareness has often turned to anger and shareholders are increasingly voting against companies' remuneration reports. In response regulators are turning their attention to the relationships between companies, remuneration committees and the consultants who advise them. While much of this attention has focused on financial firms, it is likely that innovations introduced in this industry will spread and we may expect a raft of new codes of practice in this field.

KEY POINTS

- Company directors, like the rest of us, may be motivated by personal, intrinsic factors or by extrinsic rewards. Remuneration packages for executive directors, and for non-executives in some countries, are based on the idea that extrinsic rewards are necessary.
- Remuneration committees, advised by consultants, have the job of constructing packages with an important variable component based on rewarding decisions that improve shareholder value relative to some benchmark. There are fears that some parts of the package may be inflated by the choice of comparator companies used in benchmarking.
- Performance-related bonuses are often paid in the form of shares and options, both of which make directors' wealth sensitive to shareholder value, while options may also affect directors' appetites for risk.
- In the UK most non-executive directors are paid flat fees based on their workload. In other countries they may receive performance-related payments.

- Shareholders in an increasing number of countries are being given the right to vote on directors' remuneration. While most votes are non-binding they are still influential.

CASE STUDY   Telstra: A wake-up call for a telecommunications company

Telstra can trace its history back to 1901, when the Commonwealth government established the Postmaster General's department to manage the postal, telephone and telegraph services within Australia. After several name changes it became Telstra in 1993. By that time it was already publicly listed, and the government was in the process of selling its shares to the public. Like other previously nationalised telecommunications companies, Telstra struggled to come to terms with the new telecoms market. In 2004 the resignation of the board chair, Bob Mansfield, brought boardroom struggles over restructuring into the public arena and it became clear that the company had to find new direction. Sol Trujillo, the former boss of Orange, was appointed as CEO in 2005 to oversee a five- year programme designed to modernise the company so that it could face the challenges of a changing telecoms industry.

Trujillo soon found himself embroiled in controversy over remuneration at the company. Telstra's 2006 remuneration report explained that executive directors were paid the usual mixture of base salary and short- and long-term incentive-based remuneration. Shareholders were annoyed by three aspects of the remuneration package. The first was that part of the long-term incentive payment was based on an undisclosed TSR target. The company justified this lack of disclosure by saying that to reveal it would be akin to commenting on the company's share price, yet most other companies have no such problem with revealing the TSR target. The second issue was that the revenue-growth element of the package was given twice the weight of the TSR part, meaning that the easiest way for the CEO and other board members to raise their remuneration was to go for growth rather than profit. The final issue was the fact that payments under the long-term incentive plan were available not just to board members, but to a further 213 executives. Investors found it hard to believe that this number of people could be deemed so important to the long-term success of the business. The Australian Prime Minister and the country's media encouraged Telstra's shareholders to question the company about its policy; however at the AGM they accepted the remuneration report by a majority of 79 per cent.

Telstra seemed to learn something about transparency from the media backlash in 2006, and in 2007 revealed that its TSR target was 11.5 per cent annual growth until 2010. If this were met options would be granted to a total of 260 senior executives. The conditions were slightly different for Sol Trujillo, who faced a shorter time period for his target, making him eligible for over 18 million share options at the end of the 2008/9 financial year. His total pay for 2007 was just under $12 million, including a short-term incentive of $5.2 million, which was twice that of other CEOs in the sector despite the fact that by now the company's share price was lower than it was when he joined the business. This time the shareholders showed their disapproval by voting against the remuneration report by a majority of 66 per cent. This was the first vote against a remuneration report issued by an Australian blue-chip company. While it was clearly bad news for Telstra, the vote was non-binding, so it did not prevent the company going ahead and rewarding its executives according to the recommendations of the report. The company's biggest investors publicly announced that they would be seeking discussions with the management team. Once again Telstra learned from the experience and published a new, simpler and more transparent remuneration scheme six months before its 2008 AGM, effectively ensuring that by the time the next remuneration report was published, its investors were back on side.

The Telstra case shows that while newspaper headlines may focus on how much CEOs are paid, the factor that interests investors more is how the package is made up and how many other board members and other executives receive similar packages. It also illustrates the importance of shareholder votes – even when they are non-binding they can provide a wake-up call to companies and to institutional investors, urging the two sides to work together to improve governance. Sol Trujillo left Telstra in 2009. The interim report whose publication coincided with his resignation showed that the company's share price had lost 23.3 per cent of its value since Trujillo's appointment, a fact which was trumpeted in the media when Trujillo resigned. However this compared favourably with the performance of both European and American telecommunications indices. This shows that while the media can perform a useful service in terms of highlighting corporate governance issues, they do not always tell the full story.

CASE-STUDY QUESTIONS

1 Comment on the use of revenue targets in performance-related pay packages. Do you think they do more harm than good?
2 Was Telstra right to go ahead and implement its remuneration report when its shareholders rejected it in 2007?
3 Should incentives be based on changes in share price or on total shareholder returns?

REVISION QUESTIONS

1 Do directors need monetary incentives to encourage them to make decisions in the best interest of shareholders?
2 What are the main elements of directors' remuneration packages in the UK and US, and how (if at all) does each element motivate directors to increase shareholder wealth?
3 If you were devising a remuneration package based on corporate performance, what performance measures would you use?
4 Do remuneration consultants improve the motivational aspects of reward packages or simply bid up the amount paid to directors?
5 Should executive and non-executive directors be paid in the same way?
6 Are company directors entitled to privacy over how much they are paid?

REFERENCES

Adams, J.S. (1963) 'Towards An Understanding of Inequity' *Journal of Abnormal and Social Psychology* 67 (5) 422–436

Anderson, S., Cavanagh, J., Collins, C., Pizzigati, S. and Lapham, M. (2007) 'Executive Excess 2007: the Staggering Social Cost of US Business Leadership' IPS

Bénabou, R. and Tirole, J. (2003) 'Intrinsic and Extrinsic Motivation' *Review of Economic Studies* 70 (3) 489–520

Bender, R. (2004) 'Why Do Companies use Performance-related Pay for their Executive Directors?' *Corporate Governance: An International Review* 14 (4) 521–533

Bruce, A., Buck, T. and Main, B.G.M. (2005) 'Top Executive Remuneration: A View from Europe' *Journal of Management Studies* 42 (7) 1493–1506

Buck, T., Bruce, A., Main, B.G.M. and Udueni, H. (2003) 'Long Term Incentive Plans, Executive Pay and UK Company Performance' *Journal of Management Studies* 40 (7) 1709–1727

Burns, N. and Kedia, S. (2006) 'The Impact of Performance-based Compensation on Misreporting' *Journal of Financial Economics* 79 (1) 35–67

Cadman, B., Carter, M.E. (2010) 'Compensation Peer Groups and Their Relation with CEO Pay' available at http://ssrn.com/abstract=1349997

Cai, J. and Walkling, R.A. (2009) 'Shareholders' Say on Pay: Does It Create Value?' Available at http://ssrn.com/abstract=1030925

Carter, M.E. and Zamora, V. (2009) 'Shareholder Remuneration Votes and CEO Compensation Design' AAA 2008 MAS Meeting Paper, available at http://ssrn.com/abstract=1004061

CFA (2008) 'It Pays to Disclose: Bridging the Information Gap in Executive-Compensation Disclosures in Asia' CFA

Conyon, M.J. and Murphy, K.J. (2000) 'The Prince and the Pauper: CEO Pay in the United States and the United Kingdom' *Economic Journal* 110 (467) 640–671

Conyon, M.J. and Peck, S.I. (1998) "Board Control, Remuneration Committees, and Top Management Compensation' *Academy of Management Journal* 41 (2) 146–157

Conyon, M.J., Peck, S.I. and Sadler, V.G. (2009) 'Compensation Consultants and Executive Pay: Evidence from the United States and the United Kingdom' *Academy of Management Perspectives* 23 (1) 43–55

Faulkender, M. and Yang, R. (2008) 'Inside the Black Box: The Role and Composition of Compensation Peer Groups' *Journal of Financial Economics* 96 (2) 257–270

Ferrarini, G.A., Moloney, N. and Ungureanu, M. (2009) 'Understanding Directors' Pay in Europe: A Comparative and Empirical Analysis' ECGI – Law Working Paper No. 126/2009

Ferri, F. and Maber, D. (2009) 'Say on Pay Vote and CEO Compensation: Evidence From the UK', available at http://ssrn.com/abstract=1420394

Fich, E.M. and Shivdasani, A. (2005) 'The Impact of Stock-Option Compensation for Outside Directors on Firm Value' *Journal of Business* 78 (6) 2229–2254

Gregg, P., Machin, S. and Szymanski, S. (1993) 'The Disappearing Relationship Between Directors' Pay and Corporate Performance' *British Journal of Industrial Relations* 31 (1) 1–9

HM Treasury (2009) 'A Review of Corporate Governance in UK Banks and other Financial Industry Entities: Final Recommendations' HM Treasury, 16 July

Jensen, M.C. and Meckling, W. (1976) 'Theory of the Firm: Managerial Behavior,

Agency Costs and Ownership Structure' *Journal of Financial Economics* 3 (4) 305–360

Jensen, M. C. and Murphy, K. (1990) 'CEO Incentives – It's Not How Much You Pay, But How' *Harvard Business Review* 68 (3) 138–149

Kata, T. and Kubo, K. (2006) 'CEO Compensation and Firm Performance in Japan: Evidence From New Panel Data on Individual CEO Pay' *Journal of the Japanese and International Economics* 20 (1) 1–19

KPMG (2009) 'KPMG's Survey of Directors' Compensation 2009' KPMG LLP (UK)

Main, B.G.M., Bruce, A. and Buck, T. (1996) 'Total Board Remuneration and Company Performance' *Economic Journal* 106 (439) 1627–1644

Maslow, A. H. (1943) 'A Theory of Human Motivation' *Psychological Review* 50 (4) 370–396

Merhebi, R., Pattenden, K., Swann, P.L and Zhou, X. (2006) 'Australian Chief Executive Remuneration: Pay and Performance' *Accounting and Finance* 46 (3) 481–497

Murphy, K.J. and Sandino, T. (2010) 'Executive Pay and "Independent" Compensation Consultants' *Journal of Accounting and Economics* 49 (3) 247–262

Osterloh, M. and Frey, B.S. (2004) 'Corporate Governance for Crooks? The Case for Corporate Virtue' Grandori, A. ed. *Corporate Governance and Firm Organization: Microfoundations and Structural Forms* Oxford University Press

Randøy, T. and Nielson, J. (2002) 'Company Performance, Corporate Governance, and CEO Compensation in Norway and Sweden' *Journal of Management and Governance* 6 (1) 57–81

Schaefer, S. (1998) 'The Dependence of Pay-Performance Sensitivity on the Size of the Firm' *Review of Economics and Statistics* 80 (3) 436–443

Voulgaris, G., Stathopoulos, K. and Walker, M. (2010) 'Compensation and CEO Pay: UK Evidence' *Corporate Governance: An International Review* 18 (6) 511–526

Yermack, D. (2004) 'Remuneration, Retention, and Reputation Incentives for Outside Directors' *Journal of Finance* 59 (5) 2281–2308

Zhou, X. (2000) 'CEO Pay, Firm Size, and Corporate Performance: Evidence from Canada' *Canadian Journal of Economics* 33 (1) 213–251

SUGGESTIONS FOR FURTHER READING

European Commission (2010) 'Corporate Governance in Financial Institutions and Remuneration Policies' European Commission. This green paper discusses the problems associated with the use of short-term performance measures in determining remuneration in the financial sector. It calls for greater transparency in the remuneration process and for shareholder votes on remuneration packages.

Greenbury Report (1995) 'Directors' Remuneration: Report of a Study Group Chaired by Sir Richard Greenbury' CBI. This report was commissioned in response to concerns over directors' remuneration in the UK, following the wave of privatisations in the 1980s.

http://www.aflcio.org/ This is the website of the union movement in the US. The 'Executive Paywatch' section allows user to compare their wage with the salary of their firm's CEO as well as to get more general information on executive remuneration.

http://www.financialstability.gov/about/executivecompensation.html This website brings together information on curbs on board remuneration which are part of the Troubled Asset Relief Program (TARP) in the US.

6 THE MARKET FOR CORPORATE CONTROL

LEARNING OBJECTIVES

- To understand the choices available to shareholders when companies underperform
- To understand how the threat of a hostile takeover or private equity acquisition can discipline management and alleviate the type I agency problem
- To appreciate how defences against hostile bids affect shareholder rights
- To understand the governance implications of private equity transactions
- To appreciate the empirical evidence on the effects of takeovers and buyouts on corporate performance

INTRODUCTION

While Denis (2001) highlights 1976 as the year when research began in earnest on corporate governance, the term 'the market for corporate control' has a longer history. According to Netter *et al.* (2009) it was coined by Manne in 1965 to describe the way in which an efficient stock market can lead to an improved allocation of firms' resources. If a company's management is inefficient that company will not be able to achieve its profit potential so its share price will fall, making it vulnerable to acquisition by another company whose board is keen to buy undervalued assets. The management of the acquirer will be quick to dismiss the target's management so they can take full control of the business. This implies that all rational boards of directors will do their utmost to increase shareholder value in order to keep their jobs. During the 1980s a second group of potentially hostile acquirers emerged on the scene. Buyout firms were, and still are, able to access large amounts of debt finance in order to buy listed companies using very little equity and then take them out of the stock market and reorganise their operations. The threat of acquisition by another listed company or a private equity firm should discipline management teams so that they act in the best interests of their shareholders and maximise the value of their businesses, without the need for regulation or additional incentives.

In the next section we will consider the shareholder response to poorly performing companies. After all, if shareholders will not sell their equity the mechanism described in the previous paragraph cannot act to discipline management. We will argue that while some types of shareholder will be quick to react to underperformance by selling, others will choose to retain their equity either because they feel they can influence performance or because they are not troubled by the company's track record. This implies that the numerically dominant shareholder group in a particular stock market decides whether or not it is a market for corporate control.

We will then go on to describe the merger market with a particular emphasis on the hostile takeovers which are usually associated with a change in corporate control. There is no guarantee that any individual bid will be successful, as target companies usually mount a defence which may in itself restrict shareholder rights. This means that shareholders need additional protection from inefficient managers since the stock market cannot help them. We will conclude this section by considering the empirical evidence on hostile takeovers. While some research indicates that they can substitute for internal governance mechanisms of the kind discussed in earlier chapters of this book, other research shows that target companies are not always poor performers. This too implies that the market for corporate control cannot always be relied on to solve governance problems.

In the next section we will consider the extent to which private equity deals are disciplinary. The evidence there indicates that while shareholders gain from these deals, some stakeholders may be made worse off, which rekindles the debate on which groups should be the beneficiaries of good corporate governance. Finally, in the case study that accompanies this chapter we will describe a rare creature, an attempted hostile takeover of a Japanese company. This particular transaction instigated by Steel Partners, an American hedge fund, was repelled by Bull-Dog Sauce, which used a variant on a *poison pill*, a defence which, as was hinted earlier, damages shareholder rights.

CORPORATE UNDERPERFORMANCE AND SHAREHOLDER CHOICE

Companies perform poorly for many reasons, sometimes they face economy-wide or industry problems which require policy intervention rather than individual action; at others they have internal problems that the board and top management should be able to address. When a company's performance is poor relative to the market or to its industry peers and remains so over time, its shareholders quite rightly become concerned about low dividend payments and a falling share price. The choices available to the shareholders are often described using the *exit vs. voice* framework associated with Hirschman (1970). Hirschman's much-cited book is entitled *Exit, Voice and Loyalty*, and discusses the possible responses of members of organisations when those organisations are failing. The loyalty aspect of his argument has been neglected, and instead the choice available to members is usually presented as a stark one between exit and voice. If you as a member of a club, political party or any other organisation are unhappy about its policies or performance you can simply leave and look for an alternative, or you can stay and put pressure on the governing body to change the way the organisation is run. Applying this framework to failing companies, the shareholders must decide whether they should sell their holdings in order to buy shares in better-performing companies (exit) or continue to hold their shares and attempt to influence the board to change strategy and improve performance (voice).

Shareholders are not a homogenous group. As we saw in chapter 2, many different types of people and organisations own shares and each type of shareholder faces a distinct set of costs and benefits associated with using voice to influence corporate decision-making. Regardless of identity, any shareholder owning a small proportion of equity faces an uphill struggle when using voice. They can lobby the company's investor relations department and ask questions at the AGM, but are unlikely to be able to raise interest among other investors and thereby to bring a resolution to a general meeting. Realising that their lone efforts have the characteristics of a public good, in other words, they impose costs on the individual investor while bringing benefits to others who have not paid for them; most small investors would be deterred from even attempting to use voice and would instead simply sell their shares. This is not necessarily a problem for the company itself, given that these shareholders are selling small amounts of equity, but it can become problematic if another company's management team has noticed its poor performance and believes that it could make better use of its assets. In this case it is easy for a potential acquirer to start buying equity in the market from disgruntled shareholders and thereby build a small but important holding of shares, a toe-hold, that it can use as the basis for a full takeover bid.

Financial institutions have the resources to acquire larger equity holdings, and as chapter 2 showed, they are important shareholders in the UK and US. The UK's 'Stewardship Code' based on the existing 'Code on the Responsibilities of Institutional Investors' issued by the Institutional Shareholders' Committee encourages financial institutions to be active monitors of investee companies. This includes instituting and disclosing a policy on voting and on how they will escalate matters with corporate management; this might include taking collective action with other institutions. Most financial institutions are obliged by law to hold diversified portfolios, so while they may hold valuable stakes in individual companies these stakes are likely to be small relative to the size of their portfolio. This means that despite regulators' efforts to encourage active ownership, fund managers may feel that it is simply not worth their while to take much interest in any individual failing company. This view is further encouraged by fears that a dialogue may become public knowledge and so draw attention to corporate problems and depress the share price even further. This, together with the 'trading mentality' of fund managers, implies that despite regulators' efforts, financial institutions are likely to respond to corporate underperformance by selling their shares.

Not all fund managers think in this way. Some funds use a deliberate strategy of engagement in order to make money. We saw in chapter 2 that funds like CalPERS, the pension fund for state employees in California, and the Hermes Focus Fund in the UK seek out underperforming companies and engage with their boards to bring change. In this way they are able to make abnormal gains, even taking account of the costs of intervention, as discussed by English et al. (2004) for CalPERS and by Becht et al. (2009) for Hermes. The use of focus lists in portfolio choice and a subsequent policy of intervention is a very specific type of strategy, yet Clark and Hebb (2004) believe that for pension funds in particular the tide is turning and voice will become an increasingly popular option. They note first the long-term nature of the claims made against pension funds, which must be able to generate sustainable returns in order to pay pensions in the future. They also mention the rise in *passive funds* that became popular when stock markets around the world were booming. Active fund managers realised they could not 'beat the market' and so instead chose to invest in stock market indices. Once a fund manager is locked into an index, the only way to improve the performance of that index is to use voice and work with underperforming businesses to improve their returns.

Unlike the funds discussed so far, hedge funds have no obligation to hold diversified portfolios. Some choose to use a strategy similar to that used by CalPERS and Hermes, but support it with a blockholding in the company, which makes the fund's intervention hard to resist. Brav *et al.* (2008) and Clifford (2008) both show that this strategy can be successful, reaping good returns. While hedge funds and active pension funds can make a big difference to the companies in which they invest, regulators, at least in the UK, feel that the change in mood described by Clark and Hebb (2004) has not materialised. The fact that institutional investors are now encouraged to act in accordance with the Stewardship Code (discussed further in chapter 7) indicates that most prefer to use exit rather than voice in response to corporate underperformance.

Families, governments and companies may also hold blocks of shares. They, like interventionist financial institutions, are also likely to use voice rather than exit for rather different reasons and in different ways. As was discussed in chapter 2, families and governments may be motivated by aims other than value maximisation. This means that they may actually encourage strategies that lead to underperformance in financial terms, because they allow the company to achieve other objectives such as keeping the business in the family or maintaining control of companies in strategically important industries. Where they disagree with corporate policy because it fails to encourage profitability these blockholders have the power and incentives to work with or remove management rather than to sell their shares to a rival company to get a purely short-term gain.

Companies hold shares in other businesses for many reasons. When the holding is seen as a long-term financial investment, the shareholding company has the incentive to use voice by sharing knowledge and offering expertise, as at L'Oréal, which was used as the case study in chapter 2. If the shares form a toe-hold, the shareholding institution has no incentive to intervene to improve performance because it is in its interests to see the price decline so that the transaction can be completed at a lower cost. In either case, corporate blockholders are unlikely to exit in the face of poor performance.

These observations imply that the stock market's ability to function as a market for corporate control depends on the nature of the shareholders present within it. As was discussed in chapter 2, the UK and US stock markets are dominated by financial institutions the majority of which will probably favour exit over voice, and thereby encourage the development of a market for corporate control. In contrast, continental European markets are not dominated by a single type of investor. In some cases governments, companies and families own substantial shareholdings in individual companies. These groups are unlikely to use exit as a response to problems, which means that corporate control is not likely to be traded in the stock market. As later sections will show, this prediction is borne out by international data on the incidence of hostile takeovers.

THE MERGER MARKET

Commentators often use the words merger and acquisition synonymously. While they have the same organisational implications they are rather different types of transactions. In a merger, companies A and B come together to form a new business; let's call it AB. Shares in A and B no longer exist and new equity in AB is created. In contrast, if A acquires B, it does so by buying all outstanding shares in B, which ceases to exist as an independent entity, although its brands may live on. In discussing the market for corporate control, we are interested in acquisitions rather than mergers, because in these deals there is a clear change in control from the target to the acquirer whose board has identified the opportunities offered by the transaction. Although both mergers and acquisitions take place all the time, transactions data reveal that there are distinct *merger waves* during which the number of deals of both types rises before reaching a peak and then tailing off before another wave develops.

Martynova and Renneboog (2008) discuss four completed waves, covering the early 1900s, the 1920s, 1960s, 1980s and 1990s. Each wave was preceded by some form of technological or regulatory event, and coincided with rising stock market prices, the wave then dying down as the stock market became less buoyant or the economy moved towards recession. In terms of other characteristics each wave was unique. For example, during the 1960s mergers created diversified companies which were later broken up in the de-mergers that were part of the wave of the 1980s. Hostile activity, which we will consider in more detail later in this section, was an important part of the 1981–90 wave in both the US and the UK. There was relatively little hostility in those countries during the next wave, but instead hostile takeovers became more important in continental Europe between 1993 and 2001.

Economists classify mergers and acquisitions as *horizontal*, *vertical* or *conglomerate*, depending on the nature of the activities undertaken by the two companies involved in the deal. Both horizontal and vertical transactions involve companies in the same industry. The difference is that in a horizontal deal the two companies operate at the same stage in the production process, while in a vertical deal they are at different stages in the process. If two clothing manufacturers were combined this would be a horizontal deal, while if a clothing retailer were to acquire a manufacturer that would be a vertical transaction. Horizontal deals are usually justified in efficiency terms because by bringing together two businesses doing broadly the same thing, they can exploit *economies of scale* in production and marketing, sharing fixed costs over a larger output, thereby reducing their average costs and becoming more profitable as a single entity than the two were when working independently. Vertical deals allow a company to move into other aspects of the same industry, perhaps by acquiring a company that supplies its raw materials or by buying a business that distributes its product. In each case the new company reduces transactions costs (discussed in more detail in chapter 4) and thereby raises profits. Conglomerate mergers are rather different in that the companies involved come from different industries so there are no direct cost savings from these deals. They might be justified on the grounds that they create diversified businesses and hence reduce the risks faced by shareholders, but of course shareholders can diversify risk through their choice of portfolio so the benefits of conglomerate deals to shareholders are rather dubious. In fact until recently most researchers agreed that a *diversification discount* exists, which means that the shares in conglomerate companies trade at a discount relative to the equity of more focused companies. Some more recent papers dispute this (Martin and Sayrak, 2003 provide a useful survey), but there is still evidence that de-mergers create focused companies that are more valuable, at least in the short run, than the former parent company (Veld *et al.*, 2009), indicating that the stock market favours specialisation. It is worth pointing out that while boards of directors explain their acquisition strategy as a means of creating shareholder value, despite the fact that in practice acquiring firms' share prices fall (Moeller *et al.*, 2005); the directors themselves will receive personal benefits which may influence their decisions. As was discussed in chapter 5, remuneration is higher in larger companies, so acquisitions lead to higher salaries and benefits for the key decision-makers. In addition they bring publicity and kudos to the directors, who will enjoy the extra attention as well as the possibility of enhanced career prospects.

Acquiring managers are not the only group to enjoy economic benefits from takeovers. It is well documented (Martynova and Renneboog, 2008) that the shareholders of target companies make significant positive returns on their equity when a deal is announced. This type of return is usually interpreted as good news. However in this case the good news is rather one-sided because shareholders in acquiring companies see either no benefit or indeed slight losses in the stock market when deals are announced. This indicates that the market is sceptical about the prospects that the deal will improve the acquirer's performance.

As you can see, acquisitions occur for many reasons. They may be motivated by the desire to create economies of scale, to reduce transactions costs, to gain entry to new markets, to get personal benefits for the board of directors or to avoid being acquired by another company during a merger wave. These are not the motivations associated with the disciplinary deals that are important in the market for corporate control. In these transactions the board of company A recognises that company B is undervalued due to the inefficiency of B's management. A's aim is to acquire useful assets cheaply and use them to improve profitability through improved management. This means that during the process of integrating the two companies key members of B's management will be made redundant since they are deemed responsible for B's problems. This implies that discussions of the market for corporate control should focus on hostile takeovers rather than friendly acquisitions. The next section will consider hostile bids in more detail, but first we should pause to consider the ways in which merger activity is regulated, because regulation affects the ability of the market for corporate control to discipline poorly performing management.

Regulation

Throughout the world mergers and acquisitions are subject to two forms of regulation. Governments enact *anti-trust laws* designed to ensure that horizontal mergers are not anti-competitive, in other words, to protect consumers and other stakeholders.

They may also pass securities laws designed to regulate the merger process, or empower other regulators to oversee the process, so that shareholders are protected.

Horizontal mergers concentrate market share in the hands of a single company, where before two separate entities serviced that part of the market. We have already seen that this can lead to improved efficiency by exploiting economies of scale; while this is good for the company itself this concentration of power may have detrimental effects on other market participants. When two companies merge to form a larger firm, that firm can reduce its output levels and sell its product at a higher price, making consumers worse off. It can also negotiate better deals with its suppliers, reducing their profit and having adverse effects on all companies in the supply chain. For this reason legislation usually imposes a limit on the size of mergers that can go ahead without attracting regulatory attention. 'Large' deals are investigated and may be completed if it is judged that they will not harm the market, but may be limited in scope or disallowed if an investigation reveals that they will make stakeholders worse off.

In the UK this regulation is enforced by the Office of Fair Trading, which uses two tests to decide if a deal is large enough to warrant an investigation. Size is defined according to both turnover and market share. If a deal qualifies either because the target company has annual turnover of at least £70 million or because the newly merged company would have a market share of at least 25 per cent, it is referred to the Competition Commission, which investigates and recommends whether or not it should go ahead. Large cross-border deals involving EU companies may be regulated by the European Commission rather than by national authorities. Again the Commission makes the decision according to size tests based on turnover, but if both companies generate at least two-thirds of their turnover in a single member state, that government will apply its own regulatory framework to the proposed deal. In the US the Hart–Rodino–Scott Act regulates mergers which are 'large' according to either a turnover or size of assets test. Significant cross-border deals involving American and European companies may be subject to two regulatory regimes. In this case, if one blocks the deal it cannot go ahead.

We have already seen that the stock market reaction to acquisitions is predictable in that the price of shares in the target company generally rises. This can provide opportunities to manipulate the market for profit. For this reason a second type of regulation is applied to ensure that the transaction is managed fairly from the shareholders' perspective. In the UK this is the responsibility of the Panel on Takeovers and Mergers, which enforces the City Code on Takeovers and Mergers. The Code ensures, among other things, that all shareholders get equal access to information and that no single class of shareholder gets benefits that are not available to others. Similar rules are enforced in the EU, while the situation is a little different in the US because the law there, as we will see later in this chapter, allows companies to defend against takeovers in ways that are not permitted in other countries.

HOSTILE TAKEOVERS

Hostile takeovers provoke strong reactions. At one end of the spectrum they can be seen as a valuable part of the free-market system, providing strong incentives to boards of directors to keep their shareholders happy. At the opposite extreme they are portrayed as having nothing to do with shareholder protection, but instead to be motivated by individual and corporate greed. This view tends to be expressed most openly in relation to the type of *asset-stripping* deals associated with the 1980s. These acquisitions were motivated by undervaluation as described earlier in this chapter, but in these cases the acquirer was attracted by specific assets rather than entire businesses. This meant that having acquired those assets the acquirer disposed of or closed the rest of the target company, resulting in a loss of jobs and damaging spillover effects for other businesses in the supply chain. This clash of ideas is a clash of ideals, yet another example of the debate over whether shareholders are more important than other stakeholders in governance terms.

It is not always easy to distinguish between hostile and friendly bids. One possible distinction is to say that friendly takeovers are proposed by the board of the potential acquirer to the board of the target company, while hostile ones involve a direct appeal to the target's shareholders. According to this view the takeover of Cadbury plc by Kraft Foods Inc., discussed in box 6.1, began as a friendly deal only to become hostile. Another distinction is to say that hostility is in the eye of the beholder. In 1990 the board of Continental received a takeover proposal from Pirelli. Despite the fact that this was a board-to-board suggestion, Continental interpreted it as hostile because Pirelli would not agree to the restrictions on stock trading and disclosure that it requested (Franks and Mayer, 1998). Perhaps hostility is best defined by looking at what happens once the deal is concluded. As we said earlier, if the takeover is disciplinary, the executive directors of the target will lose their jobs. The prospect of job loss as a result of takeover means that the mere threat of a hostile bid should be enough to make boards behave in the best interests of their shareholders. In this way the market for corporate control becomes a means of reducing the type I agency problem, and so is an important corporate governance mechanism that can substitute for the kind of internal or firm-level governance mechanisms described in this book.

Box 6.1 The takeover of Cadbury plc by Kraft Foods, Inc.

John Cadbury began to sell cocoa and drinking chocolate in 1824, going on to open his first manufacturing plant in 1831. The company went from strength to strength, becoming known not just for its popular product range but also for its ethical approach to business. It developed a worldwide presence through acquisitions yet was still thought of as a British business, despite the fact that by the first decade of the twenty-first century most of its employees were based abroad and one-third of its shares were in American hands. In September 2009 the board of Kraft Foods, Inc., an American company, approached Cadbury's board with a takeover proposal. The board turned it down, at which the point the bid became hostile. While Cadbury's shareholders were open to a deal at a better price the company's stakeholders were quick to voice their disapproval. Politicians, trade unions and consumers were worried about the deal, and there were calls to amend takeover regulation to prevent the foreign acquisition of British companies. The takeover went ahead in January 2010, showing that shareholder exit is more powerful than stakeholder voice.

While hostile takeovers could be an important governance mechanism, they can only achieve their potential if the acquisitions market is allowed to function without interference. We have already seen that mergers are regulated so as to protect the interests of both shareholders and stakeholders. Large horizontal mergers that could be disciplinary may be blocked. In addition, in some jurisdictions target managers can use creative methods to defend against hostile bids, again limiting the ability of the stock market to operate as a market for corporate control.

Defences against hostile bids

Regulation is not the only factor that impedes the efficiency of the market for corporate control. The board of a target company has clear incentives to protect itself by defending against a hostile bid. The simplest and cheapest means of defence is for the target management to contact shareholders to defend their recent behaviour, explain that any poor performance was due to circumstances beyond their control and point out the potential disadvantages of the deal, one of which is usually that it undervalues the company. Targets often set up dedicated areas of their corporate websites for this purpose. Other defences include raising dividends to boost shareholder morale and hopefully the share price, revaluing assets so as to make the company appear more valuable and restructuring the business, for instance by selling off poorly performing divisions in an attempt to raise the share price or even by buying other businesses in order to increase value. These defences are available in all countries, but the strategy that has prompted most interest in the corporate governance literature is an (almost) exclusively American phenomenon – the poison pill. It is interesting to note here that while commentators often talk about the UK and the US as being very similar in governance terms, there are important differences, one of which is the nature of takeover regulation. As Armour and Skeel (2007) point out, regulation in the UK was motivated by the investment community which introduced effective self-regulation through the City Code on Takeovers. In contrast, in the US it was corporate management that was the driving force behind the use of the law to regulate takeovers. This explains why in the UK regulation is designed to protect shareholders' interests while in the US it tends to protect (target) management's interests.

A poison pill, or to give it its correct name, a shareholder rights plan, is a legal right that is triggered only when a hostile acquirer announces a bid having already bought a proportion of the firm's shares. A flip-in plan gives shareholders other than the bidder the right to buy new shares in the company at less than the market price. The aim is to make the company much harder to swallow. A flip-over plan also gives rights to the target shareholders, but this time they are entitled to buy shares in the acquirer if it goes ahead and buys the company. Here the aim is to change the ownership of the acquirer so that some equity owners are antagonistic to the company's strategy, making life uncomfortable for the management team. While the name of the defence is accurate in that it does give new rights to shareholders in the event that a hostile bid is made, many authors argue that shareholder rights plans are bad for shareholders, because they protect poor managers from the discipline of the market for corporate control, allowing them to continue to make decisions that do not create shareholder value.

This is illustrated in the growing literature on corporate governance or shareholder rights indices that originated with Gompers *et al.* (2003). Given that much empirical work on corporate governance has yielded inconclusive results when governance variables are measured individually, many researchers now create governance indices designed to capture the combined effects of governance measures. In these indices, if two companies are identical in governance terms except that one has a shareholder rights plan, that firm would rank lower in terms of shareholder protection. Some companies, like Disney and Motorola, have taken note of this mood and dismantled their poison pills. Meanwhile, in Japan, a country not usually associated with hostile takeovers, *warrants* have been issued so as to have the effect of a poison pill, as the Bull-Dog Sauce case illustrates.

Greenmail is another controversial defence associated with the American takeover market. The board of the target company makes an offer to the hostile acquirer to buy at a premium the toe-hold it has already acquired in the market. If this defence works it shelters the incumbent management from disciplinary takeovers while simultaneously diverting the company's cash reserves from profitable uses, making it doubly bad for shareholders. The practice may also encourage pseudo-bids from companies that can afford to buy toe-holds in the hope of making a profit by selling them back to the target companies. This possibility seems to have motivated the judgement by the Tokyo High Court in a ruling discussed in the case study at the end of this chapter.

The literature on the market for corporate control assumes that a free market is good for shareholders, but it says little about other stakeholders. Kacperczyck (2009) argues that according to the shareholder model of corporate governance, the pursuit of shareholder wealth is good for all stakeholders, therefore if a company is protected against takeovers its decision makers are free to pursue their own aims at the expense of both shareholders and stakeholders. On the other hand, stakeholder theory would assert that protection against takeovers frees decision makers from thinking about short-term fluctuations in their company's share price, and allows them to think about the long term. This is good for stakeholders like employees and members of the supply chain because they would like to have a long-term relationship with the company. Qiu and Yu (2009) consider debtholders only, but also suggest that takeover protection can have ambiguous results. If companies are protected from the threat of takeover their decision makers become less careful and so-called *managerial slack* builds up. This lowers corporate value and increases risk and the cost of debt. On the other hand, when a company is under threat of a leveraged takeover that increases the risk faced by existing debtholders, which means they would prefer companies to defend against these bids.

Empirical evidence

Earlier we suggested that hostile takeovers are more likely to occur in countries where share ownership is dispersed among individuals and financial institutions rather than held in blocks by families or the state. Dispersed share ownership has long been associated with the US and UK, and it is well known that hostile takeovers are more common in these countries than in other parts of the world. Schneper and Guillén (2004), for example, report that there were 478 attempted hostile bids in the US between 1988 and 2003. During the same period 273 hostile bids were announced in the UK, but only 19 in France, 18 in Norway, 7 in Germany and 3 in Japan. This is why all the evidence reported here focuses on research undertaken in the US and UK.

Having established that hostile takeovers have the potential to be an important governance mechanism, we can turn to the empirical evidence on the functioning of the takeover market to see if it in fact contributes to sound governance. Holstrom and Kaplan (2001) do this by contrasting the acquisitions and governance environments of the 1980s and 1990s in the US. It is well known that the 1980s saw a huge merger wave, together with the rise of leveraged buyouts and the birth of the junk bond market. They argue that this was encouraged by deregulation and the introduction of new technologies which enabled investors to see that the companies they owned were not performing well. Investor dissatisfaction made it easy for hostile bidders and buyout companies to acquire firms and restructure them so as to make a profit. Restructuring took three main forms during this period. Many conglomerates were broken up now that it was recognised that too much diversification destroys rather than creates value. In some industries managers eliminated excess capacity to reduce costs, and boards that had previously protected stakeholders at the expense of shareholders were replaced. Governance changed radically in the 1990s. Boards became smaller and more active. Managerial remuneration changed with the widespread introduction of stock options and financial institutions began to take an active interest in the companies whose shares they held. At the same time the merger wave subsided and hostility decreased. This contrast leads Holstrom and Kaplan (2001) to conclude that the market for corporate control and internal governance mechanisms are substitutes. However, this is a broad-brush analysis which does not look at the characteristics of the companies that were involved in the merger boom.

Over the years there has been a lot of research into specifically hostile takeovers, with the aim of determining whether or not they are disciplinary and are therefore evidence that the market for corporate control operates effectively. Researchers, like companies, define hostility in slightly different ways. Sinha (2004) adopts a definition offered by Martin and McConnell (1991), who treat takeovers as hostile if they lead to CEO turnover. This seems sensible given that the CEO is ultimately responsible for corporate performance, and would be unwelcome in the acquiring company if the target were performing poorly before the deal. While their definitions are the same, their conclusions are different. Sinha (2004) finds that the probability of a hostile takeover is not influenced by target underperformance in UK firms; this implies that deal makers see hostility as a form of negotiation rather than a means of taking control of poorly managed assets. Martin and McConnell (1991) find that the targets of American hostile bids perform worse that their industry competitors and therefore conclude that hostile bids are disciplinary. Denis and Kruse (2000) agree with this result even though they come to the question from a slightly different starting point. They begin by compiling a sample of underperforming companies, then investigate whether or not they are subject to more disciplinary events than otherwise similar firms. They find that underperforming companies in the US are more likely to be targeted by hostile bidders.

In contrast, Agrawal and Jaffe (2003) and Franks and Mayer (1996) take a different view of hostility. They define as hostile any bid that is at first rejected by the target management. Franks and Mayer (1996) conclude that pre-bid under-performance is not an important feature of UK target companies, so hostile bids are not disciplinary. Agrawal and Jaffe (2003) find some evidence of market under-performance in their sample of American firms, but this underperformance comes eight years prior to the bid, which suggests an extremely slow response by potential acquirers. They also examine the operating performance of their sample and find that targets are not poor performers, so they conclude that hostile takeovers do not have a useful disciplinary function.

This mixed evidence on the performance of target companies casts doubt on the idea that the market for corporate control is an effective corporate governance mechanism, and other analysis is even less supportive of the idea. Lysandrou and Stoyanova (2007) point out that the vast majority of equity sales in the UK are unconnected with the market for corporate control. Stock market turnover is dominated by transactions involving the constituents of the FTSE100 index, a group of companies that is relatively unlikely to be the subject of a control trans-action. Further, if we accept that hostile takeovers are the deals most likely to have corporate governance implications, they constitute a small proportion of all merger and activity. In the US and the UK less than 1 per cent of all mergers and acquisi-tions are hostile (Armour and Skeel, 2007). This implies either that few companies need to reform their governance practices, or that hostile takeovers are not an effi-cient way of reforming corporate governance from the standpoint of shareholders.

As far as stakeholders are concerned, the little evidence that exists suggests that different groups of stakeholders are affected in different ways. While all types of merger and acquisitions activity are feared by employees, who believe it will lead to job losses, Kacperczyk (2009) finds that the market for corporate control has no impact on corporate attention to employees and customers. However, she finds that companies take better care of their communities and the environment when they are protected from takeover, in other words, a free market for corporate control is bad for these groups. By way of contrast, Qiu and Yu (2009) find that a free market is good for bondholders, reducing the risk they face.

PRIVATE EQUITY

The market for corporate control is often treated as synonymous with hostile takeovers involving two listed companies, but private equity deals also change control, and in addition have important implications for governance. The key differences between these and other control transactions is that private equity deals involve the purchase of a company using large amounts of debt rather than equity, and remove the target company from the stock market. Both aspects of these deals have important governance implications, as is shown in the following subsections. While private equity backed deals come in many varieties, the most common are the leveraged buyout (LBO) and the management buyout (MBO). The key differ-ence between the two is that an MBO is led by incumbent managers who bring in a private equity team to support the deal, while in an LBO the private equity firm itself leads the deal.

The mechanics of private equity

Private equity funds raise money from financial institutions such as pension funds and other types of mutual fund, and use it, along with large amounts of debt, to buy either individual divisions of listed companies, or entire firms. The firm that is acquired in this way becomes a private limited company, owned by a holding company which holds the equity in the operating business as an asset matched by its own equity and the debt used to buy the operating company's shares. The holding company receives dividends from the operating company and uses them to pay interest on its debt. The operating company is under pressure to increase its cash flow in the future so that the debt can be repaid. This involves being more efficient than before, cutting wasteful spending and seeking projects that generate a positive net present value. In other words, the debt disciplines management to focus on value-creation and so solves the type I agency problem. Of course, simply being conscious of the need to create value is unlikely to generate sufficient cash to pay off the debt, so the operating company may have to sell assets such as real estate to generate cash to pay down debt. Clearly the company needs these assets, so must lease them back in order to continue operations. This, in turn, gives the management team the additional incentive to work efficiently so that there is enough cash to pay the new leasing costs.

The aim of the private equity deal is to create a leaner, fitter business that can generate enough cash to repay its debt and then be sold at a profit three to five years after purchase, providing a return for the investors in the private equity fund. It is hard to argue against the aim of promoting efficiency that benefits share-holders, but private equity deals are controversial in some circles because of their effects on other stakeholders, notably the government and employees. A highly levered holding company pays no tax because the dividends it receives from the operating company are dwarfed by the interest costs it faces, so it makes a loss. It can therefore enjoy all the services provided by the state without making any financial contribution to it. Trade union leaders are concerned about the potential for job losses as companies cut costs. They also recognise that many LBOs end in liquidation, so they are risky for pension funds as providers of finance for the private equity firms. If pension funds invest in risky ventures this creates additional problems for the workers, who rely on the funds to provide retirement benefits.

Governance implications

Private companies have far more freedom to choose appropriate governance mechanisms than do their listed counterparts. In chapter 7 we will explain how laws and codes of corporate governance have been adopted around the world in an attempt to improve the governance in, and ultimately the performance of companies listed on the stock market. Many recent reforms have focused on the composition and operation of boards of directors. Boards are expected to include a significant number of independent directors who serve on specialist sub-committees covering areas such as remuneration, nomination, audit and risk. Private limited liability companies do not have to comply with this type of regulation, so they are free to operate with very different board structures. In addition, companies which have been taken private through private equity deals have fewer shareholders and much more concentrated ownership than the typical listed company. These two features mean that governance changes dramatically when a listed company is acquired by private equity; the Alliance Boots case outlined in box 6.2 is a good illustration of this.

Box 6.2 Board changes at Alliance Boots

The Boots Group has a long history dating back to 1849, when John Boot opened a shop selling herbal remedies. The business expanded to become probably the best-known chain of chemist's shops in the UK. In 2007 Boots merged with Alliance Unichem, another company with a long history, to form Alliance Boots. Within a year the business made history by becoming the first FTSE100 company to be taken over through a private equity deal; the transaction was organised by Kohlberg Kravis Roberts (KKR) working closely with Stefano Pessina, then the executive deputy chair of Alliance Boots. Just before the private equity deal the board was made up of 13 directors, 7 of whom were non-executives, as prescribed by UK corporate governance regulation. Having left the stock market the company was no longer subject to this regulation. The board size was reduced to 10, 4 of whom had been executive members of the old board, and 4 new executives and 2 KKR representatives were added. Interestingly, the 2010 board is the same size as the old plc board, including 6 executives, 3 KKR representatives and 4 non-executives. Given that most private equity targets are disposed of three to five years after acquisition, these non-executives may be in place to attract investors to a reverse LBO or simply to offer useful independent contributions to decision-making. Time will tell.

Cornelli and Karakas (2008) compare board sizes before and after private equity targets are acquired and de-listed. They find that boards become smaller and that the existing independent directors are replaced by directors supplied by the private equity fund. This strengthens the connection between the owners and the company and ensures that the new directors have in-depth knowledge of the business gained during the deal process. This allows far better board monitoring than in most listed companies. Masulis and Thomas (2009) argue that in addition to playing a general monitoring role, these directors have specialist skills in understanding the risks associated with derivatives, making them a particularly valuable resource in companies that undertake significant derivatives transactions.

Empirical evidence

The global evidence on private equity deals shows that they bring abnormal gains to shareholders at the time of the deal (Lehn and Poulsen, 1989) and, on average, they improve the operating performance of the companies involved (Kaplan, 1989, for the US; Harris *et al.*, 2005, for the UK; Boucly *et al.*, 2009, for France and Bergström *et al.*, 2007, for Sweden). Nikoskelainen and Wright (2007), looking at the UK data, argue that the size of gains depends on the mix of corporate governance mechanisms implemented at the time the company goes private. They highlight the importance of the levels of managerial ownership, gearing and loan syndication. Some gains come because LBO firms tend to invest less in research than their quoted counterparts (Long and Ravenscraft, 1993), which boosts short-term performance through the retention of cash flows. As far as the long term is concerned, it is tempting to suggest that LBO firms are storing up problems for the future, but of course it may be the quoted companies that are doing this by over-investing in 'pet projects' and being less careful with cash than their private counterparts. Trade unions oppose private equity deals because of their effect on stakeholders such as labour and the government. Reducing the size of the work-force is an obvious way to reduce costs and retain cash to service debt. There is evidence that employment increases more slowly in LBO targets than in quoted companies in the US (Kaplan, 1989) and that wages rise more slowly in British LBO firms (Amess and Wright, 2007), while employment levels are consistent with those of listed companies. French LBOs buck these trends (Boucly *et al.*, 2009) by providing higher employment growth and wage increases than listed companies. So far we have made no distinction between types of buyout, but it is worth pointing out that the effects described so far come from buyouts that are instigated by outsiders. Bruining *et al.* (2005) using data on the UK and the Nether-lands, and Amess *et al.* (2007) looking only at the UK report that employees gain in MBOs. Not only do employment and wage levels rise, but employees are given more control over their working practices.

All this evidence suggests that private deals are good for shareholders and both the pre-buyout owners and the post-buyout owners, but potentially bad for employees, who may lose their jobs or receive relatively low wages in the case of an LBO, and for the government, which loses revenue because of the tax-shield effects of debt financing. Before concluding that private equity deals solve the type I agency problem we must sound several notes of caution. First, like all empirical results, the ones highlighted here are based on the average performance of a partic-ular sample. While the average LBO firm in these samples becomes leaner, fitter and more profitable, some have to be liquidated because the debt burden is too much or because their poor performance cannot be improved. Private equity firms typically retain their investment in individual companies for three to five years. After that they sell them to other buyers or take them back to the stock market. Evidence on reverse-LBOs shows that companies manipulate their earnings figures just before the deal to make the equity offering more attractive (Chou *et al.*, 2006), casting doubt on some of the performance figures reported.

CONCLUSION

The idea that the stock market can function as a market for corporate control is beguiling. It implies no need for the explicit regulation of corporate governance because boards of directors and private equity specialists are always looking out for companies which are undervalued due to poor management. When a board spots such a company it will buy it and replace the existing management, gener-ating improved profits through efficiency gains. Knowing that acquisitive boards are hunting for targets, every management team will realise that the only way to stay in post is to maximise shareholder value. The type I agency problem is solved by the mere threat of a takeover. This is the theory. In practice the market for corporate control is often imperfect because of competition law and the existence of takeover defences which protect inefficient management teams. This may explain why the empirical evidence has not reached a consensus on the question of whether or not hostile takeover targets are poorly performing companies in need of better management.

The private equity market can also play a role in disciplining poor performers. Private equity companies can identify under-priced firms in exactly the same way as listed acquirers do. They may make more organisational and governance changes to the acquired business because they have to unlock cash in order pay down debt and because the operating company is not listed and therefore subject to lighter regulation. A key difference between a company acquired through private equity and one bought by another operating company is that the former will be resold three to five years after its acquisition. The sale may take it back to the stock market or place it in a group of operating companies. This feature does not diminish its potential role as a disciplinary force, but does reinforce the idea that LBOs are motivated by the greed of a small number of private equity investors who are not interested in creating long-term value.

While hostile takeovers are associated with the US and the UK, private equity companies are active in continental Europe and Asia, as well as in Anglo-Saxon countries. If acquisition or the threat of acquisition were sufficient to resolve agency problems, regulators in these countries would be silent on corporate governance. Instead, the last 20 years have witnessed intense interest in and action on governance regulation around the world. It seems, then, that while the market for corporate control can contribute to the solution of governance problems, it cannot tackle them all. We need other forms of intervention. In the next chapter we will discuss how regulation emanating from governments, public-sector agencies and stock markets has affected the way companies are governed.

KEY POINTS

- The stock market can act as a market for corporate control when acquisitions are motivated by under-pricing due to poor management of the target company. The acquisitions that are most likely to be part of this mechanism are hostile takeovers.
- Friendly acquisitions are negotiated by the two boards of directors while hostile takeovers may involve the acquiring board going direct to the target shareholders. A key feature of a hostile deal is the removal of key members of the target board once the deal is complete.
- Hostile takeovers occur most frequently in stock markets where share ownership is dispersed rather than being held in significant blocks.
- If the stock market is an effective market for corporate control we would expect the targets of hostile bids to perform less well than other companies. While some research confirms this, other evidence disagrees.
- Acquisitions by private equity firms may also have a disciplinary effect. They certainly change the structure and composition of boards and therefore affect governance.

CASE STUDY   Bull-Dog Sauce: How to leave a nasty taste in the mouth of a potential acquirer

The Bull-Dog Sauce Company is a Japanese business that was founded in 1902 as a wholesale supermarket. It started manufacturing sauces in 1905. Today it is still best known as a manufacturer of sauces and condiments, but it also has a real-estate division. It was first listed in 1973, and gained some notoriety in 2007 when it became the target of a hostile takeover bid. The Japanese corporate governance system is often depicted as having a stakeholder orientation stemming from the importance of debt finance and monitoring by banks and cross-holdings of shares. This feature makes hostile takeovers rare.

Steel Partners is an American hedge fund founded in 1990 with an interventionist style, operating a number of funds including the Japan Strategic Fund. By May 2007 the Japan Strategic Fund owned 10.25 per cent of the equity in Bull-Dog Sauce. On 18 May the fund made a tender offer of ¥1,584 per share. The Bull-Dog board responded by questioning Steel Partners about how they would run the company if the bid were successful. Unhappy with the responses, they rejected the offer on 7 June on the grounds that it was not in the shareholders' interests. They then went on to put a special resolution before the general shareholders' meeting on 24 June. The resolution would authorise the company to issue discriminatory warrants to the company's shareholders. Specifically, all other shareholders who owned shares on 10 July would receive three warrants for every share owned, warrants which could be exercised during September at a price of ¥1. This meant that the number of shares in issue would quadruple as long as every shareholder exercised their warrants, leaving Steel Partners with just 2.82 per cent of outstanding shares. In order to ensure the dilution of Steel Partners' shareholding, the company would exercise any unused warrants in exchange for three shares. Bull-Dog Sauce would purchase Steel Partners' warrants for ¥396 each. This would allow Steel Partners to return to the stock market and purchase sufficient shares to take their holding back to its pre-warrant percentage, avoiding accusations of unfairness towards this individual shareholder. Finally, the resolution stated that if Steel Partners were to withdraw its tender offer before 5 July the warrants would not be issued. In other words, the warrants had all the characteristics of a poison pill except that the issue was authorised after a bid was made. In the jargon, this made the warrants a *morning-after pill*.

Two years earlier Nippon Broadcasting System had attempted a similar issue in response to a bid from Livedoor. In this case the Tokyo High Court ruled that the issue of warrants was unfair unless the bidder intended to sell back the equity to the company at a premium, to transfer intellectual property, to liquidate the business in order to repay debts or to sell off non-core assets to pay a special dividend. Given this precedent Steel Partners went to the Tokyo District Court to seek an injunction against the issue of warrants by Bull-Dog Sauce. By the time the court ruled on the issue the shareholders' meeting had voted in favour, with a majority of 83.4 per cent. The court rejected Steel Partners' request on the grounds that the issue treated all shareholders equally, since Steel Partners would be paid for its warrants. Further, the decision to issue the warrants had been made at a general shareholders' meeting, which is the ultimate decision-making body within the firm. Steel Partners appealed to the High Court which ruled in favour of Bull-Dog Sauce. The High Court went further than the District Court in that it decided that this was an abusive acquisition because Steel Partners was a hedge fund with a duty to its clients and hence would not be motivated by the best interests of Bull-Dog Sauce. Steel Partners remained undaunted and appealed to the Supreme Court, which rejected the appeal, arguing that unless a shareholders' meeting is procedurally unfair, its decision must stand.

Japan is a country where hostile bids are rare. Their very rarity might lead one to suppose that they are proposed for sound economic reasons, yet this ruling makes it almost impossible for any hostile bid to succeed. This contrasts both with countries where hostility is rare and where it is commonplace. The Japanese and German systems are often spoken of in the same breath as if they are very similar, yet the European Commission is against the use of poison pills. In the US, companies are under pressure from shareholders to dismantle poison pills so as not to interfere with the market for corporate control. Japan apparently stands alone in allowing companies to protect themselves so completely from hostile bids. It is impossible to say what would have happened to Bull-Dog Sauce if Steel Partners had been able to acquire the company, but it is clear that the company has had problems since 2007. The company's gross profits have fallen each year since 2007, and thanks to large 'unusual' costs, it made net losses in 2008 and 2009. Steel Partners continued to look for Japanese acquisitions but its attempt to gain a controlling stake in Sapporo Holdings, Japan's third largest brewery, finally failed in February 2009. During 2008–9 the fund sold shares worth around ¥150 billion (Reuters, 17 February 2009). Analysts believe the fund is returning money to investors who have made losses during the financial crisis, rather than winding down its interests in Japan.

CASE-STUDY QUESTIONS

1 Explain how the issue of warrants acts as a poison pill.
2 In the Livedoor case the High Court established a number of situations in which the issue of warrants to defend against a hostile takeover would be deemed 'fair'. Explain why the issue would be fair in these cases by explaining the effects of the various situations on shareholders.
3 Do you agree with the view expressed by the High Court that hedge funds act in the best interests of their clients rather than of the companies whose shares they hold?

REVISION QUESTIONS

1 How would you distinguish between a 'friendly' and a 'hostile' acquisition?
2 When faced with a choice between using 'exit' or 'voice' in response to corporate underperformance, why might a shareholder choose to exit?
3 What is a 'poison pill', and why is it associated with poor governance?
4 Do you agree that the threat of hostile acquisitions is sufficient to discipline managers?
5 Why do some corporate stakeholders oppose private equity deals?
6 Do you agree that board governance in companies owned by private equity firms is better than in listed companies?

REFERENCES

Agrawal, A. and Jaffe, J.F. (2003) 'Do Takeover Targets Underperform? Evidence from Operating and Stock Returns' *Journal of Financial and Quantitative Analysis* 38 (4) 721–746

Amess, K., Brown, S. and Thompson, S. (2007) 'Management Buyouts, Supervision and Employee Discretion' *Scottish Journal of Political Economy* 54 (4) 447–474

Amess, K. and Wright, M. (2007) 'The Wage and Employment Effects of Leveraged Buyouts in the UK' *International Journal of Economics and Business* 14 (2) 179–195

Armour, J. and Skeel, D.A. (2007) 'Who Writes the Rules for Hostile Takeovers, and Why? – The Peculiar Divergence of U.S. and U.K. Takeover Regulation' *Georgetown Law Review* 95 (6) 1727–1794

Becht, M., Franks, J. Mayer, C. and Rossi, S. (2009) 'Returns to Shareholder Activism: Evidence from a Clinical Study of the Hermes UK Focus Fund' *Review of Financial Studies* 22 (8) 3093–3129

Bergström, C. Grubb, M. and Jonsson, S. (2007) 'The Operating Impact of Buyouts in Sweden: A Study of Value Creation' *Journal of Private Equity* 11 (1) 22–39

Boucly, Q., Sraer, D. and Thesmar, D. (2009) 'Leveraged Buyouts – Evidence From French Deals' World Economic Forum *The Global Economic Impact of Private Equity Report 2009* 47–61

Brav, A., Jiang, W., Partnoy, F. and Thomas, R. (2008) 'Hedge Fund Activism, Corporate Governance, and Firm Performance' *Journal of Finance* 63 (4) 1729–1775

Bruining, H., Boselie, P., Wright, M. and Bacon, N. (2005) 'The Impact of Business Ownership Change on Employee Relations: Buyouts in the UK and the Netherlands' *International Journal of Human Resource Management* 16, 345–365

Chou, D. Gombola, M. and Liu, F. (2006) 'Earnings Management and Stock Performance of Reverse Leveraged Buyouts' *Journal of Financial and Quantitative Analysis* 41 (2) 407–438

Clark, G.L. and Hebb, T. (2004) 'Pension Fund Corporate Engagement: The Fifth Stage of Capitalism' *Industrial Relations* 59 (1) 142–171

Clifford, C.P. (2008) 'Value Creation or Destruction? Hedge Funds as Shareholder Activists' *Journal of Corporate Finance* 14 (4) 323–336

Cornelli, F. and Karakas, O. (2008) 'Private Equity and Corporate Governance: Do LBOs Have More Effective Boards?' World Economic Forum *The Global Economic Impact of Private Equity 2008* 65–84

Denis, D.K. (2001) 'Twenty-five Years of Corporate Governance Research … and Counting' *Review of Financial Economics* 10 (3) 191–212

Denis, D.J. and Kruse, T.A. (2000) 'Managerial Discipline and Corporate Restructuring Following Performance Declines' *Journal of Financial Economics* 55 (3) 391–424

English, P.C., Smythe, T.I. and McNeil, C.R. (2004) 'The "CalPERS Effect" Revisited' *Journal of Corporate Finance* 10 (1) 157–174

Franks, J. and Mayer, C. (1998) 'Bank Control, Takeovers and Corporate Governance in Germany' *Journal of Banking and Finance* 22 (10–11) 1385–1403

Franks, J. and Mayer, C. (1996) 'Hostile Takeovers and the Correction of Managerial Failure' *Journal of Financial Economics* 40 (1) 163–181

Gompers, P.A., Ishii, J.L. and Metrick, A. (2003) 'Corporate Governance and Equity Prices' *Quarterly Journal of Economics* 118 (1) 107–155

Harris, R., Siegal, D.S. and Wright, M. (2005) 'Assessing the Impact of Management Buyouts on Economic Efficiency: Plant Level Evidence from the United Kingdom' *Review of Economics and Statistics* 87 (1) 148–153

Hirschman, A. O. (1970) *Exit, Voice, and Loyalty: Responses to Decline in Firms, Organizations, and States* Harvard University Press

Holstrom, B. and Kaplan, S.N. (2001) 'Corporate Governance and Merger Activity in the United States: Making Sense of the 1980s and 1990s' *Journal of Economic Perspectives* 15 (2) 121–144

Kacperczyk, A. (2009) 'With Greater Power Comes Greater Responsibility? Takeover Protection and Corporate Attention to Stakeholders' *Strategic Management Journal* 30 (3) 261–285

Kaplan, S.N. (1989) 'The Effects of Management Buyouts on Operating Performance and Value' *Journal of Financial Economics* 24 (2) 217–254

Lehn, K. and Poulsen, A. (1989) 'Free Cash Flow and Stockholder Gains in Going Private Transactions' *Journal of Finance* 44 (3) 771–787

Long, W.F. and Ravenscraft, D.J. (1993) 'LBOs, Debt and R&D Intensity' *Strategic Management Journal* 14 (S1) 119–135

Lysandrou, P. and Stoyanova, D. (2007) 'The Anachronism of the Voice-Exit Paradigm: Institutional Investors and Corporate Governance in the UK' *Corporate Governance: An International Review* 15 (6) 1070–1078

Manne, H. (1965) 'Mergers and the Market for Corporate Control' *Journal of Political Economy* 73 (2) 110–120

Martin, J. D. and Sayrak, A. (2003) 'Corporate Diversification and Shareholder value: A Survey of Recent Literature' *Journal of Corporate Finance* 9 (1) 37–57

Martin, K.J. and McConnell, J.J. (1991) 'Corporate Performance, Corporate Takeovers and Management Turnover' *Journal of Finance* 46 (2) 671–687

Martynova, M. and Renneboog, L. (2008) 'A Century of Corporate Takeovers: What Have We Learned and Where Do We Stand?' *Journal of Banking and Finance* 32 (10) 2148–2177

Masulis, R.W. and Thomas, R.S. (2009) 'Does Private Equity Create Wealth? The Effects of Private Equity and Derivatives on Corporate Governance' *University of Chicago Law Review* 76 (1) 219–260

Moeller, S.B., Schlingemann, F.P. and Stultz, R.M. (2005) 'Wealth Destruction on a Massive Scale? A Study of Acquiring–Firm Returns in the Recent Merger Wave' *Journal of Finance* 60 (2) 757–782

Netter, J., Poulsen, A. and Stegemoller, M. (2009) 'The Rise of Corporate Governance in Corporate Control Research' *Journal of Corporate Finance* 15 (1) 1–9

Nikoskelainen, E. and Wright, M. (2007) 'The Impact of Corporate Governance Mechanisms on Value Increase in Leveraged Buyouts' *Journal of Corporate Finance* 13 (4) 511–537

Qiu, J. and Yu, F. (2009) 'The Market for Corporate Control and the Cost of Debt' *Journal of Financial Economics* 93 (3) 505–524

Schneper, W.D. and Guillén, M.F. (2004) 'Stakeholder Rights and Corporate Governance: A Cross-national Study of Hostile Takeovers' *Administrative Science Quarterly* 49, (2) 253–295

Sinha, R. (2004) 'The Role of Hostile Takeovers in Corporate Governance' *Applied Financial Economics* 14 (18) 1291–1305

Veld, C. and Veld-Merkoulova, Y.V. (2009) 'Value Creation Through Spin-offs: A Review of the Empirical Evidence' *International Journal of Management Reviews* 11 (4) 407–420

SUGGESTIONS FOR FURTHER READING

Froud, J. and Williams, K. (2007) 'Private Equity and the Culture of Value Extraction' *New Political Economy* 12 (3) 405–420. This paper explains how private equity deals work, concluding that they capture rather than create value, which implies that some stakeholders are damaged by these transactions.

Kini, O., Kracaw, W. and Mian, S. (2004) 'The Nature of Discipline by Corporate Takeovers' *Journal of Finance* 59 (4) 1511–1552. The authors contrast two decades, one characterised by poor internal governance of companies, but an active market for corporate control, the other witnessing improvements in governance and little hostile takeover activity. They conclude that the market for corporate control is useful when other governance mechanisms fail to safeguard shareholders' interests.

http://www.calpers-governance,org/ This section of the CalPERS website explains the pension fund's approach to investment and its thoughts on the use of 'voice'.

http://www.evca.eu The website of the European Private Equity and Venture Capital Association includes links to data and research on the impact of private equity in Europe.

7 REGULATION

⬢ **LEARNING OBJECTIVES**

- ▮ To appreciate the variety of laws and other forms of regulation that affect the corporate governance arrangements of companies
- ▮ To understand why corporate governance codes based on the comply or explain principle have become so popular
- ▮ To appreciate the similarities and differences between the codes issued in different countries
- ▮ To understand the implications of the Sarbanes–Oxley Act 2002 for the governance of companies listed in the US
- ▮ To appreciate the empirical evidence on the impact of codes and laws on the companies they regulate

INTRODUCTION

As we have seen at many points in this book, the corporate governance system in any country emerges due to the interplay of legal, market and cultural influences on corporate behaviour. This means that governance is affected by laws and regulations on issues as diverse as securities transactions, accounting standards, employment rights and mergers. While the terms 'law' and 'regulation' are sometimes used synonymously, here we use them in different ways. By 'law' we mean a set of rules that are embodied in a statute. When these rules are breached it is up to the state to decide whether or not to bring the case to a trial. By 'regulation' we mean a set of rules or principles for behaviour laid down by a stock exchange, professional or trade association. When these rules are breached there are no legal consequences, but the rule-making authority may impose its own sanctions which might include adverse publicity for the company or a fine.

Regulation of this type has become very popular in the field of corporate governance, with many countries adopting codes based on the 'comply or explain' principle. These codes have been issued by a variety of organisations, including stock exchanges, governments and associations of directors and investors. The most influential have become part of the stock exchange listing requirements, which means that in the event the company neither complies nor explains the stock exchange can, as a last resort, de-list the company's securities. These codes usually offer recommendations on the role, composition and remuneration of boards of directors and may also describe shareholder and stakeholder rights where these are not stipulated by law or other regulation. Companies can decide whether to accept all the code's recommendations, in which case they simply report their compliance in their annual report or some other statement, or they can choose to explain why they have chosen to adopt some other practice. The requirement to explain in this way gives companies the freedom to adapt the recommendations to their individual situations as well as allowing the market to judge the implications of the departure from the code. In this way codes offer a flexibility that laws cannot, as well as delegating decisions on the seriousness of non-compliance to the stock market rather than to the legal system, thus saving public resources.

In the next section we will offer a general introduction to the development and diffusion of codes around the world before focusing on the situation in the UK. We will outline the history of the UK Corporate Governance Code and the new Stewardship Code before describing their main recommendations. We will then go on to compare the codes issued in 36 countries on the basis of the board features they prescribe, before discussing some of the many academic studies on the impact of codes on corporate policy.

While the US has a history of producing corporate governance codes, commentators on the state of American governance usually ignore them and highlight the importance of the Sarbanes–Oxley Act of 2002. This is a wide-ranging piece of legislation, so in this description we will focus on those elements which are most closely related to corporate governance issues. Any new legislation brings compliance costs as well as benefits. Many people have speculated that the costs of this Act outweigh its benefits, so we will offer a flavour of the research on this question. One of the features of the Sarbanes–Oxley Act 2002 is that it appears to place responsibility for financial transparency firmly on the shoulders of the CEO and CFO while increasing the penalties they face for any wrongdoing in their company. It is this feature of the Act which comes under scrutiny in the case that accompanies this chapter, where we look at the facts surrounding the prosecution of Richard Scrushy, the first CEO to face a trial under the Sarbanes–Oxley Act.

CODES OF CORPORATE GOVERNANCE

Today codes based on the 'comply or explain' principle are the standard way of regulating corporate governance. At least 77 countries[3] have codes, indicating their importance in regulation. Some of these codes are based on the OECD Principles of Corporate Governance, which we will discuss in chapter 9 in the context of emerging markets; here we will concentrate on national codes. The first corporate governance code was issued in 1978 by the Business Roundtable, an organisation representing the CEOs of major American businesses. In their report the Business Roundtable (1978) notes that boards were often made up of directors with very similar backgrounds, sometimes hand-picked by the CEO. They recommend that boards should become more diverse but do not propose a particular ratio of executive to non-executive members, although they do suggest that outside members should do the bulk of the committee work relating to audit, compensation and nominating procedures. This code stood alone until 1989 when the Hong Kong

Stock Exchange published a very short set of guidelines on governance which were followed two years later by a code issued by the Irish Association of Investment Managers, which has continued to publish guidelines in this area. Given their early interest in corporate governance it is strange that, as box 7.1 explains, Ireland is the only country in the EU that does not have its own code. The development that really ignited interest in the use of codes to regulate corporate governance was the publication in the UK in 1992 of the Financial Aspects of Corporate Governance, usually known as the Cadbury Report. As the next section will explain, the Cadbury Report led to the formation of a succession of other committees each of which published its own report, culminating in the issue of the Combined Code of Corporate Governance in 1998. This provoked a flurry of activity in other parts of the world, so that by the end of 2005 144 codes had been issued, 95 of which were published after 2000 (Zattoni and Cuomo, 2008).

Box 7.1 Corporate governance in Ireland

Ireland is unusual in corporate governance terms. Despite the fact that both the Irish Association of Investment Managers and the Corporate Governance Association of Ireland have published guidance on corporate governance, the country's stock exchange requires listed companies to comply with or explain their deviations from the UK Corporate Governance Code. This makes it the only country in the EU which does not have its own code. The accounting firm Grant Thornton publishes an annual review of corporate governance in Ireland. The latest survey indicates that the proportion of companies in full compliance with the code fell from 51 to 36 per cent between 2008 and 2009. This would not be a problem if those firms that do not comply give adequate explanation of their reasons. However the survey shows that some firms do not give enough information to enable investors to fully understand why the companies have chosen their own governance arrangements. Grant Thornton recommends that some aspects of corporate governance regulation, such as the separation of the roles of CEO and chair of the board, should become the subject of legislation, since the 'comply or explain' framework which is so popular around the world does not seem to work in the case of Ireland.

The beauty of the principle of 'comply or explain' is that companies can choose to comply with all the requirements of the relevant code, in which case a simple statement to that effect can be made in the annual report or corporate governance statement; or if instead a company decides that it does not want to comply with a particular requirement of the code, it can adopt an alternative practice but has to explain why, thereby drawing attention to the deviation. This is useful from the investors' point of view because it makes it easy to spot divergences from the code and allows them to determine the gravity of the divergence. A serious deviation will be punished by the market as investors sell their shares and the firm's stock market value falls. Actions by investors make life simpler for regulators since they do not have to take any formal action against companies unless they fail to explain their non-compliance.

While codes are used in every continent, empirical research on their adoption and content indicates that different legal systems are associated with different adoption patterns and diverse content. Legal systems are usually classified according to whether they are based on common or civil law. Countries like the UK and US have a common-law framework in which judges set precedents in court and those precedents affect future judgements. In contrast, continental Europe has a civil-law framework which relies instead on statutes and codes to determine the content of the law. One would expect that corporate governance codes would fit more easily in a civil law framework, but on the contrary, Aguilera and Cuervo-Cazurra (2004) find that codes are more likely to be adopted in common-law countries. This is confirmed by Zattoni and Cuomo (2008), who find that in addition to being early adopters of codes, common-law countries also issue more of them. The UK is an excellent example of this phenomenon, since it is a common-law country which has issued six versions of its code along with numerous reviews. Codes are also more likely to be adopted in markets where foreign investors are important (Aguilera and Cuervo-Cazurra, 2004). This is supported by the data presented in the tables in chapter 2 of this book. They indicate that overseas equity ownership is significant in the UK and in continental European countries where codes have become an important part of the governance environment. In contrast, foreign ownership is relatively unimportant in the US market, where legislation in the form of the Sarbanes–Oxley Act has been introduced. One area in which the codes themselves differ is in the extent to which they specify the composition of the board of directors. In countries with a dual board system and where codetermination is practised, the law already specifies how boards should be composed, while in countries with the unitary board system codes recommend how boards should be composed.

The development of codes in the UK

The late 1980s saw a number of high-profile scandals and business failures in the UK, including the Bank of Credit and Commerce International (BCCI), Mirror Group Newspapers and Polly Peck. The BCCI and Polly Peck collapses were due to fraud at the highest levels of the organisation while the scandal at Mirror Group Newspapers involved the flouting of pension fund rules. A common feature of both Mirror Group Newspapers and Polly Peck was that the companies were headed by strong CEOs who also chaired and dominated their boards (Wearing, 2005). The Cadbury Committee was formed in 1991 to investigate the causes of such failures and to suggest ways in which they could be avoided in future. The committee was sponsored by the Financial Reporting Council, the London Stock Exchange and the accountancy profession. These sponsors were concerned about the loss of confidence in financial reporting and doubts over the ability of auditors to provide adequate reassurance to investors. These concerns, together with the report's title, 'The Financial Aspects of Corporate Governance', gave the impression that the recommendations would be in the area of accounting and auditing. However, while the Cadbury Report included a section on auditing, its ideas on board composition and accountability formed the heart of the report, which recommended the adoption of a code of best practice which would then be implemented by the London Stock Exchange on a comply or explain basis. The report recommended that boards should be headed by a chair who is not also the CEO of the company, and should include at least three non-executive directors, the majority of whom should be independent of the business in that they had no personal or business links with its management. It should set up three subcommittees with specific responsibilities for financial reporting and audit matters, designing remuneration contracts and ensuring that the board is refreshed with new talent. The non-executive directors should take all the seats on the audit committee and form the majority of the remuneration and nomination committees.

Further committees were established to continue the work on corporate governance. In 1995, following widespread public concern over directors' pay, the Greenbury Report focused on the relationships between directors' remuneration and both their individual and corporate performance. It added to the guidance on the operation of remuneration committees. Later that year the Hampel Committee was set up to review the implementation of the previous reports. When it reported in 1998 it endorsed the two earlier reports and recommended that the Financial Reporting Council, an independent regulator, should continue to update previous recommendations. It did this when it brought together the three reports in the Combined Code on Corporate Governance, which was then updated in 2000 and further revised in 2003, 2006, 2008 and 2010. The latest version, the UK Corporate Governance Code, has separated out the recommendations on active involvement by financial institutions, which are now offered in the Stewardship Code for Institutional Investors.

The UK Corporate Governance Code

The principles of the UK Corporate Governance Code are laid out in five sections covering leadership, effectiveness, accountability, remuneration and relations with shareholders. Additional schedules discuss the design of remuneration contracts and disclosure of governance practices. The first two sections highlight the collective responsibility of the board for decision-making and specify the composition of boards, allowing some variation, dependent on the size of the firm. All companies should separate the roles of CEO and Chair, appointing an independent chair of the board. The majority of other board members should be independent, and one of these should take the role of Senior Independent Director, who is responsible for relations with shareholders in the event that other communication channels have broken down. The independent directors should take the lead in matters relating to the integrity of financial information, remuneration and succession planning through their work on the audit, remuneration and nomination committees, each of which should have at least three members. The nomination committee is the only one on which executive directors can sit, but even this committee must have a majority of independent members. New directors should go through an induction process, and then be subject to annual re-election. The effectiveness of the board as a group should be evaluated each year. Smaller companies, defined as those outside the FTSE350 index, must have at least two independent directors, may have smaller committees and can re-elect directors at three-year intervals.

This brief summary highlights the importance of independent directors to the governance system in the UK. The Code requires the board to identify in the annual report those directors it considers to be independent based on their relationships with the company. It goes on to list seven aspects of that relationship which would undermine independence: having been employed by the company during the last five years; having had a material business relationship with it during the previous three years; having received any remuneration apart from a director's fee; having a family tie to an adviser, director or senior adviser of the company; having business links with other directors through cross-directorships or involvement in other organisations; representing a major shareholder or having served on the board for more than nine years. Of course, the mere fact of being independent is not enough to make a director valuable to a specific board. The Code emphasises the need for a balance of skills on the board, for a good induction process when new members join and for the continuous provision of relevant information to board members so that they can discharge their duties effectively.

The Code highlights the fact that good corporate governance includes communication with shareholders over how the company is governed. The annual report is the vehicle for communicating information on the composition and remuneration of the board, the remit and composition of the individual committees and details of the number of meetings held and directors' attendance. This has contributed to the increase in the length of annual reports, which will be discussed in more detail in chapter 8. As an indicator of this, taking the 2010 Annual Report of Marks and Spencer plc as an example, the corporate governance section accounts for 28 per cent of the length in pages, not far behind the financial statements section, which accounts for 35 per cent of the length. This is a good indicator of the importance that corporate governance reporting has assumed in the UK, thanks to the Code. This particular report is also an example of good practice in disclosure, having been short-listed for the 2010 ICSA Hermes Transparency in Governance award.

The board's accountability for business and financial decisions, including risk management, is covered in the third section of the Code. It emphasises the board's collective responsibility in determining the level and type of risk the company should take in order to achieve its objectives, in explaining how the company achieves those objectives and thereby creates value and in preparing the annual report and accounts. Some of its requirements are highly specific, suggesting where in the annual report certain material should be located and directing the board to additional guidance on subjects such as going-concern risk. It also describes the role of the audit committee in reviewing the company's internal control procedures, its relationship with the external auditors, the effectiveness of the internal audit and the provisions for *whistle-blowing* within the organisation.

As we saw in chapter 5, remuneration packages should be designed by the independent directors on the remuneration committee so as to attract, retain and motivate directors. The committee may be advised by remuneration consultants, and where this is the case the board must report on whether or not the consultants have other connections with the company. Executive directors' pay should be significantly influenced by both personal and corporate performance. No director should be able to influence their own pay, so the payments made to non-executives should be determined by the board or in some cases the shareholders, to reflect their time commitment to the company. Payments to non-executives should not be related to corporate performance, because this would take away their independence.

While the Code appears to lay down many rules for behaviour, in the preface the FRC is at pains to point out that simple compliance with the Code is not enough to ensure sound governance. It emphasises the importance of the spirit of the code which implies careful thought about what governance is and how good governance can be achieved, and involves open and frank communication between directors who are dedicated to the companies they serve; none of this can be mandated by a set of rules.

The Stewardship Code

The Stewardship Code is designed to govern the way in which institutional investors consider and report on their stewardship role with respect to the companies in which they invest. Like the UK Code of Corporate Governance it is based on the 'comply or explain' principle, although it is not obvious what sanction exists for those institutional investors which choose to do neither. This is a short code including just six pages of text, offering guidance on seven principles. These are that institutional investors should: determine and disclose a policy explaining how they fulfil their responsibilities as stewards; formulate and disclose a policy on how they will manage conflicts of interest; monitor the companies in which they invest; produce guidelines on how they will escalate their monitoring activities should this be required; be willing to act alongside other institutions to bring change; formulate and disclose a policy on voting and produce periodic reports on their stewardship and voting practices.

It is clear from the way the code is written that the FRC sees stewardship as a natural part of the exercise of a financial institution's fiduciary duty to its retail investors. We have met the concept of fiduciary duty already in this book in terms of the relationship between corporate boards and shareholders, and potentially between boards and both lenders and employees. Financial institutions have the fiduciary duty to safeguard the interests of the people who delegate investment decisions to them; this means seeking the best possible return subject to maintaining risk levels at a level that is appropriate for those retail investors. The Code is clear that stewardship is part of this fiduciary duty irrespective of the fund's investment style, in other words, whether the fund is passively invested in an index or seeks to beat the market. This is interesting given that the literature discussed in chapter 6 implies that the managers of passive funds are more likely than their active counterparts to be interested in governance issues. The code discusses a variety of forms of investor engagement with corporate management, ranging from voting at general meetings, giving careful consideration to the explanations given by boards when they choose to explain rather than comply, through to meeting with corporate directors when they feel that there are major problems. The code recognises that fund managers may fear this course of action because it might lead to them receiving inside information and hence being unable to trade the company's securities. It states that they will not expect companies to give them access to this type of information.

Just as the UK Code of Corporate Governance emphasises the need for disclosure of governance practices, so the Stewardship Code is keen to encourage institutional investors to disclose information concerning the application of the principles on their websites. Given that it is so recent there have been no academic studies of the impact on the Code on investor behaviour. However, a highly unscientific search for information conducted by this author and reported in box 7.2 indicates that disclosure is not high on institutions' agendas. The FRC is keen not to impose further duties on the overseas investors who are such important holders of

Box 7.2 Early signs of compliance with the Stewardship Code

A quick search of the websites of a variety of well-known institutions reveals rather patchy stewardship reporting, at least as at the end of October 2010. Not surprisingly, given its commitment to shareholder activism, the Hermes website has links to an article on the Code on the front page of its website. The UBS Asset Management website revealed an impressive page offering links to the Code itself as well as to various statements of its voting records. However, to access those statements the user must be willing to accept a statement that they are a professional rather than a retail customer. Jupiter Asset Management has a section on the Code, together with a statement that it supports the principles and will report on its compliance at a later date. The author found no references to the Code on the websites of AVIVA, Scottish Widows or Standard Life. This of course does not mean that there is nothing available, rather that these institutions are not making it easy for retail clients to gain information on what the FRC sees as an important aspect of corporate governance.

equity in UK firms. The Stewardship Code states that any disclosures they make in line with their own domestic regulation should satisfy the UK requirements. Interestingly, British institutional investors are urged to apply the Code's requirements to all their investments, not just to their holdings in the UK. If they comply with this, it could have important implications for the way in which governance practices are transmitted across the world, a subject we shall return to in chapter 9.

A Comparison of Codes

It is often said that corporate governance systems around the world are converging. This may be due to contagion effects, as regulators in one part of the world learn from good practice elsewhere or because overseas investors encourage regulators to import systems that have proved useful elsewhere. In emerging markets the influence of the OECD Principles, which will be discussed in more detail in chapter 9, may also encourage regulators to adopt similar practices. Zattoni and Cuomo (2008) note that most codes emphasise the importance of reforming boards of directors, which includes discouraging duality, encouraging the use of non-executive directors, creating committees dominated by non-executives and introducing procedures for evaluating the work of boards. Here we will compare a variety of codes of corporate governance based on the extent to which they incorporate these elements. The codes are chosen on the grounds that they were issued in countries using the unitary board system (for ease of comparison) and that English translations are available via the European Corporate Governance Institute (ECGI) website. In the following tables we indicate the date of each code, which was the most recent version available at the time of writing (October 2010) and the type of organisation that issued it. Stock exchanges and securities commissions are the most prolific providers of codes, followed by standing corporate governance committees. By the time you read this we are sure many codes will have been updated, so you can check on that website to see how much regulation has changed in the intervening period!

Table 7.1 compares the codes in operation in European countries. The key characteristics used in the comparison are the recommendation to separate the roles of chair and CEO, for the majority of directors to be independent, to establish audit, remuneration and nomination committees and to put in place a system for board evaluation. As you would expect, a tick indicates that the code makes that recommendation and a cross that it does not. In the 'majority of board independent' column, NED means that the recommendation on composition is made with reference to non-executive rather than independent directors. As the table indicates, the need to evaluate the board is the principle on which most counties agree. Of the 14 country codes mentioned in the table, only one, the Greek code, is silent on this point. There are 11 countries that require companies to establish committees to deal with audit, remuneration and nomination issues. In those countries where fewer than three committees are advocated, it is the nomination committee which is usually omitted, although Greece is unusual in also not recommending an audit committee. It is worth pointing out that most of the codes appearing in this table were issued after 2005. If one excludes the earlier codes issued in Greece, Malta, Russia and Turkey, the remainder would agree that all three committees should be in place. Nine countries regulate against duality. Those that tolerate the practice of duality are a mixed group. Greece, Romania and Spain are EU members while Russia and Switzerland are not, but are unalike in economic terms. Recommendations on board composition are far from uniform in Europe. Norway must be regarded as a special case, because all board members must be non-executives. Of the remaining countries in the table, five require the majority of members to be independent, three instead seek a majority of non-executives while the others offer no guidance.

Table 7.1 A comparison of corporate governance codes in Europe

Country	Separation of CEO/chair	Majority of board independent	Three subcommittees	Board evaluation
Belgium (2009)[2]	✔	NED	✔	✔
Finland (2008)[1]	✔	✔	✔	✔
Greece (2001)[4]	✘	✘	remuneration	✘
Iceland (2009)[4]	✔	✔	✔	✔
Luxembourg (2009)[1]	✔	✘	✔	✔
Malta (2005)[3]	✔	✘	audit and remuneration	✔
Norway (2009)[2]	✔	NED[5]	✔	✔
Romania (2009)[1]	✘	✘	✔	✔
Russia (2002)[2]	✘	✘	audit and remuneration	✔
Spain (2006)[1]	✘	✘	✔	✔
Sweden (2010)[2]	✔	✔	✔	✔
Switzerland (2008)[2]	✘	NED	✔	✔
Turkey (2005)[1]	✔	NED	✔	✔
United Kingdom (2010)[2]	✔	✔	✔	✔

Notes:
1 Code issued by the stock market or securities commission
2 Code issued by a corporate governance committee
3 Code issued by other regulator
4 Code issued by directors' organisation or trade body
5 Boards in Norway do not include any company executives. The majority of the members elected by shareholders should be independent

Table 7.1 excludes several major European economies because companies in those countries operate the dual-board system described in chapter 4. While this structure is fundamentally different from the unitary board, many of the governance features associated with the codes summarised in table 7.1 also form a part of the codes issued in countries like Austria and Germany, which have dual boards. As we saw in chapter 3, employee representatives sit on the supervisory boards of Austrian and German companies, but the codes of both countries require that at least some of the remaining board members be independent. The Austrian code states that the majority of the members elected by the general meeting should be independent. It also stipulates that the supervisory board should set up audit, nomination and remuneration committees, while the German code requires only audit and nomination committees. The French code allows companies to choose either the unitary or dual-board system. Where the unitary board is chosen, it must be headed by a chair who is not the CEO, it must set up audit, remuneration and nomination committees and one-third of its members must be free from conflicts of interest.

Table 7.2 compares the codes issued in the two North American countries, Canada and the US. Both agree that the majority of board members should be independent, and that boards should have audit, nomination and remuneration committees. The Canadian guidelines say nothing specific about board evaluation, and the American code permits duality. There has been some debate about this within American corporate governance circles. The consensus seems to be that there is no harm in allowing one person to take both roles as long as the board appoints a senior independent director as a check on the concentration of power in the hands of a single individual.

Table 7.2 A comparison of corporate governance codes in North America

Country	Separation of CEO/chair	Majority of board independent	Three subcommittees	Board evaluation
Canada (2006)[1]	✔	✔	✔	✘
US (2008)[2]	✘	✔	✔	✔

Notes:
1 Code issued by the stock market or securities commission
2 Code issued by directors' organisation or trade body

Table 7.3 compares a selection of countries from the Asia-Pacific region. The codes issued in this region tend to be older than European and North American codes, just 3 of the 12 were published after 2005, and to imply different governance patterns. While 10 of the 12 codes separate the roles of chair and CEO, only 3 require the majority of board members to be independent. This may reflect the difficulty of finding truly independent directors in relatively small stock markets where most business leaders are known to one another, although this is not the whole story, given that the code in Bangladesh requires independence, despite there being fewer listed companies there than in Thailand, which does not even require the majority of board members to be non-executives. The audit committee has been adopted throughout the region, but only one-half of the countries included in the table require both a nomination and a remuneration committee as well. Of the 12 codes, 7 stipulate regular evaluations of the board.

Table 7.3 A comparison of codes of corporate governance in the Asia-Pacific Region

Country	Separation of CEO/chair	Majority of board independent	Three subcommittees	Board evaluation
Australia (2010)[1]	✔	✔	✔	✔
Bangladesh (2004)[2]	✔	✔	audit	✔
Hong Kong (2004)[1]	✔	✘	✔	✘
Malaysia (2007)[1]	✔	✘	✔	✘
New Zealand (2004)[1]	✔	NED	audit	✔
Pakistan (2002)[1]	✘	✘	audit	✘
Singapore (2005)[2]	✔	✘	✔	✔
South Korea (2003)[2]	✔	✔[3]	✔	✔
Sri Lanka (2005)[1]	✔	✘	audit and remuneration	✘
Taiwan (2002)[1]	✔	✘	audit	✘
Thailand (2006)[1]	✔	✘	✔	✔
The Philippines (2002)[1]	✘	✘	audit	✔

Notes:
1 Code issued by the stock market or securities commission
2 Code issued by a corporate governance committee
3 This provision does not apply to very small companies or to those where a blockholder has more that 50 per cent of the shares

The final table, table 7.4, compares eight governance codes issued in the Middle East and Africa. While these countries vary dramatically in their wealth and stage of development, they display unanimity in requiring the separation of the roles of chair and CEO. None of these countries demands a majority of independent directors on the board, but half advocate a majority of non-executives. As was hinted in the context of Asia, this may say more about the available pool of independent directors than about the desire to improve governance. They also agree that companies should appoint members to audit and remuneration committees, while five of the eight recommend a nomination committee as well. Finally, three of the eight recognise the need for regular board evaluations.

We began this section by suggesting that corporate governance systems are converging. By taking an overview of the four tables discussed here we may be able to get a better idea of whether or not this is true. Of the 36 countries included in the tables, 6 are similar in that they ticked each of the four governance characteristics highlighted. Two of these, Australia and the UK share a common language and historical ties, so it is not surprising that they share common governance characteristics. Finland, Iceland and Sweden might also be regarded as similar. Table 2.3 in the chapter on shareholders indicates that in 2006 Iceland and Sweden had similar patterns of equity ownership by all groups, apart from the public sector and non-bank financial institutions. Overseas investors were the largest single group in each country, which as Aguilera and Cuervo-Cazurra (2004) indicate, is important in terms of the adoption of codes. South Korea is the outlier in terms of geography, but it too has ticked all four boxes. If in describing board composition we were to substitute non-executives for independent directors, Bahrain, Belgium, Norway, South Africa and Turkey would join the group of countries ticking four boxes, taking the total to 11 of this sample of 36. In other words, nearly one-third of this sample agrees on how boards should be composed, what subcommittees they should have and on the need for self-evaluation.

Table 7.4 A comparison of codes of corporate governance in the Middle East and Africa

Country	Separation of CEO/chair	Majority of board independent	Three subcommittees	Board evaluation
Bahrain (2010)[3]	✔	NED	✔	✔
Egypt (2006)[4]	✔	NED	audit and remuneration	✗
Kenya (2002)[2]	✔	✗	✔	✔
Nigeria (2003)[1]	✔	✗	audit and remuneration	✗
Saudi Arabia (2006)[3]	✔	✗	✔	✗
South Africa (2009)[2]	✔	NED	✔	✔
Tunisia (2008)[4]	✔	✗	✔	✗
United Arab Emirates (2007)[1]	✔	NED	audit and remuneration	✗

Notes:
1 Code issued by the stock market or securities commission
2 Code issued by a corporate governance committee
3 Code issued by other regulator
4 Code issued by directors' organisation or trade body

The tables also include eight nations which are alike in that they ticked fewer than two of the four governance characteristics listed. Two country codes do not record a tick against any characteristic. These are the Greek and Pakistani codes. These codes are silent on board leadership, composition and evaluation but the code in Greece requires companies to have a remuneration committee while the code in Pakistan requires an audit committee. Russia, Sri Lanka. Taiwan, The Philippines, Egypt and Nigeria have issued codes that include one of the four features mentioned by Zattoni and Cuomo (2008). However, a relaxation of the criterion on independence to non-executives would exclude Egypt from the list. Of the remainder, Russia, Sri Lanka and Nigeria score a tick on either composition or evaluation and also require boards to establish audit and remuneration committees.

While the forgoing analysis of the tables implies that governance systems, by which we mean the collection of individual mechanisms used in particular economies, still vary, a simple count of the codes advocating each of the four mechanisms offers a rather different picture. Of the codes listed in the tables 78 per cent agree that the roles of CEO and chair of the board should be held by different people; 67 per cent agree that the board should evaluate its work regularly and create subcommittees to oversee the audit, remuneration and nomination functions; 25 per cent of the codes recommend that the majority of board members should be independent, but that figure rises to 50 per cent if we change the requirement to independent or non-executive. Clearly regulators around the world agree that certain governance mechanisms are important, principally the separation of the roles of chief executive and chair of the board. However, most give companies discretion over how they arrange their own governance structures, so even if regulated governance structures are not wholly convergent, economic and investor pressures may lead to greater voluntary convergence.

Evidence on the implementation and effects of codes

As we have already seen, corporate governance codes based on the principle of 'comply or explain' have been adopted all over the world. International organisations like the OECD are keen to see wider implementation of existing principles. This suggests that regulators are convinced that compliance with codes will bring tangible benefits to investors, firms and even economies. In this section we turn to the evidence on the implementation of codes and their effect on corporate performance.

As we saw earlier, the UK Code has been through several revision processes. The best test of the impact of any code is to look at the situation before and after some major change. For that reason, even recently published papers on compliance with the Code have concentrated on the introduction of the Cadbury Report, rather than on the refinements that have taken place since then. There is general agreement that most companies have chosen to comply rather than explain, in that the proportion of companies appointing a chair who is not also the CEO rose significantly following the publication of the Cadbury Report, and more companies included at least three non-executives on the board and introduced remuneration committees (Weir and Laing, 2000). However there is less agreement on the benefits of compliance with the Code. Some of the differences may stem from the rather different methodologies used to look at the relationship between compliance and performance.

Weir and Laing looked at the effects of compliance in two rather different ways. In a paper published in 2000 they looked at the relationship between corporate performance, measured in both accounting and market terms, and four groups of explanatory variables. One group of variables represented compliance with the Cadbury Report; the others represented ownership, control variables such as debt, size and risk, and finally lagged performance. The authors examined the relationship using two groups of 200 randomly chosen companies from the *Times* 1000. Data were collected for 1992 for the first group and for 1995 for the second. They found that the changes embodied in the Cadbury Report had not had the positive impact one would have expected. Neither performance measure was significantly affected by duality, which is interesting given that regulators in so many countries have chosen to separate the roles of the chair and CEO. According to this evidence the presence or absence of duality is irrelevant to both stock market returns and return on assets. Return on assets is also unaffected by the presence of a remuneration committee. The number of non-executive directors is important, but in an unexpected way. The results show that in 1992 an increase in the number of non-executives had a significantly negative effect on return on assets, while in 1995 those boards including three non-executives experienced a reduction in returns. Before concluding that non-executives actually harm performance we should note that the lagged performance variable was consistently positively significant. This means that poor performance in one year leads to poor performance in the next, so some of these companies may have increased the number of non-executives as a response to problems. Without a time series we cannot comment on whether or not this brought future benefits. The only Cadbury-related variable to have any effect on stock market returns was the presence of a remuneration committee which was positively related to returns in both years.

Their later paper used a different methodology, but reached similar conclusions. In their paper published in 2001 Weir and Laing took a group of 320 UK companies and looked at their governance in 1995 and their performance a year later. They found that the majority of companies complied, but when the companies were ranked in terms of their performance, there was a pattern in non-compliance. The best performers had more instances of duality than the other groups and also had smaller proportions of non-executives on the board. These findings may suffer from the kind of endogeneity issues already mentioned, but even so, do not encourage the reader to conclude that compliance is conducive to good performance.

A second team of authors, Dahya and McConnell (2007) and Dahya *et al.* (2002), provide results which are more encouraging for regulators. In their 2007 paper Dahya and McConnell focus on a specific element of the Cadbury Report, the requirement to have at least three non-executives on the board. They divide their sample of companies into three groups according to whether they complied with this even before the report and continued the practice, whether they complied when the report was published or did not comply following publication of the report. The results obtained by looking at the companies that became compliant are particularly interesting. These companies experienced positive abnormal returns in the stock market following the announcement that they had become compliant. They then went on to record significant improvements in return on assets due to higher revenue growth and slower growth in both the cost of goods sold and in operating expenses. This implies that they implemented better internal controls once their boards had a larger independent element. In their paper with Travlos, published in 2002, they tackled the effects of compliance in a different way, looking at how it affected top management turnover. An anticipated benefit of more independent boards is their ability to root out inefficient management. Those boards that became Cadbury-compliant did indeed see a significant increase in CEO turnover, and the turnover rate became more sensitive to corporate performance. These findings indicate that an independent board is an important element in ensuring sound corporate governance, leading to improved performance.

The continental European literature on the relationship between corporate performance and compliance with codes is small. However the few published papers, while using different methodologies, support the idea that compliance leads to improved performance. For Germany Goncharov *et al.* (2006) examine the relationship between both stock market prices and returns and a measure of relative compliance with the German Code. German companies publish a Declaration of Conformity, allowing the researchers to measure the number of deviations from the code made by their sample of firms. They create a dummy variable, taking the value 1 if the company has made the same or fewer deviations than the median number, or 0 otherwise. Using an econometric specification that takes account of endogeneity, they find that their corporate governance variable is positive and significant in explaining both prices and returns.

Beiner *et al.* (2006) measure compliance with the Swiss Code in an absolute sense rather than the relative one just described. They base their index of compliance on the results of a survey in which firms rate their compliance by answering 38 questions. Rather than simply stating that they do or do not comply they rate the strength of compliance from 1 (low) to 5 (high). The results are added up, then the number is normalised across firms so that compliance varies from 0 to 100. Controlling for endogeneity by estimating a simultaneous equations model, they find that causation runs from compliance to firm value, and the relationship between the two is statistically significant.

Alves and Mendes (2004) also measure compliance using a questionnaire submitted by Portuguese firms. They find that compliance increases over time, but that only certain types of compliance are value-relevant. They measure corporate performance using both abnormal and raw stock market returns. They find that both types of return are positively and significantly affected by compliance with regulations concerning the structure and functioning of the board. Regulations concerning best practice on internal control and on voting and shareholder representation have no impact on either measure of returns. The surprising result is that compliance with information disclosure rules has a significantly negative impact on raw returns, which loses its significance but remains negative when abnormal returns are used. This seems odd, given that investors should value information. Perhaps in this case the information disclosed was unfavourable. On balance the evidence shows that codes of corporate governance have had a positive impact on the value of European companies.

The even smaller amount of evidence on Asian corporate governance is also supportive. Nowland (2008) reports that disclosure has improved in Hong Kong, Indonesia, Malaysia, the Philippines, Singapore, South Korea, Taiwan and Thailand since those countries introduced corporate governance codes. Further, companies' forecast errors have improved, along with analysts' forecast errors, when the codes have emphasised the importance of good disclosure practices. Individual country studies for Malaysia (Abdul Wahab et al., 2007) and Thailand (Kouwenberg, 2006) also indicate that the adoption of codes improves companies' market value.

THE SARBANES–OXLEY ACT

The Public Company Accounting Reform and Investor Protection Act of 2002, or the Sarbanes–Oxley Act, as it is usually known, was passed soon after the Enron scandal. To some it seemed like a knee-jerk reaction to the Enron debacle, yet Romano (2005), in examining the events that led to the passage of the bill, argues that the legislature's appetite for reform had waned after the investigations into Enron and the bill was not seen as urgent until WorldCom collapsed. While the Act brought in many detailed rules, the best-known sections relate to the establishment of the Public Company Accounting Oversight Board (PCAOB), the introduction of new rules governing the relationship between companies and their auditors, improved disclosure of off-balance sheet items and greater accountability of top management for fraud in their companies. Given the nature of the Enron scandal, the company's extensive use of special-purpose vehicles that do not appear on the balance sheet, and the close relationship between the company and its auditors Arthur Andersen, it is easy to see how the Act appeared to be designed to ensure that there would never be another Enron.

While the Sarbanes–Oxley Act is often described as corporate governance legislation, a glance at the contents of the Act[4] reveals that it covers matters that are very different from those included in the codes described earlier in this chapter. While codes focus on board matters, the emphasis in the Act is on auditing, financial disclosure and fraud, although it does deal with the audit committee and the responsibilities of the CEO and CFO with regard to financial statements.

As we saw in chapter 4, audit committees were common in American companies before they were adopted elsewhere. The SEC recommended their use in 1940, but it was rather later, in 1977, that the New York Stock Exchange demanded that every listed company should have an audit committee. The Sarbanes–Oxley Act amended the Securities Exchange Act of 1934 to include the requirement that each listed company establish an audit committee made up of independent directors, including one financial expert, to which the auditor should report. While this could hardly be called an innovation, the section introducing corporate responsibility for financial reports gave new responsibilities to CEOs and led to the first prosecution under the Act, which is outlined in the case at the end of this chapter. Now when a corporate officer signs the firm's financial statements they assert that the statements and accompanying report, whether annual or quarterly, contain no untrue facts or material omissions and therefore fairly represent the financial and operating positions of the company. Further, the signing officers take responsibility for establishing and testing the company's internal controls as well as for reporting any changes or deficiencies, along with any fraud, to the auditors and the audit committee. On the face of it these measures should make it impossible for any CEO or CFO to plead ignorance of financial problems or fraud within their organisations. Further, if a company fails to comply with the reporting requirements and has to restate its figures, the CEO and CFO have to return any incentive-based remuneration and profit made from trading the company's securities during the 12-month period following the filing of inaccurate accounts. To reinforce the responsibilities of the CFO the Act also requires companies to introduce codes of ethics for senior financial officers. These ethics codes are supposed to promote ethical behaviour, timely and understandable disclosures and compliance with rules; aspects of behaviour which are normally seen as part of professional ethics, rather than matters that are legislated. Interestingly this aspect of the Act, together with the requirement for a financial expert to sit on the audit committee, is not mandatory; companies can choose to explain why they deviate from the practice, making these provisions similar to the recommendations included in codes of corporate governance.

While some people saw the passage of the Sarbanes–Oxley Act as a decisive step towards improved corporate governance and accountability, others saw it as the imposition of costly rules which would reduce the profitability of companies and even prompt some to leave the stock market. Early academic studies of the impact of the Act supported these concerns. Zhang (2007) used event-study methodology to investigate the effects of the Act. She found that companies experienced negative abnormal returns, that is, declining stock price, around key legislative events, indicating that the market saw the Act as bad news. Engel *et al.* (2007) reported an increase in going-private transactions after 2002.

Other researchers have questioned the validity of these findings. Leuz (2007) suggests that it is difficult to interpret the evidence on key events because other important issues, such as the likelihood of war with Iraq and the creation of the Department of Homeland Security, were also affecting confidence in the American economy at that time. Further, he notes that even before the Act was passed there was a trend towards de-listing thanks to the activities of private equity investors and the availability of debt. Piotroski and Srinivasan (2008) analyse the costs of the Act by concentrating on the effects it had on firms' choice of exchange. They concentrate on the choice between listing on the London Stock Exchange or in an American market. They find that the Act made no difference to the choices made by large firms, but did affect the decisions made by smaller firms. Smaller firms became more likely to choose London's Alternative Investment Market than NASDAQ once the Act was in force.

As we said earlier, unlike codes of corporate governance the Sarbanes-Oxley Act says little about corporate boards. However, some researchers have noticed that boards of directors have changed following the passage of the Act. Linck *et al.* (2009) and Valenti (2008) agree that the incidence of duality has decreased since the Act and that more accountants now sit on boards. In addition, Linck *et al.* (2009) report an increase in the number of lawyers and academics sitting on American boards, part of a trend towards greater independence. However, this has come at a cost both to the individual directors and to the companies on whose boards they sit in that directors' workload and risk have increased and so, not surprisingly, directors' remuneration has also risen.

CONCLUSION

During the last 20 years we have seen an explosion of interest in, and regulation of corporate governance. While the major innovations in the UK and US have been very different in form, in both cases they came as a response to corporate scandals involving fraud and audit practices that did not warn shareholders of impending dangers. In Britain the sponsors of change were the FRC, the London Stock Exchange and the accountancy profession, which together set up the Cadbury Committee. This committee recommended that companies should comply with or explain deviations from a code of corporate governance designed to suggest improvements in governance practices while at the same time allowing companies to choose mechanisms suited to their own situations. This approach has gained widespread approval in the UK and beyond, and countries all over the world have adopted their own codes, which often share common features such as the separation of the roles of the chair and CEO and the use of board sub-committees to oversee the audit, remuneration and nomination processes. Investors generally welcome codes, and there is evidence that they have been made better off as a result of the changes they bring.

In the US the government has legislated on some aspects of corporate governance in the Sarbanes-Oxley Act of 2002. When the Act was passed there were fears that the costs of complying with the legislation would outweigh its benefits. While early evidence suggested this was true, later empirical work has shown the Act in a more positive light. It would be misleading to characterise the Sarbanes-Oxley Act as pure governance regulation. It also had major implications for the relationship between companies and their auditors and on the nature of companies' financial disclosures. Given the importance of communication in governance, the next chapter discusses the ways in which companies disclose important information to their major stakeholders.

- In recent years we have seen a proliferation of codes of corporate governance based on the 'comply or explain' principle. This type of regulation sets standards of corporate governance while allowing companies the flexibility to choose whether or not to adopt specific governance practices.
- While codes differ around the world differ because of the influence of other regulation and legislation, most include recommendations on board composition, structure and evaluation.
- Evidence shows that compliance increases over time and can be associated with improved shareholder wealth.
- In the US the Sarbanes-Oxley Act 2002 has introduced important changes to the accountability of corporate officers.

CASE STUDY Richard Scrushy and the accountability of the CEO under the Sarbanes–Oxley Act 2002

Richard Scrushy may not be well known outside the US, but there he is infamous, following a clutch of highly publicised court appearances. He is currently serving a six-year jail sentence for bribery, having donated funds to a political campaign run by former governor Don Siegelman in exchange for a seat on a state hospital board. In 2009 he was ordered to pay compensation of $2.7 billion to HealthSouth, having been found liable for the fraud that nearly destroyed the company. Richard Scrushy has another dubious claim to fame, having been the first CEO to be charged under the provisions of the Sarbanes-Oxley Act 2002.

Scrushy's mother was a nurse who came to specialise in respiratory care. Richard followed in her footsteps, qualifying as a respiratory therapy technician and teaching the subject before going on to work at Lifemark, a company which managed hospitals. The company was unable to implement his innovative ideas on the use of rehabilitation centres in respiratory treatment, so he left to found HealthSouth in 1984, becoming the chair and chief executive officer. According to Aaron Beam, a former CFO, Scrushy persuaded his colleagues to fraudulently manipulate the company's earnings in 1996 when it appeared that the company would not be able to realise its projected figures. The manipulation of income figures became routine until 2003, one year after the Sarbanes-Oxley Act entered the statute books.

For years Weston Smith, the company's CFO, had signed off the company's fraudulent quarterly earnings figures. When the time came for him to do so once again in 2003, he resigned from the company, fearing the tougher penalties for white-collar crime that the Act had introduced. This drew the attention of the SEC and led to the prosecution he feared. He and a group of executives, including Richard Scrushy, faced multiple fraud charges in relation to the $2.7 billion of non-existent income in the company's financial statements. For Scrushy the charges included violation of the Sarbanes-Oxley Act, which requires CEOs to vouch for the accuracy of their company's financial statements.

Prior to the passage of the Sarbanes-Oxley Act corporate officers could be personally liable for misreporting only if it could be shown that they had breached their fiduciary duty. The Act requires CEOs and CFOs to certify that they have read each financial report, that each provides a true picture in which no material facts are excluded and that the financial statements present a fair picture of the state of the firm's operations. By taking part in the certification process the officers also confirm that they have complied with the legislation and informed their auditors of any weaknesses in the firm's internal controls.

Richard Scrushy's lawyers began their defence claiming that the Sarbanes-Oxley Act is unconstitutional because the certification requirements include phrases such as 'fairly presents' 'willfully [sic] certifies' and 'material respects'. The use of the word 'wilful' is particularly important because the penalties for wilfully signing off false statements are much higher than for knowingly signing them. While some legal commentators agree that the distinction between doing something knowingly and wilfully is unhelpful (Taylor, 2005), the trial judge dismissed the claim that these phrases made the Act unconstitutional because their meaning has been clarified by case law. The lawyers then went on to rely on the very simple defence that Richard Scrushy was unaware of the fraud. The jury believed that the five corporate officers who stated in court that he knew exactly what was going on were lying, and acquitted him.

The acquittal shocked many people. The wording of the Act seems to make it clear that CEOs should understand the internal controls and procedures that lead to the publication of its financial statements, and in this case should be aware of the potential for fraud. A common view (Stock, 2006 and Taylor, 2005) was that Scrushy would have been found guilty if the trial had been held in New York rather in his home state of Alabama, where his local celebrity and philanthropy worked in his favour. The civil case was heard without a jury. Thus time the judge found him guilty. It seems odd that two trials based on the same facts can lead to opposite conclusions. This case calls into question the idea that the criminal law is the best vehicle to use in cases of fraud, and also raises the issue of whether or not it is appropriate to legislate on matters of corporate governance.

CASE-STUDY QUESTIONS

1 HealthSouth is one of many companies which ran into difficulties having appointed its CEO as the chair of the board. Does this lead you to believe that governments should legislate against duality?
2 Is reasonable to expect both CEOs and CFOs to attest to the accuracy of financial statements?
3 Do you believe that corporate governance regulation of any kind can deter fraud and other criminal acts?

REVISION QUESTIONS

1 Advocates of the 'comply or explain' approach believe that it makes corporate governance flexible. Do you agree or do you think it is a lazy approach to regulation?
2 Which governance topics are included in the UK Code of Corporate Governance?

3 Do you think the UK Code of Corporate Governance gives independent directors too much responsibility?

4 Would it make sense for the EU to impose a single corporate governance code on all member states?

5 What contribution has the Sarbanes-Oxley Act 2002 made to corporate governance in the US?

6 If you were devising corporate regulation from scratch would you choose to pass a law or implement a code?

REFERENCES

Abdul Wahab, E.A., How, J.C.Y. and Verhoeven, P. (2007) 'The Impact of The Malaysian Code on Corporate Governance: Compliance, Institutional Investors and Stock Performance' *Journal of Contemporary Accounting and Economics* 3 (2) 106–129

Aguilera, R., and Cuervo-Cazurra, A. (2004) 'Codes of Good Governance Worldwide: What is the Trigger?' *Organization Studies* 25 (3) 417–446

Alves, C. and Mendes, V. (2004) 'Corporate Governance Policy and Company Performance: The Portuguese Case' *Corporate Governance: An International Review* 12 (3) 290–301

Association Française de la Gestion Financière (2010) 'Recommendations on Corporate Governance' Association Française de la Gestion Financière

ASX Corporate Governance Council (2010) 'Marked-up Amendments dates 30 June 2010 to the Second Edition August 2007 of the Corporate Governance Principles and Recommendations' ASX

Austrian Working Group for Corporate Governance (2009) 'Austrian Code of Corporate Governance' Austrian Working Group for Corporate Governance

Bangladesh Enterprise Institute (2004) 'The Code of Corporate Governance for Bangladesh: Principles and Guidelines for Best Practice in the Private Sector, Financial Institutions, State-owned Enterprises and Non-governmental Organisations' Bangladesh Enterprise Institute

Beiner, S., Schmid, M.M., Drobetz, W. and Zimmermann, H. (2006) 'An Integrated Framework of Corporate Governance and Firm Valuation' *European Financial Management* 12 (2) 249–283

Belgian Corporate Governance Committee (2009) 'The 2009 Belgian Code on Corporate Governance' Belgian Corporate Governance Committee

Bucharest Stock Exchange (2009) 'Corporate Governance Code' Bucharest Stock Exchange

Business Roundtable (1978) 'The Role and Composition of the Board of Directors of the Large Publicly Owned Corporation' *The Business Lawyer* 33, 2083–2113

Capital Market Authority (2002) 'Corporate Governance Regulations in the Kingdom of Saudi Arabia' Capital Market Authority

Capital Markets Board of Turkey (2005) 'Corporate Governance Principles' Capital Markets Board of Turkey

Comisión Nacional del Mercado de Valores (2006) 'Report of the Special Working Group on the Good Governance of Listed Companies' Comisión Nacional del Mercado de Valores

Confederation of British Industry (1995) 'Directors' Remuneration: Report of a Study Group Chaired by Sir Richard Greenbury' Confederation of British Industry

Coordination Council for Corporate Governance (2002) 'Corporate Governance Code' Coordination Council for Corporate Governance

Council on Corporate Disclosure and Governance (2005) 'Code of Corporate Governance' Council on Corporate Disclosure and Governance

Dahya, J. and McConnell, J.J. (2007) 'Board Composition, Corporate Performance, and the Cadbury Committee Recommendations' *Journal of Financial and Quantitative Analysis* 42 (3) 35–564

Dahya, J., McConnell, J.J. and Travlos, G. (2002) 'The Cadbury Committee, Corporate Performance, and Top Management Turnover' *Journal of Finance* 57 (1) 461–483

Economiesuisse (2008) 'Swiss Code of Best Practice for Corporate Governance' Swiss Business Federation

Egyptian Institute of Directors (2006) 'Guide to Corporate Governance Principles in Egypt' Egyptian Institute of Directors

Emirates Securities and Commodities Authority (2007) 'Corporate Governance Code for Joint-stock Companies and Institutional Discipline Criteria' Emirates Securities and Commodities Authority

Engel, E., Hayes, R.M. and Wang, X. (2007) 'The Sarbanes–Oxley Act and Firms' Going-private Decisions' *Journal of Accounting and Economics* 44 (1–2) 116–145

Federation of Greek Industries (2001) 'Principles of Corporate Governance' Federation of Greek Industries

Financial Reporting Council (1992) 'The Financial Aspects of Corporate Governance' FRC

Financial Reporting Council (2010) 'The UK Corporate Governance Code' FRC

Financial Reporting Council (2010) 'The UK Stewardship Code' FRC

Goncharov, I., Werner, J.G. and Zimmermann, J. (2006) 'Does Compliance with the German Corporate Governance Code Have an Impact on Stock Market Valuation? An Empirical Analysis' *Corporate Governance: An International Review* 14 (5) 432–445

Government Commission on the German Corporate Governance Code (2010) 'German Corporate Governance Code' Government Commission on the German Corporate Governance Code

Grant Thornton (2009) 'ISEQ Corporate Governance Review 2009' Grant Thornton

Iceland Chamber of Commerce, NASDAQ OMS Iceland and SA-Confederation of Icelandic Employers (2009) 'Corporate Governance Guidelines' Iceland Chamber of Commerce, NASDAQ OMS Iceland and SA-Confederation of Icelandic Employers

Institute of Chartered Accountants of Sri Lanka and Securities and Exchange Commission of Sri Lanka (2006) 'Rules on Corporate Governance for Listed Companies' SEC

Institute of Directors South Africa (2009) 'King Code of Governance for South Africa 2009' Institute of Directors South Africa

Kingdom of Bahrain Ministry of Industry and Commerce (2009) 'Corporate Governance Code: Kingdom of Bahrain' Ministry of Industry and Commerce

Korea Corporate Governance Service (2003) 'Code of Best Practices for Corporate Governance' Korea Corporate Governance Service

Kouwenberg, R. (2006) 'Does Voluntary Corporate Governance Code Adoption Increase Firm Value in Emerging Markets? Evidence from Thailand' http://www.set.or.th/en/regulations/cg/files/CG_research_Paper_DrRoy.pdf

Leuz, C. (2007) ''Was the Sarbanes–Oxley Act of 2002 Really this Costly? A Discussion of Evidence from Event Returns and Going-private Decisions' *Journal of Accounting and Economics* 44 (1–2) 146–165

Linck, J.S., Netter, J.M. and Yang, T. (2009) 'The Effects and Unintended Consequences of the Sarbanes–Oxley Act on the Supply and Demand for Directors' *The Review of Financial Studies* 22 (8) 3287–3328

Luxembourg Stock Exchange (2009) 'Corporate Governance: The Ten Principles of Corporate Governance of the Luxembourg Stock Exchange' Luxembourg Stock Exchange

Malta Financial Services Authority (2005) 'Code of Principles of Good Corporate Governance' Malta Financial Services Authority

Marks and Spencer plc (2010) 'Annual Report' available at http://annualreport.marksandspencer.com/downloads/M&S_AR10.pdf

National Association of Corporate Directors (2008) 'Key Agreed Principles to Strengthen Corporate Governance for U.S. Publicly-traded Companies' National Association of Corporate Directors

New Zealand Securities Commission (2004) 'Corporate Governance in New Zealand; A Handbook for Directors, Executives, and Advisers' Securities Commission, New Zealand

Norwegian Corporate Governance Board (2009) 'The Norwegian Code of Best Practice for Corporate Governance' Norwegian Corporate Governance Board

Nowland, J. (2008) 'The Effect of National Governance Codes on Firm Disclosure Practices: Evidence From Analyst Earnings Forecasts' *Corporate Governance: an International Review* 16 (6) 475–491

OECD (2004) 'Principles of Corporate Governance' OECD

Piotroski, J.D. and Srinivasan, S. (2008) 'Regulation and Bonding: The Sarbanes–Oxley Act and the Flow of International Listings' *Journal of Accounting Research* 46 (2) 383–425

Private Sector Corporate Governance Trust (2002) 'Principles for Corporate Governance in Kenya and a Sample Code of Best Practice for Corporate Governance' Private Sector Corporate Governance Trust

Republic of the Philippines Securities and Exchange Commission (2002) 'Code of Corporate Governance' Republic of the Philippines Securities and Exchange Commission

Romano, R. (2005) 'The Sarbanes–Oxley Act and the Making of Quack Corporate Governance' *The Yale Law Journal* 114 (7) 1521–1611

Securities and Exchange Commission Nigeria (2003) 'Code of Corporate Governance in Nigeria' Securities and Exchange Commission Nigeria

Securities and Exchange Commission of Pakistan (2002) 'Code of Corporate Governance' Securities and Exchange Commission of Pakistan

Securities Commission Malaysia (2007) 'Malaysian Code on Corporate Governance' Securities Commission Malaysia

Securities Market Association (2008) 'Finnish Corporate Governance Code 2008' Securities Market Association

Stock, W. (2006) '*UNITED STATES V SCRUSHY* and its Impact on Criminal Prosecutions under the Certification Requirements of Sarbanes–Oxley' *Texas Wesleyan Law Review* 13 (1) 239–264

Stock Exchange of Hong Kong (2004) 'Conclusions on Exposure Draft on Corporate Governance Practices and Corporate Governance Report' Hong Kong Exchanges and Clearing Limited

Stock Exchange of Thailand (2006) 'The Principles of Good Corporate Governance for Listed Companies 2006' Stock Exchange of Thailand

Swedish Corporate Governance Board (2010) 'The Swedish Corporate Governance Code' Swedish Corporate Governance Board

Taiwan Stock Exchange Gre Tai Securities Market (2002) 'Taiwan Corporate Governance Best-practice Principles – 2002' Taiwan Stock Exchange Gre Tai Securities Market

Taylor, J. (2005) 'Fluke or Failure: Assessing the Sarbanes–Oxley Act after *United States V. Scrushy*' *UMKC Law Review* 74 (2) 411–434

TSX (2006) 'TSX Guide to Good Disclosure for National Instrument 58–101 *Disclosure of Corporate Governance Practices* (NI 58–101) and Multilateral Instrument 52–110 – *Audit Committees* (MI 52–110)' TSX

Valenti, A. (2008) 'The Sarbanes–Oxley Act of 2002: Has it Brought About Changes in the Boards of Directors of Large U.S. Corporations?' *Journal of Business Ethics* 81, 401–412

Wearing, R. (2005) *Cases in Corporate Governance* Sage

Weir, C. and Laing, D. (2000) 'The Performance-Governance Relationship: The Effects of Cadbury Compliance on UK Quoted Companies' *Journal of Management and Governance* 4 (4) 265–281

Weir, C. and Laing, D. (2001) 'Governance Structures, Director Independence and Corporate Performance in the UK' *European Business Review* 13 (2) 86–95

Zattoni, A. and Cuomo, F. (2008) 'Why Adopt Codes of Good Governance? A Comparison of Institutional and Efficiency Perspectives' *Corporate Governance: An International Review* 16 (1) 1–15

Zhang, I.X. (2007) 'The Economic Consequences of the Sarbanes–Oxley Act of 2002' *Journal of Accounting and Economics* 44 (1–2) 74–115

SUGGESTIONS FOR FURTHER READING

Andres, C. and Theissen, E. (2008) 'Setting a Fox to Keep the Geese – Does the Comply-or-Explain Principle Work?' *Journal of Corporate Finance* 14 (3) 289–301. This paper provides an interesting insight into the interplay between the operation of binding legislation and voluntary codes.

Coates, J.C. (2007) 'The Goals and Promise of the Sarbanes–Oxley Act' *Journal of Economic Perspectives* 21 (1) 91–116. This paper offers a well-balanced view of the Act, explaining its main provisions and offering early evidence on the costs and benefits associated with it.

http://www.ecgi.org/codes/all_codes.php The website of the European Corporate Governance Institute offers an index of codes published all round the world, not just in Europe. This is a useful resource, allowing the user to check the provenance of codes and see how they have developed over time.

http://www.frc.org/corporate/ukcode.cfm The corporate governance section of the Financial Reporting Council's website explains the philosophy behind the codes issued in the UK as well as links to the codes themselves and reviews and consultations on those codes.

8 COMMUNICATION AND DISCLOSURE

LEARNING OBJECTIVES

- To appreciate the ways in which corporate reporting has evolved in the UK.
- To understand why companies have incentives to both conceal information and to disclose information that is not required by regulation.
- To appreciate why auditors do not always detect fraud.
- To recognise why companies use a variety of disclosures and media to manage their reputations.

INTRODUCTION

It has never been easier or quicker to communicate across long distances. E-mail, texting, tweeting and real-time chat in social networking sites have all but replaced handwritten letters as far as social communication is concerned. In business, e-mail and increasingly texts are used to communicate with customers. Efficient search engines allow us to use the internet with ease and give us a bewildering choice of sites to trawl for the information we seek. These developments are not always helpful. Very short messages cannot always convey what the sender wants to say, and internet users cannot be certain that the information they gather is accurate. While it appears we are better informed than ever before, each new financial or business scandal leaves us asking, 'Why didn't we know about this?' Why didn't we know about the 'toxic assets' held by banks in 2007, or about Enron's inflated earnings in 2001? Should we blame the decision-makers who concealed or even falsified information, or the auditors who failed to uncover the truth? Maybe as a society we have forgotten that communication is more than simply the dissemination of information. Perhaps we have failed to consider the relevance of reliability of the data we are given, accepting them at face value and not bothering to ask the questions or provide the feedback that is an essential part of the communication process.

In this chapter we will consider the ways in which companies communicate with their shareholders and stakeholders and the type of information they supply. For many companies their stakeholders are overlapping rather than discrete groups. An individual may own shares in Tesco and buy their groceries from a Tesco store, which means they are exposed to the company's financial and promotional information. Both types of information are relevant in forming the company's image, but that image will not be the same for every stakeholder; each forms a different view of the company based on their experience of dealing with it.

The section on communication with shareholders will discuss the way in which financial and non-financial information are presented in annual accounts. We will look at the impact of International Financial Reporting Standards (IFRS), and consider companies' incentives to manipulate or hide information so as to present an unduly optimistic picture of the business, and also to provide additional information to signal good news that is real but hard to discern. We will also discuss the nature of the audit process and attempt to explain why auditors do not always spot fraudulent transactions. In discussing the way in which companies communicate with their stakeholders we will return to the theme of changing communications technology and the way this has empowered stakeholders. We will also consider routine communication which seeks to build a good reputation and reactions to crises which threaten to destroy corporate reputation. The chapter ends with a case study of Satyam Computer Services Ltd, an Indian company whose CEO was able to manipulate the company's revenues and inflate its asset values; this will take us back to the issue of what auditors look for when they examine a company's records and processes.

COMMUNICATION WITH SHAREHOLDERS

One of the hallmarks of a good corporate governance system is that shareholders behave as owners of companies rather than simply as owners of securities. In order to do this they must have access to accurate and timely information about the companies whose shares they hold. This explains why disclosure is an important element in both voluntary codes like the UK Corporate Governance Code and in legislation like the Sarbanes–Oxley Act in the US. Traditionally the annual report was the primary means by which companies provided their shareholders with information, which is why we will discuss it in some detail later in this chapter. Clearly it is not enough to provide information once a year, so companies also publish quarterly financial information which will be reported by the media and increasingly use their own websites to provide a continuous flow of information to their shareholders and, given the nature of the internet, any other interested party.

Regular communication

As we have seen in other chapters, the 1980s were something of a turning point in corporate governance. This was the era of hostile takeover bids and leveraged buyouts, both of which contributed to the re-energising of the shareholder as a business owner. This was also the decade during which companies woke up to the fact that they had to become more open and transparent and to communicate effectively with their shareholders. This is illustrated by the rise in importance of the investor relations function within companies. In 1985 just 16 per cent of

Fortune 500 companies had investor relations departments; by 1989 the proportion had risen to 56 per cent (Laskin, 2009) and today no corporate website is complete without an investor relations section. In a recent survey Laskin (2009) discovered that most Fortune 500 companies (65 per cent in his sample) have dedicated investor relations departments; where this is not the case, investor relations are handled either by the finance or treasury function (27 per cent) or more rarely by the communications or public relations department (8 per cent). Key activities for people working in this area are organising conferences, giving presentations and handling queries from shareholders, principally institutional investors, and from analysts. As we saw in the previous chapter, corporate governance codes around the world stress the importance of good communication, often giving a key role to the chair of the board or senior independent director. They also encourage the use of corporate websites to provide information to shareholders at the same time it is given to analysts.

Marks and Spencer plc has been mentioned in this book in both a negative (see the case study in chapter 4) and a positive light (see the reference to its annual report in chapter 7). This company's corporate website is a good example of just how much regular disclosure large British companies make to their shareholders. The investor section of the site includes not just a library of annual reports, but also interim management statements, quarterly trading statements webcasts on interim results and access to all press releases made by the company. This type of disclosure means that shareholders and indeed other interested parties have access to all the latest information about the company.

The annual report

Statutory content: UK

While communication is a two-way process, we know far more about the information provided by companies to their shareholders that we do about the reactions of those shareholders. One of the best ways of finding out about a company is through its annual report. While the financial data included are of necessity backward-looking, the narrative sections give an indication of the company's current and future activities and may hint at the culture of the business. A typical annual report is a mixture of information required by statute, by accounting standards and provided on a voluntary basis by the company concerned. In the UK, the Companies Act 2006 (s. 471) requires all quoted companies to include their financial statements, a directors' report, a report on the remuneration received by directors together with an auditor's report commenting on the financial statements and the auditable parts of both the directors' report and the directors' remuneration report.

The financial accounts must give a true and fair view of the company's financial situation (s. 292) and be prepared on the basis of international accounting standards (s. 395). The directors' report must include a business review (s. 417) which describes how the business has developed during the financial year, the nature of the risks and uncertainties it faces, any trends likely to affect its future development, an analysis of key performance indicators as well as sections on employees and environmental and social issues. The directors' remuneration report must include details of directors' gains on exercising options, the income received from long-term incentive plans, severance payments and other benefits. The auditor's report should explain which financial statements were subject to audit and the standards used in the audit process. It should go on to comment on whether or not the financial statements were prepared in accordance with relevant standards and with the Act and say if they give a true and fair view (s. 495). It must also comment on the consistency of the directors' report with the annual accounts (s.496) and say if the remuneration report has been prepared in accordance with the Act.

In 2009 the Accounting Standards Board (ASB) undertook a survey of companies to see how well they were complying with the narrative requirements of the Act. Not surprisingly the results indicated that larger companies were more compliant than smaller ones, but very few companies achieved the maximum score indicating that they used best practice in their choice of content and method of communication. Compliance scores were highest for the financial review section, but even there only 10 per cent of firms were given the best practice score. A recurrent theme in the discussion of the findings is the issue of how the information is provided. The companies achieving the highest scores all used graphs and charts to summarise the data. This may indicate that the ASB is particularly interested in the perceptions of retail investors, since Penrose (2008) presents evidence that naïve investors show particular interest in the narrative and graphical elements of annual reports while analysts focus on the financial statements.

Box 8.1 Awards and prizes for financial reporting

Most of us associate the phrase 'awards ceremony' with glamorous show-business events like the academy awards, or for those with literary inclinations, the Man Booker prize. You might be surprised to discover just how many awards are available for the writers of a very particular type of non-fiction – the annual report. Prizes are organised all over the world by groups like the New Zealand Institute of Chartered Accountants, the Norwegian Society of Financial Analysts and associations of Chartered Secretaries in both the UK and Australia.

While the ceremonies associated with the awards may be an excuse for a good night out, the fact that the awards exist surely points to huge differences in reporting standards, especially in relation to narrative reporting by companies in areas like governance, audit and risk management, which are the subjects of some of the more specialist awards. If you are wondering what makes a good annual report you should read the report issued by BAE Systems plc in 2009. This won a prize for innovation in governance disclosure and prompted the kind of judges' comments that we would expect to see on the back cover of a paperback novel. It is clearly written and includes many diagrams, charts and text boxes. You can access it through the 'Investors' section of the company's website (http://www.baesystems.com/).

International Financial Reporting Standards

In 2002 the EU decided that as of 2005 all European companies should prepare their consolidated financial statements in accordance with IFRS rather than local Generally Accepted Accounting Principles (GAAP). The perceived benefits of this harmonisation include improved disclosure, improved international comparability of the statements and better international capital flows leading to a lower cost of equity for companies (Lee *et al.*, 2008). Prior to this, academic accountants were concerned that accounting numbers were losing their value relevance. In other words, measures such as accounting profit were unrelated to share prices. There was a suspicion that this was because intangible assets were playing an increasingly important role in the generation of profit, but the accounting treatment of intangibles did not reflect this. Traditionally, tangible and intangible assets had been treated in different ways for accounting purposes. Tangible assets were shown in the balance sheet at their historic cost net of depreciation, and depreciation also appeared in the income statement as a charge for the use of the asset. In contrast, because of the difficulty of valuation, and the uncertainties associated with intangible assets like research and development, trademarks and brands, the full costs associated with them were charged to the income statement during the year in which they were incurred, and so they did not appear in the balance sheet. The empirical evidence on the value-relevance of intangibles is mixed. While some authors find that the value-relevance of earnings figures is lower for high-technology companies (Kwon, 2001) or for R&D-intensive companies (Lev and Zarowin, 1999), others (Francis and Schipper, 1999) find the decline in value-relevance has affected all companies regardless of the technology they use.

Problems associated with the valuation of intangibles should be alleviated by the implementation of IFRS, because this system is focussed on the balance sheet, and begins by valuing assets, including some intangibles (such as trademarks and licences) that were not capitalised under most national GAAP. Unlike GAAP, it makes more use of the concept of 'fair value', particularly in valuing financial assets such as derivatives. For assets that are traded regularly the fair value would be the market price; where this cannot be observed, it must be modelled. Once assets and debt have been valued, equity is valued as a residual, which means that changes in equity require more explanation than under GAAP.

IFRS require group companies to produce four financial statements. These are the income statement, the balance sheet, the statement of changes in equity and the statement of cash flows. The income statement or profit and loss account lists the operational and non-operational revenues received and costs incurred during the financial year in order to arrive at the final profit figure. Companies can report their income statement in one of two formats. In the first, the company presents an income statement and a statement of changes in equity which itself is in two parts, a statement of recognised income and expense and a statement of changes in equity. The statement of recognised income and expense includes items that are non-operational, such as property revaluations and changes in the fair value of assets that are available for sale. The second part of the statement of changes in equity summarises the way in which income, dividends and other transactions with shareholders have been attributed to shareholders in the parent company. In the second format the company produces a statement of comprehensive income which includes the items from the statement of recognised income and expense; in this case the statement of changes in equity includes only the changes in equity relating to income and transactions with shareholders. The cash flow statement indicates how the company generated cash (as opposed to profit) from its operating, investing and financing activities. The balance sheet may now be known instead as the statement of financial position. Unlike the other statements, it does not summarise a set of transactions made during the year. Instead it provides a picture of the assets held at the end of the financial year, together with a statement of the equity and liabilities financing those assets.

At the time of the adoption of IFRS the expectation was that it would have most impact on companies listed in countries with a stakeholder rather than a shareholder orientation. This would apply, for instance, in Germany, where the accounting system had been based on tax requirements. Consistent with expectations, Jermakowicz *et al.* (2007) find that the adoption of IFRS in Germany has been associated with an increase in the value-relevance of earnings figures. Gjerde *et al.* (2008) find the opposite for Norwegian firms, but when they classify their sample according to the extent to which the firms rely on intangible assets, they find that the value relevance of earnings is improved for those companies that rely on intangibles, which is not surprising, given the fact that IFRS are built around the measurement of asset values. Lee *et al.* (2008) highlight the impact of the adoption of IFRS on the cost of equity, and are surprised to find that the greatest reduction was felt in the UK, rather than in those European countries where companies rely heavily on debt. It seems, then, that the introduction of IFRS has had a beneficial impact throughout Europe. These standards are also being adopted in both developed and developing countries across the world, including the US, which for some time had been sceptical about changing its GAAP, but is now moving towards harmonisation with IFRS.

Narrative reporting and voluntary disclosures

As was stated earlier, annual reports include not just the general information demanded by statute and the accounting information required by standard-setters. Companies have discretion over the extent to which they provide additional information and also over how it is presented. The annual reports of British companies have changed a great deal over the years. They have become much longer, their size increasing by 108 per cent between 1965 and 1988 (Lee, 1994) and then by another 100 per cent between 1994 and 2002 (Davison and Skerratt, 2007). While the increase in length is partly due to additional required content, an average of 47 per cent of the content in annual reports in 2002 was added voluntarily by companies. The voluntary element includes information on the company's products, brands, markets, management, workforce and customers. In addition to the annual report, 65 per cent of companies in the FTSE 100 in 2002 also published a shorter document, often called an annual review, in which some of the financial information was repeated, along with information on corporate governance and important developments in the company's history. While the provision of additional information could be useful and interesting to investors, a potential problem with issuing two annual statements is that readers may be confused about which is the more important, especially since 28 per cent of annual reviews had front covers that are identical to the cover of the annual report and 64 per cent had matching covers. Readers who look only at the annual review may miss out on important information or get too rosy a picture of how the company is performing, since the company itself can choose the information presented there. Inter-industry comparisons show that companies with relatively high levels of intangible assets are more likely to produce an annual review and to use pictures in their publications. The impact of IFRS on this choice remains to be seen.

In the UK the Companies Act 2006 requires all listed companies to make their annual reports available on their websites. In other countries this may be required by either corporate law or corporate governance regulation. This means that in most countries annual reports are freely available to any interested stakeholder, not only to the shareholders for whom annual reports have traditionally been written. It is important that annual reports are written clearly so that they convey relevant information to the wide range of users who have access to them, so a number of academic researchers have investigated the language used in various sections of the annual report. Geppart and Lawrence (2008) concentrate on the content of the letter to shareholders written by the chair or CEO. They base their analysis on the *variety index*, which is measured simply as the number of different words used in the text divided by the total number of words. A low variety index is associated with a relaxed writing style and with truthfulness. Having measured the variety index for 39 American firms, they went on to see how the index was related to reputation as measured by the Fortune survey, the Harris Interactive survey and Business Ethics magazine's 100 best corporate citizens. They found that firms with better reputations have a lower variety index in their letter to shareholders; they also use shorter words, more words conveying desirable corporate attributes and use the present tense more than firms with lower reputations. Not surprisingly, when the chair or CEO of a company with a good reputation communicates with the shareholders they can do so in a relaxed and frank way. Rutherford (2005) also focuses on one section of the annual report, this time the operating and financial review in British reports. The paper uses *genre analysis* to consider the type of words used by profitable and loss-making companies. He finds that both types of firm use the word 'loss' to the same extent, but the firms which make losses make more references to revenue and other items near the top of the income statement than do profitable companies. Li (2008) examines the 'readability' of the annual report as a whole. Readability is measured using both the *fog index* and the length of the report. The fog index measures complexity on the assumption that, all else equal, a document is harder to read the more multi-syllabic words it contains and the longer are its sentences. The index is summarised in a measure of how many years of education are required to read the document. Li (2008) finds that the Management Discussion and Analysis section, together with the notes to the accounts, are easier to read than the report as a whole. This is likely to draw the reader's attention to the views of management and to enable them to better understand the implications of the financial statements. Li (2008) also finds that the readability of the annual report is positively related to company earnings. Like Geppart and Lawrence's findings, this suggests that companies feel able to communicate in a relaxed way when they have good news to convey.

We have already seen that a large proportion of the information included in companies' annual reports is published voluntarily. Research in this area usually explains voluntary disclosure using either agency theory or signalling theory. Agency theory has come up in many parts of this book already, so there is no need to say too much here. The relevant aspect in this context is bonding. Managers realise that investors have good reason to suspect them of acting in their own interests. In order to reassure investors that they are acting in good faith, managers may choose to disclose information that is not mandated by regulators. This could be in the form of additional financial information such as financial ratios, or segment analysis in some jurisdictions, or it could be non-financial information relevant to a range of stakeholders. In the UK environmental and CSR reporting would have come under this heading before the implementation of the Companies Act 2006. The key thing is that managers incur additional costs in producing the information and by doing so reassure shareholders that they are acting openly and can therefore be trusted. If voluntary disclosures are in fact a bonding mechanism, we would expect them to be used by those companies that are most likely to suffer from the type I agency problem, in other words, the companies with dispersed ownership and/or weak governance structures.

The implications of signalling theory are similar to those of agency theory, but the approach begins from a different starting point. While agency theory states that there is tension between shareholders and managers because managers have incentives to behave opportunistically, signalling theory explores the problems that arise because managers have more information about the company than its shareholders do. In general terms, signalling theory looks at situations where the two parties to a transaction have different amounts of information about the product or service being sold. This can occur in any market, but has been discussed extensively in relation to employers who have insufficient information about job applicants (Spence, 1973), consumers who have insufficient information about durable goods (Akerlof, 1970) and shareholders who have insufficient information about companies (Ross, 1977 and Miller and Rock, 1985, among many others). When buyers cannot distinguish between good and bad products they may make costly mistakes by buying inferior products which break down or simply do not perform as expected. In extreme situations this can lead to a complete collapse of the market, with buyers becoming so cautious that they do not buy anything. The information asymmetry can be overcome in two ways. The buyer can search for information, adding to their purchase costs, or the seller can signal information, in which case they bear the costs. Many types of activity can be used as signals. The key point is that a signal must be credible, in other words it must be something which, over time is associated with good quality. As we have already said, this requires that the action must be costly, but more than that, it must be more expensive for a low-quality seller to perform than for a high-quality seller. Education is often viewed as a signal in labour markets, guarantees can be signals in product markets and in financial markets dividend payments and borrowing may signal company quality. Notice that the signal itself does not lead to good quality, but indicates underlying quality.

The provision of voluntary disclosures is certainly costly for all companies, because it requires the collection and presentation of additional data. There is also the issue that the additional data may give an unfavourable picture of the firm, so in that sense it is more costly for weaker companies. If voluntary disclosure is used to alleviate information asymmetries it should be associated with stronger financial performance by the companies that issue non-statutory information. There is a substantial empirical literature on the determinants of voluntary disclosure, but it is not always easy to compare papers since by its nature, voluntary disclosure covers many and varied types of information. Birt *et al.* (2006) focus on the disclosure of segment information by Australian companies. Segment reporting involves a breakdown of a company's financial results by market segment. They find that the companies that voluntarily reported segment data were those in more competitive industries and those with more concentrated ownership. This is the opposite of what would be expected if voluntary disclosure were used as a bonding mechanism. However, it could occur because controlling owners encourage greater disclosure by managers. Eng and Mak (2003) look at the effect of different types of share-holders on voluntary disclosure in Singapore. They include a range of voluntary disclosures of both financial and non-financial data in a disclosure index. They find that there is no relationship between the level of disclosure and ownership by blockholders, but government ownership encourages, while managerial ownership discourages disclosure. The relationship between government ownership and voluntary disclosure is not surprising, since the state would probably like to encourage the dissemination of information by management. However, in this study disclosure is also negatively related to the proportion of outside directors on the board, which is surprising, given that outside directors are supposed to be a part of good governance, which itself should encourage the provision of addi-tional information. The opposite result is found by Cheng and Courtenay (2006) for Singapore and Donnelly and Mulcahy (2008) for Ireland. Both look at the effect of board composition on voluntary disclosure. Cheng and Courtenay (2006) measure independence by the proportion of independent directors while Donnelly and Mulcahy (2008) use non-executives. Both find that greater disclosure goes hand-in-hand with greater independence. Donnelly and Mulcahy (2008) also find that disclosure varies directly with firm size, which probably reflects the impor-tance of cost in deciding whether or not to provide information.

UK evidence is consistent with results from the US indicating that voluntary disclosure of information is greater in particular industries. Discretionary envi-ronmental reporting is relatively high in the chemicals and pharmaceuticals indus-tries (Brammer and Pavelin, 2006 and Murray *et al.*, 2006). This could be simply due to the fact that companies in these industries are more likely to cause envi-ronmental damage or because they suffer greater informational asymmetries than others. There is some support for the first explanation from Brammer and Pavelin (2006), who find that companies which have been recently for fined for breaches of environmental standards go on to produce higher-quality environmental infor-mation in subsequent annual reports. Such companies clearly feel the need to regain their reputation by disclosing verifiable data or reporting on targets for future behaviour. Dedman *et al.* (2008) provide some support for the second explanation by looking at the abnormal returns of pharmaceutical and biotech-nology companies. Clearly these companies are subject to a great deal of uncer-tainty because a huge proportion of their research activity will never result in a tangible product. The accounting conventions applied to research and develop-ment at the time of the study meant that spending on these activities was expensed in the year in which it took place, rather than being capitalised. This depressed earnings, making earnings figures less informative than they are in other sectors. Dedman *et al.* (2008) confirm that the stock market reaction to an announcement about drug trials is higher than its reaction to an earnings announcement in these industries. In a rare direct test of the relationship between information asymmetry and disclosure in Denmark, Petersen and Plenborg (2006) find that information asymmetry is negatively related to voluntary disclosure of financial and non-financial information. This agrees with previous American studies and indicates that even in very different types of stock market voluntary disclosure works to overcome informational asymmetries between companies and their investors.

Earnings management, fraud and auditing

While there is plenty of evidence to suggest that companies seek to publish financial and non-financial information that can be used by investors to correctly value businesses, there is also a substantial body of literature that shows that companies may also manipulate or manage their earnings figures in order to give a good impression. In extreme cases earnings and other accounting data are manipulated to hide fraudulent activity. One aim of corporate governance regulation is to improve the transparency of financial disclosures so that investors can trust the information they receive from companies. Researchers usually measure earnings management using abnormal accruals. The concept of accruals is central to accounting. Accounting statements recognise transactions when they occur rather than when cash changes hands. This process involves matching costs with revenues and deciding when to allocate costs and to depreciate assets. The use of accruals accounting tends to produce earnings numbers that are much smoother than the underlying cash flows (Dechow and Skinner, 2000). Companies that believe their investors prefer smooth or rising earnings have an incentive to change the point at which transactions are recognised in order to manipulate their reported profit. There is plenty of evidence to suggest that earnings manipulation is associated with weak corporate governance.

Leuz *et al.* (2003) classify a sample of 8000 companies according to whether they come from countries where investor protection is high, medium or low. High protection is associated not just with strong legal protection and enforcement but also with outside influence on boards of directors, while weak protection is associated with poor enforcement of laws and dominance of companies by insiders. They find that earnings management is more prevalent in countries with weak investor protection. Directors' independence is also relevant to earnings manipulation in single-county studies. In companies whose boards are dominated by executive directors there is greater management of earnings in the US (Bowen *et al.*, 2008) and Australia (Davidson *et al.*, 2005). Discretionary accruals are also associated with companies whose boards hold relatively few meetings, whose boards interlock with those of other companies and where bonuses are a relatively important element of the remuneration package (Bowen *et al.*, 2008). For the US, Klein (2002) finds similar results by focusing on the composition of the audit committee rather than the entire board. There, earnings management is reduced when independent directors make up the majority of the committee.

While academic researchers are confident that they can identify accruals that are made in order manipulate earnings, these practices and even more serious fraudulent activities often continue unchecked in companies until an insider blows the whistle, as was the case at WorldCom, or makes a public confession, as happened at Satyam Computer Services, which is discussed at the end of this chapter. The question that always seems to arise in these cases is, 'Where were the auditors?' The fact that people ask this question is at one level evidence of the so-called *expectations gap* that exists in auditing. The detection of fraud is commonly believed to be an important part of the audit process. In fact the primary aim of an audit is to check that the company has followed the relevant framework for financial reporting and that the financial statements give a materially fair view. The word 'materially' implies that while reporting is not done to the last penny no important transactions have been missed. It was only in 1997 that the American auditing profession made any mention of auditors having a role in the detection or prevention of fraud. While auditors recognise that they do have a role to play in this area, they perceive this role to be less important than other people do. For example Hassink *et al.* (2009) found that in the Dutch context both auditors and company managers believe that auditors should detect material fraud not involving collusion by executives, but only managers believe that they should also detect non-material fraud.

Certainly auditors plan their work according to the risks they perceive at the company in question. Blay *et al.* (2007) looked at a sample of audits carried out in the US by one of the 'Big 4' audit companies. They found that when the auditor identified a risk of material misstatement they planned a different style of audit, with activity concentrated towards the end of the financial year and the use of more independent forms of evidence than was usual in other situations. Evidence obtained through interviews with American auditors indicates that they use corporate governance mechanisms as indicators of risk. Of the auditors interviewed by Cohen *et al.* (2002), 67 per cent indicated that they look at a company's existing corporate governance structures when deciding whether or not to take it on as a client. In every case corporate governance is an input into the audit planning process, indicating that not only can auditing be seen as part of the governance process, but that auditors believe that their role is conditioned by other governance mechanisms. The importance of risk in the audit process is borne out by case-based evidence such as that presented by Weil (2004) on HealthSouth (discussed in chapter 7). There the auditor believed that the risk of fraud was low so they did fewer tests, choosing to ignore individual assets whose value changed by less than $5000. The HealthSouth fraud was accomplished through the so-called contractual adjustments account, which measured the difference between the amount billed to a client and received from the health insurer. Judicious use of this account enabled the company to inflate revenue, which was then reflected in assets whose balance sheet value changed by less than $5000 during the year, allowing the fraud to go undetected. The fraud at Waste Management involved misstatements of tax, insurance and deferred costs over a period of five years. While their auditor detected the fraud and reported it to management, they did not report it more widely because each individual amount they found was immaterial (Rezaee, 2005). No wonder, then, that Dutch managers believe that auditors should be interested in small problems as well as large ones.

Cullinan and Sutton (2002) note that in a drive to make the audit process more cost-effective many audit firms have moved away from practices based on individual accounts towards a method in which they look at processes and information systems. They point out that by concentrating on processes auditors are more likely to detect low-level fraud carried out by relatively junior employees. However, most fraud is committed by senior management and goes undetected because they ensure that accounting adjustments are made so that this year's figures are similar to last year's, and therefore do not appear unusual or suspicious to the auditors. It is easy to continue in this way for years when the managers involved are particularly powerful or when the relationship between the company and the audit firm is close. Both conditions applied at Enron.

When an auditor spots a problem within a company they have the duty to report it to the board. When the problem is material it may result in the auditor issuing a qualified audit report. Qualified reports can be issued for a number of reasons, including uncertainty over some of the figures reported, disagreements with management over the procedures used, and the special case of a going-concern qualification in which the auditor expresses the view that the company is suffering from such a high degree of financial distress that it may not remain solvent throughout the coming year. This last type of qualified report sounds damning, but empirical evidence suggests that going-concern qualifications are not good predictors of bankruptcy because they focus on firm-level data and ignore economic conditions that contribute to the probability of insolvency (Lennox, 1999). The issue of any type of qualified audit report is likely to lead to a deterioration of the relationship between the company and the auditor and could lead to the auditor's removal. This is particularly damaging if the audit company provides non-audit services to the client, as was the case at Enron, where Arthur Andersen supplied a range of services in addition to auditing and, perhaps for that reason, chose not to question Enron's methods. Less dramatic evidence in favour of the hypothesis that audit reports are affected by the package of services supplied to clients is provided by Basioudis *et al.* (2008). They find that financially distressed firms are less likely to receive going-concern qualifications when their auditors also supply non-audit services. No wonder, then, that regulation like the Sarbanes–Oxley Act attempts to reinforce auditor independence.

When an auditor has extreme concerns about a company's financial practices, which may or may not include worries over criminal activity, they may choose to resign rather than to issue a qualified report. While audit reports seem to convey little information to the market, auditor resignations explained with reference to fundamental disagreements over accounting policy or internal controls have a significant effect. Beneish *et al.* (2005) find that these resignations lead to negative abnormal returns to the affected companies, in other words, their share prices fall significantly. Interestingly, this form of resignation can have beneficial spin-offs for remaining audit clients. Client firms which are similar to those from which the auditor resigns see a significant increase in their market returns following explained resignations. Perhaps surprisingly, the market ignores auditor resignations that are not explained.

Both corporate law and accounting regulation aim to ensure that companies provide timely, high-quality information to users of financial statements. Companies themselves choose to provide additional information when they feel that investors need to be reassured about the motives of the management team, or when the company's achievements cannot be measured in purely financial terms. The audit report should act as a safeguard that the company's accountants have prepared the financial statements in an appropriate way so that they give an accurate picture of the state of the business. Unfortunately for the audit profession, while the public is quick to notice and comment on those occasions when they fail to spot serious problems, most of the time their work goes unnoticed, despite the fact that it is an important part of the governance process.

COMMUNICATION WITH STAKEHOLDERS

In chapter 3 we discussed two definitions of stakeholders. They may be characterised narrowly as individuals or organisations with the power to affect the firm or more broadly as individuals or organisations that are affected by it. The latter definition can include many constituents, such as local communities and the environment, and starts to move us into the realm of corporate social responsibility. We have so far resisted saying too much about the broad range of stakeholders implied by the second definition, but it is hard to ignore them when considering communication. Until fairly recently the subject of communication with stakeholders would have included advertising as a means of informing and persuading consumers, internal newsletters and other forms of communication with employees and the disclosure of relevant financial information to lenders. Today the growing literature on corporate social reporting and the observed use of the internet as a campaign tool by ethical consumer groups and coalitions of protesters have broadened the scope of corporate communication.

The advent of the internet has also focused attention on the fact that communication is a two-way process. While we have always known this to be true, Gonring (2008) argues that until the late 1990s companies were free to think about communication as their choice to disclose information to particular groups. They received little unsolicited feedback from those groups, and what they did get was communicated privately. Today stakeholders are able to use technology to provide very public feedback to companies. Protesters have used websites to campaign against environmental damage caused by major companies (for example, http://www.cokejustice.org), to organise consumer boycotts (for instance http://www.jeboycottedanone.com) and even to encourage consumers to download specific songs in order to prevent the winner of a TV talent show from reaching the number one position in the music charts (the campaign against the 2009 winner of the X-Factor was run from Facebook). The internet has changed the balance of power between companies and their stakeholders. Of course it is not all bad for companies. Take the example of Southwest Airlines (Gonring, 2008), a company which enjoys a loyal customer base. During an airport delay one of its employees played the ukulele to entertain waiting passengers, one of whom filmed the performance and posted it on YouTube. This created free advertising for the airline, further strengthening its image. Companies are now realising that loyal customers and employees are valuable *brand champions* able to promote companies in novel and credible ways. This creates new incentives to communicate effectively with stakeholders.

In this section we will consider a variety of ways in which companies communicate with their stakeholders, both routinely and in response to crises, considering the way in which communication affects reputation. Reputation is a tricky concept. Like it or not, each of us has a reputation, sometimes deserved and sometimes not. Reputation depends on a mixture of impressions and hard evidence. It may take years to build a good reputation but it can be destroyed overnight following adverse publicity. This means that companies must always be aware of the way they are perceived by the public.

Communication and reputation

Hutton *et al.* (2001) surveyed Fortune 500 companies, asking about the different forms of communication used, how much money was spent on each and the rationale behind the chosen methods. They found that firms in their sample spent more money on advertising than any other form of corporate communication. The magnitude of the difference was huge, with spending on advertising being four times the spending on communications with employees, five times bigger than spending on investor relations, 11 times the amount spent on annual and quarterly reports and 26 times greater than spending on industry relations. At first sight this spending pattern implies that companies are particularly keen to advertise as part of their sales strategy. However, when asked what they hoped to achieve through their corporate communication, respondents ranked support of sales at the bottom of a list of eight possible outcomes. The most important aim was corporate reputation management. The researchers went on to see if different types of communication spending were correlated with reputation as measured by the Fortune survey of most admired companies. This survey asks corporate executives how they perceive various aspects of corporate behaviour and puts these together to measure reputation. Perhaps surprisingly, the correlation between reputation and spending on advertising, the area attracting the greatest expenditure, was negative but statistically insignificant. The spending categories that had a positive and significant impact on reputation were foundation funding, investor relations (but this result was driven by the data on a single company), executive outreach and media relations. The authors were quick to point out that their results contradicted those obtained from earlier surveys; but to suggest that this may have been driven by unusual step changes in the reputation of some of the companies in the sample. An interesting feature of these results is the way they indicate that while individuals and companies can choose what and how to communicate, they cannot control the way it is perceived by others.

This research also raises the question, 'Why did the companies in the survey believe that advertising would improve their reputation?' It is important here to distinguish between the reputation of products or brands and the reputations of the companies that make them. Taking the example of Procter and Gamble, you probably know that they make household products but might not be able to match the company to some of its best-known brands like Cushelle toilet tissue, Crest toothpaste and Pampers nappies. The advertising for these brands focuses on the qualities of the product, and does not mention the company that makes them. In contrast, you cannot help associating Cadbury with Dairy Milk, Fruit and Nut and a range of other products. The Cadbury signature logo features prominently on all product packaging and the name Cadbury appears in all advertising. In fact, some advertisements say very little about individual products, focusing instead on the company name. This is an example of corporate-image advertising which, as the name implies, does not seek to promote a particular product but instead to promote the company itself. By promoting the company this type of advertising is aimed at a range of stakeholders, not just at consumers (Balmer and Greyser, 2002). The results of Hutton *et al.*'s (2001) survey might indicate that corporate image advertising is becoming increasingly important for American companies.

Companies with good brand images can expect to have good relationships with other companies in their supply chains, to get repeat and referred business from their customers and to have a loyal workforce. The word 'image' in itself highlights the importance of the perceptions of the person or organisation that is looking at the company. Each stakeholder brings their own set of expectations to their relationship with the company, and can therefore be said to 'co-create' the company's image. Companies must therefore be aware of their stakeholders' expectations and use effective communication to ensure that unrealistic expectations are altered, and that expectations of a good relationship are fulfilled. While corporate-image advertising can be valuable in this regard, it is interesting to note that different stakeholding groups are exposed to different media (Fiedler and Kirchgeorg, 2007), indicating that while the company wants to convey a single image to all its stakeholders it should convey the message in different ways to different groups. A good illustration of this is provided by a paper by Dyck *et al.* (2008). The paper looks at the tactics used by the Hermitage Fund, a Russian institution that uses a strategy of engagement with the companies whose shares it holds. It uses the media to draw attention to poor corporate governance in the hope that either the management team will change its policies or that regulators will apply pressure for change. Dyck *et al.* (2008) find that companies are more likely to reverse decisions or policies that are made public in American or British news media than in Russian media, indicating that Russian managers care about their reputation abroad, so are best reached this way.

Analysts should be considered separately from other stakeholders because they act as intermediaries between the company and the stock market. Their reports and recommendations affect the decisions of retail investors, which means that this group of stakeholders has unique influence over shareholders. Aerts *et al.* (2007) argue that the role and importance of analysts differs significantly according to national governance characteristics. They suggest that analysts have a greater role to play in countries like the US where share ownership is dispersed and investors rely on analysts to interpret corporate disclosures. In countries where ownership is more concentrated and blockholders are important, management will communicate directly with them. This means they will disclose less information, giving analysts less to work with. This fits with their evidence on voluntary, web-based disclosures by North American and continental European companies. In North America such disclosures reduce the dispersion of analysts' forecasts, especially with regard to companies that rely on intangible assets. In contrast, voluntary, web-based disclosures have no impact on analysts' forecasts in Europe.

While voluntary disclosures over the internet lead to consensus among American analysts, a general increase in the availability of information does not have the same result. In 2000 the US SEC approved Regulation Fair Disclosure, a requirement that companies make public all information given to analysts. This requirement for more general disclosure resulted in an increase in voluntary disclosures by companies (Bailey *et al.*, 2003; Heflin *et al.*, 2003) and to an increase in the dispersion of analysts' forecasts (Bailey *et al.*, 2003). In contrast, when Asian countries introduced codes of corporate governance recommending increased disclosure, companies complied and analysts' forecast errors fell, while the dispersion of their forecasts was unchanged. (Nowland, 2008). Clearly analysts are affected by the volume of information available, but existing evidence does not allow us to say with certainty that it brings consensus within this stakeholding group. This may have something to do with the range of information considered by analysts. We tend to think of them focusing on 'hard' financial information, yet research by Gabbioneta *et al.* (2007) reveals that Italian analysts are also influenced by governance factors, as well as by the leadership and vision of corporate management. This implies that the disclosure of 'soft' information that is open to a variety of interpretations may lead to greater disagreement among the analyst community.

So far we have considered routine communication with stakeholders. It has become apparent that companies disclose a wide variety of information using different media to appeal to their various stakeholders and to maintain or enhance their reputations. It is also interesting to see how companies react to crises that threaten to destroy their reputations. As a rule of thumb the best response to a crisis is quick and honest, using an approach that gets to the heart of the problem. A good example of this is Johnson and Johnson's response to the Tylenol crisis. In October 1982 five people in the Chicago area died, having taken the painkiller Tylenol, which had been laced with cyanide. The company immediately responded by withdrawing the batches of the drug that contained the contaminated bottles. The Food and Drug Administration (FDA) quickly determined that the company was not implicated in the tampering, and that the contaminated bottles had been deliberately placed in the shops where they were bought. A few days later more contaminated Tylenol was discovered, this time in California, where the product killed another two people. The company immediately responded by withdrawing all supplies of the drug across the US. While the company's honesty and full cooperation with the FDA were exemplary and enhanced its reputation, in the short run the affair was costly to the company and to its shareholders. Earnings fell by $50 million and $2313 million was wiped off the company's value during October 1982. However, the company's speedy and ethical response enabled it to regain almost all its former market share within one year of the contamination (Greyser, 2009).

While Johnson and Johnson took swift action to restore public confidence, Danone SA entered a protracted legal battle against the organisers of a boycott of its products in 2001. Danone's problems began on 10 January of that year, when *Le Monde* published a story about the company's plans to shed 1700 jobs in France and a further 1300 in the rest of Europe. The company confirmed that it had excess capacity in the biscuit part of its business, but declined to say more, because French law required companies to provide information to their trade unions before making public announcements. When the company finally announced its plans on 29 March, it published a generous package of measures which went beyond its legal requirements to its employees. The package included a choice of alternative roles for employees whose jobs were redundant, help finding work elsewhere if the employees preferred this, relocation expenses and even help for spouses to find work if they lost jobs as a result of relocation. Despite the generosity of the package, consumers started a boycott fuelled by the decision of the editor of Technikart to create a website devoted to the boycott. The website featured Danone's logo prompting the company to take the protest group to court. This was the beginning of a legal battle that would last for two years, with a victory for one side quickly followed by a counter-claim by the other. In the end the protesters emerged as the winners. Perhaps if Danone had used the media rather than the courts to challenge the protesters the boycott would lost steam much more quickly than it did. Instead the company lost sales and saw its value decline by 29 per cent between 2001 and 2003 (Hunter *et al.*, 2008).

While these crises were caused by actual events, rumours can also wreak havoc on a company's reputation. Fombrun (1996) gives the example of Procter and Gamble which, during the 1980s, was rumoured to be donating some of its profits to Satanists. The rumour was supported by claims that the company's logo, which depicts the moon and 13 stars, was a symbol used by Satanists. Rather than responding immediately, the company attempted to find the source of the rumour, threatened lawsuits against the person or group and sent press releases to the newspapers. This approach failed to dismiss the rumour, which persisted for some time. Procter and Gamble's approach can be contrasted with that of Entenmann's Bakery when, in 1991, it was claimed that the company was owned by the founder of the Unification Church. As soon as the rumour surfaced, the chair held a press conference in which he discussed the company's history and family ownership, effectively crushing the allegations. These examples show that the danger of saying nothing is that others interpret silence as agreement with others' statements. In other words, lack of communication can in itself communicate unwanted messages.

The keys to crisis management are speed and honesty. A company facing an image crisis must react quickly, and that reaction must come from top management as an indication that the problem is being taken seriously. The reaction must be honest, and if the company is at fault it must admit its fault. If it does not, it is likely to be caught out by journalists or bloggers, and that can only lead to further problems and to the destruction of reputation.

CONCLUSION

Recent years have witnessed events which have had a huge impact on the amount of information that is provided to shareholders and stakeholders and on the way it is communicated. Financial scandals like the ones at BCCI in the UK and Enron in the US have been a catalyst for the introduction of corporate governance codes and legislation. Disclosure is a feature of both forms of regulation as well as of recent changes in company law in the UK. Companies have to disclose increasing amounts of financial and governance information to their shareholders, which is why they are publishing longer annual reports and choosing to establish investor relations departments to manage the flow of information. The additional information is not always useful; in fact the value-relevance of fundamental accounting numbers such as net profit has been questioned in recent years. The decline in value-relevance has been blamed on the accounting treatment of intangibles and on companies' own actions in manipulating their earnings figures. This may explain why many companies choose to disclose information not required by law, and why investors use these voluntary disclosures in valuing firms.

Just as the investor relations department has become important in terms of communicating with shareholders, so the public relations department has developed to improve communication with stakeholders. Companies are using a variety of different media to promote both individual products to consumers and the firm itself to a wider group of stakeholders. The aim is to create or maintain a good reputation, an intangible asset which is vital to business success. Changing communications technology has increased the vulnerability of reputation to attack. It is now vital for companies to respond quickly and honestly to all allegations of wrongdoing as well as to regularly communicate a positive image. This both nurtures good relationships with stakeholders and protects the value of shareholders' investment in the firm.

KEY POINTS

- The accounting information provided by law to shareholders has not always been relevant in valuing companies. The recent introduction of IFRS has improved the value-relevance of financial statements.
- Companies may choose to disclose additional financial and non-financial information in order to signal their value to investors.
- While some companies use earnings management techniques to smooth their earnings and impress the market, this is less likely to happen in well-governed firms.
- The creation and maintenance of reputation is a key motivating factor behind corporate information disclosures to stakeholders. This may explain why some companies choose to advertise their corporate image rather than to promote individual products.
- The rise of the internet has allowed stakeholders to communicate quickly and publicly with companies. It is therefore vital that companies respond with speed and frankness when stakeholder campaigns threaten their reputation.

CASE STUDY — Satyam Computer Services Ltd: The search for truth in corporate reporting

Satyam Computer Services Ltd was founded by Ramalinga Raju in 1977. 'Satyam' is the Sanskrit word for 'truth'. For many years the company's reputation tallied with its name and it grew to become the fourth largest IT services company in India, boasting an impressive global client list including Ford Motor Company, General Electric and Nestlé. In 2008 the World Council for Corporate Governance named it as one of the world's best-run companies. Everything changed on 7 January 2009 when Ramalinga Raju, now the chairman of the board, sent an extraordinary letter of resignation to his fellow board members. In the letter he explained that a small difference between the company's actual and reported profit had grown over the years, accompanied by an increasingly overstated asset position. During the second quarter of 2008 the company had reported revenues of 27 billion rupees when they were in fact 21.12 billion; this was reflected in a fictional increase in cash holdings of 5.88 billion rupees in that quarter. A series of such overstatements had led to the balance sheet as at 30 September 2008 showing a non-existent cash balance of 50.4 billion rupees, or $1.04 billion. This was the number that grabbed the newspaper headlines, but of course the accounting manipulation had resulted in other fictitious items, such as 4.9 billion rupees of non-existent debtors and 3.76 billion rupees of non-existent accrued interest.

Having stated the bald facts of the accounting manipulation, Raju went on to explain that he had attempted to replace the fictitious assets with real ones by purchasing Maytas Properties and Maytas Infrastructure, companies operated by members of the Raju family. His plan had been to show the assets in the balance sheet while delaying payment. When analysts saw the details of the proposed deals in December 2008 they realised that they overstated the value of both companies. Maytas Properties was valued at nearly six times its net worth, and this led to a shareholder revolt. Notice that 'Maytas' is 'Satyam' spelt backwards, the play on words perhaps unintentionally indicating that truth was absent in the proposed deal. Satyam was forced to drop the acquisitions and five board members resigned during the month. In his letter Raju pointed out that he alone was responsible for the fraud, and none of the other board members knew anything about it. He went on to suggest that the company could still recover by acquiring other companies and said that Merrill Lynch, which had been engaged ten days earlier to explore possible merger opportunities, should carry on with that work. What he didn't know was that a few hours before, Merrill Lynch had terminated its agreement with Satyam, having noticed financial irregularities at the company.

If the team from Merrill Lynch had been able to spot the fraud, why hadn't the directors or auditors seen it? The directors who resigned in the wake of the failed acquisitions were not available for comment, so we have no way of knowing if they resigned because they were concerned about the over-valued deals, or because they suspected that something more was going on. Given that one was a professor at Harvard Business School and another a former dean of the Indian School of Business, one would expect them to have been vigilant in their roles. The audit partner at Price Waterhouse resigned even though he was not involved with the Satyam audit, and while the firm refused to make a detailed statement it did say that the fraud had been designed to avoid detection during an audit, and the audit itself had used appropriate evidence. While audits are not organised specifically to detect fraud, they are designed to ensure that the financial statements are an accurate reflection of the transactions undertaken by the company. When those transactions result in assets appearing on the balance sheet, evidence should be sought. In this case one would imagine that the firm's bank statements should have revealed whether or not the cash on its balance sheet actually existed. Perhaps the emphasis on process discussed earlier in this chapter meant that the auditors did not check individual accounts. As you would expect, Raju was arrested within days of sending his resignation letter, and other arrests, including those of two auditors and several company executives, followed a year later.

The case became known as India's Enron. At one level there are striking similarities. Both companies were well-known, highly respected and had won plaudits for the quality of their boards and corporate governance in general. Both had long-standing relationships with respected audit companies which did not spot the problems with their accounting statements. However, the epilogue to the Satyam fraud provides an interesting example of how the public and private sectors can work together to resolve a crisis. The Ministry of Corporate Affairs acted quickly, protecting stakeholders by replacing the board and appointing KPMG and Deloittes to restate the company's accounts. The board decided that an acquisition was the best way forward, and in April 2009 Venturbay Consultants Private Ltd, a subsidiary of Tech Mahindra, acquired a controlling stake in Satyam. Satyam Computers has now emerged as Mahandra Satyam, which managed to stem the flow of clients leaving in search of other suppliers and, as the major provider of IT services to the 2010 World Cup in South Africa, it is once again raising its international profile.

CASE-STUDY QUESTIONS

1 What role, if any, should the independent directors of Satyam have played in spotting the fraud?
2 If shareholders cannot trust audited financial statements, what other types of information should they seek?
3 Should the Indian government respond to this case by introducing legislation similar to the Sarbanes–Oxley Act?

REVISION QUESTIONS

1 What is earnings management and how does it affect investors?
2 What is a signal, and why might the voluntary disclosure of non-financial information act as a signal?
3 What contribution does agency theory make to our understanding of voluntary disclosures?
4 Why doesn't the audit process necessarily uncover fraudulent transactions?
5 What benefits can a company expect to get if it creates a good reputation?
6 Give examples of good and bad crisis management by firms.

REFERENCES

Accounting Standards Board (2009) 'A Review of Narrative Reporting by UK Listed Companies in 2008/2009' Financial Reporting Council

Aerts, W., Cormier, D. and Magnan, M. (2007) 'The Association Between Web-based Corporate Performance Disclosure and Financial Analyst Behaviour Under Different Governance Regimes' *Corporate Governance: An International Review* 15 (6) 1301–1329

Akerlof, G. A. (1970) 'The Market for "Lemons": Quality Uncertainty and The Market Mechanism' *Quarterly Journal of Economics* 84 (3) 488–500

Bailey, W., Haitao, L., Mao, C. and Zhong, R. (2003) 'Regulation Fair Disclosure and Earnings Information: Market, Analyst, and Corporate Responses' *Journal of Finance* 58 (6) 2487–2514

Balmer, J.M.T. and Greyser, S.A. (2002) 'Managing the Multiple Identities of the Corporation' *California Management Review* 44 (3) 72–86

Basioudis, I.G., Papakonstantinou, E. and Geiger, M.A. (2008) 'Audit Fees, Non-audit Fees and Audit Going-concern Reporting Decisions in the United Kingdom' *Abacus* 44 (3) 284–309

Beneish, M.D., Hopkins, P.E., Jansen, I.P. and Martin, R.D. (2005) 'Do Auditor Resignations Reduce Uncertainty About the Quality of Firms' Financial Reporting?' *Journal of Accounting and Public Policy* 24 (5) 357–390

Birt, J.L., Bilson, C.M., Smith, T. and Whaley, R.E. (2006) 'Ownership, Competition, and Financial Disclosure' *Australian Journal of Management* 31 (2) 235–263

Blay, A.D., Sneatthen, L.D. and Kizirian, T. (2007) 'The Effects of Fraud and Going-concern Risk on Auditors' Assessment of the Risk of Material Misstatement and Resulting Audit Procedures' *International Journal of Auditing* 11 (3) 149–163

Bowen, R.M., Rajgopal, S. and Vekatachalam, M. (2008) 'Accounting Discretion, Corporate Governance and Firm Performance' *Contemporary Accounting Research* 25 (2) 351–405

Brammer, S. and Pavelin, S. (2006) 'Voluntary Environment Disclosures by Large UK Companies' *Journal of Business Finance and Accounting* 33 (7) & (8) 1168–1188

Cheng, E.C.M. and Courtenay, M. (2006) 'Board Composition, Regulatory Regime and Voluntary Disclosure' *International Journal of Accounting* 41 (3) 262–289

Cohen, J., Krisnamoorthy, G. and Wright, A.M. (2002) 'Corporate Governance and the Audit Process' *Contemporary Accounting Research* 19 (4) 573–594

Cullinan, C.P. and Sutton, S.G. (2002) 'Defrauding the Public Interest: A Critical Examination of Reengineered Audit Processes and the Likelihood of Detecting Fraud' *Critical Perspectives on Accounting* 13 (3) 297–310

Davidson, R., Goodwin, J. and Kent, P. (2005) 'Internal Governance Structures and Earnings Management' *Accounting and Finance* 45 (2) 241–267

Davison, J. and Skerratt, L. (2007) *Words, Pictures and Intangibles in the Corporate Report* Institute of Chartered Accountants of Scotland

Dechow, P.M. and Skinner, D.J. (2000) 'Earnings Management: Reconciling the Views of Accounting Academics, Practitioners, and Regulators' *Accounting Horizons* 14 (2) 235–250

Dedman, E., Lin, S.W., Prakash, A.J. and Chang, C. (2008) 'Voluntary Disclosure and its Impact on Share Price: Evidence From The UK Biotechnology Sector' *Journal of Accounting and Public Policy* 27 (3) 195–216

Donnelly, R. and Mulcahy, M. (2008) 'Board Structure, Ownership, and Voluntary Disclosure in Ireland' *Corporate Governance: An International Review* 16 (5) 416–429

Dyck, A., Volchkova, N. and Zingales, L. (2008) 'The Corporate Governance Role of the Media: Evidence from Russia' *Journal of Finance* 63 (3) 1093–1135

Eng, L.L. and Mak, Y.T. (2003) 'Corporate Governance and Voluntary Disclosure' *Journal of Accounting and Public Policy* 22 (4) 352–345

Fiedler, L. and Kirchgeorg, M. (2007) 'The Role Concept in Corporate Branding and Stakeholder Management Reconsidered: Are Stakeholder Groups Really Different?' *Corporate Reputation Review* 10 (3) 177–188

Fombrun, C.J. (1996) *Reputation: Realizing Value From the Corporate Image* Harvard Business School Press

Francis, J. and Schipper, K. (1999) 'Have Financial Statements Lost Their Relevance?' *Journal of Accounting Research* 37 (2) 319–352

Gabbioneta, C., Ravasi, D. and Mazzola, P. (2007) 'Exploring the Drivers of Corporate Reputation: A Study of Italian Securities Analysts' *Corporate Reputation Review* 10 (2) 99–123

Geppart, J. and Lawrence, J.E. (2008) 'Predicting Firm Reputation Through Content Analysis of Shareholders' Letter' *Corporate Reputation Review* 11 (4) 285–307

Gjerde, Ø., Knivsflå, K. and Sætton, F. (2008) 'The Value-relevance of Adopting IFRS: Evidence from 145 NGAAP Restatements' *Journal of International Accounting, Auditing and Taxation* 17 (2) 92–112

Gonring, M.P. (2008) 'Customer Loyalty and Employee Engagement: An Alignment for Value' *Journal of Business Strategy* 29 (4) 29–40

Greyser, S.A. (2009) 'Corporate Brand Reputation and Brand Crisis Management' *Management Decision* 47 (4) 590–602

Hassink, H.F.D., Bollen, H.D., Meuwissen, R.H.D. and de Vries, M.J. (2009) 'Corporate Fraud and the Audit Expectations Gap: A Study of Business Managers' *Journal of International Accounting, Auditing and Taxation* 18 (2) 85–100

Heflin, F., Subramanyam, K.R. and Zhang, Y. (2003) 'Regulation FD and the Financial Information Environment: Early Evidence' *Accounting Review* 78 (1) 1–37

Hunter, M.L., Le Menestrel, M. and De Bettignies, H. (2008) 'Beyond Control: Crisis Strategies and Stakeholder Media in the Danone Boycott of 2001' *Corporate Reputation Review* 11 (4) 335–350

Hutton, J.G., Goodman, M.B., Alexander, J.B. and Genest, C.M. (2001) 'Reputation Management: the New Face of Corporate Public Relations?' *Public Relations Review* 27 (3) 247–261

Jermakowicz, E.K., Prather-Kinsey, J. and Wulf, I. (2007) 'The Value Relevance of Accounting Income Reported By DAX-30 German Companies' *Journal of International Financial Management and Accounting* 18 (3) 151–191

Klein, A. (2002) 'Audit Committee, Board of Director Characteristics and Earnings Management' *Journal of Accounting and Economics* 33 (3) 375–400

Kwon, S.S. (2001) 'Value Relevance of Financial Information and Conservatism: High-tech Versus Low-tech Stocks' http://ssrn.com/abstract=285346

Laskin, A.V. (2009) 'A Descriptive Account of the Investor Relations Profession: A National Study' *Journal of Business Communication* 46 (2) 208–233

Lee, T.A. (1994) 'The Changing Form of the Corporate Annual Report' *Accounting Historians Journal* 21 (1) 215–232

Lee, E., Walker, M. and Christiansen, H.B. (2008) *Mandating IFRS: Its Impact on the Cost of Equity Capital in Europe* ACCA Research Report no. 105 Certified Accountants Educational Trust

Lennox, C.S. (1999) 'The Accuracy and Incremental Information Content of Audit Reports in Predicting Bankruptcy' *Journal of Business Finance and Accounting* 26 (5/6) 757–778

Leuz, C., Nanda, D. and Wysocki, P.D. (2003) 'Earnings Management and Investor Protection: An International Comparison' *Journal of Financial Economics* 69 (3) 505–527

Lev, B. and Zarowin, P. (1999) 'The Boundaries of Financial Reporting and How to Extend Them' *Journal of Accounting Research* 37 (2) 353–358

Li, F. (2008) 'Annual Report Readability, Current Earnings, and Earnings Persistence' *Journal of Accounting and Economics* 45 (2–3) 221–247

Miller, M.H. and Rock, K. (1985) 'Dividend Policy Under Asymmetric Information' *Journal of Finance* XL (4) 1031–1051

Murray, A., Sinclair, D., Power, D. and Gray, R. (2006) 'Do Financial Markets Care About Social and Environmental Disclosure? Further Evidence and Exploration From The UK' *Accounting, Auditing and Accountability Journal* 19 (2) 228–255

Nowland, J. (2008) 'The Effects of National Governance Codes on Firm Disclosure Practices: Evidence From Analyst Earnings Forecasts' *Corporate Governance: An International Review* 16 (6) 475–491

Penrose, J.M. (2008) 'Annual Report Graphic Use' *Journal of Business Communication* 45 (2) 158–180

Petersen, C. and Plenborg, T. (2006) 'Voluntary Disclosure and Information Asymmetry in Denmark' *Journal of International Accounting, Auditing and Taxation* 15 (2) 127–149

Rezaee, Z. (2005) 'Causes, Consequences, and Deterrence of Financial Statement Fraud' *Critical Perspectives on Accounting* 16 (3) 277–298

Ross, S.A. (1977) 'The Determination of Financial Structure: The Incentive Signalling-Approach' *Bell Journal of Economics* 8 (1) 23–40

Rutherford, B.A. (2005) 'Genre Analysis of Corporate Annual Report Narratives' *Corporate Reputation Review* 42 (4) 349–378

Spence, M. (1973) 'Job Market Signaling' *Quarterly Journal of Economics* 87 (3) 355–374

Weil, J. (2004) 'Behind Wave of Corporate Fraud: A Change in How Auditors Work' *Wall Street Journal* March 25, 2004

SUGGESTIONS FOR FURTHER READING

Ferri, F. and Sandino, T. (2009) 'The Impact of Shareholder Activism on Financial Reporting and Compensation: The Case of Employee Stock Option Expensing' *Accounting Review* 84 (2) 433–466. This paper examines the reaction to the SEC's introduction of regulation allowing shareholders to vote on accounting matters for the first time in 2003. Their votes had a significant impact on both accounting and corporate governance practices.

Sweeny, L. and Coughlan, J. (2008) 'Do Different Industries Report Corporate Social Responsibility Differently? An Investigation Through the Lens of Stakeholder Theory' *Journal of Marketing Communications* 14 (2) 113–124. The authors look at the CSR reporting found in the annual reports of companies in the FTSE4Good index. They find that companies choose to report in line with stakeholders' expectations, which they take as evidence that CSR reporting is a form of marketing.

http://www.ir-soc.org.uk/ The website of the Investor Relations Society includes resources available to download in the IR Best Practice section.

http://www.cipr.co.uk/ The website of the Chartered Institute of Public Relations includes articles on public relations and reports on various aspects of communication in the Research and reports section of the site.

9 CORPORATE GOVERNANCE IN EMERGING MARKETS

- To appreciate the range of governance problems facing companies and investors in emerging and developing economies
- To understand why governance has implications for economic development
- To appreciate the roles of a variety of international agencies in promoting good governance
- To appreciate the scope of the OECD Principles of Corporate Governance
- To gain an understanding of the empirical evidence on the impact of sound governance on companies in emerging economies

INTRODUCTION

In this chapter we will explore the governance problems faced by investors and companies in emerging markets. The term 'emerging markets' is usually used to describe those countries that have recently emerged from central planning and have moved or are moving towards a market economy. Under this definition the focus would be on China and Eastern Europe. Here we are including in the term those countries sometimes described as 'developing' or 'less developed'. This means that much of South America, Africa and Asia are also included in the definition. In terms of the choice of specific countries we have been guided by the classification used by *Emerging Markets Monitor* which looks at issues affecting Emerging Europe, Asia, Latin America and the Middle East and Africa.

We have encountered emerging economies in other parts of this book, notably in chapter 7 on regulation. We saw there that codes of corporate governance are a popular form of regulation in emerging markets, just as they are in more developed countries. What is interesting about this observation is the fact that governance has become an issue in the West long after its economies were classified as developed. In the less developed parts of the world corporate governance reforms are being made as those economies grow. In this chapter we will begin by considering the kind of economic problems faced in emerging markets and how these relate to governance issues. We will go on to consider the response of international organisations like the World Bank and the OECD. These organisations see improvements in corporate governance as a vital element in encouraging economic growth, hence the observation that governance initiatives are embedded in growth strategies, whereas in more developed nations they have emerged long after industrialisation and development have been achieved. It is envisaged that improved governance will lead to better access to finance, the development of capital markets, improved corporate performance and lower risk. We will consider each of these claims here, using relevant country-level data and empirical evidence on corporate performance. Finally, the case study considers Natura, a Brazilian company which has taken advantage of stock market reforms to mark itself out as an example of sound governance in a country which suffers from public-sector corruption, and where the legal rights of lenders and borrowers are poorly protected.

ECONOMIC PROBLEMS IN EMERGING MARKETS

As was stated in the introduction, we are using the term 'emerging markets' to cover a large part of the globe. The countries we will consider face a variety of problems and challenges as they implement new corporate governance arrangements. Countries that have recently moved from a centrally planned to a market system, as is the case in emerging Europe and in China, tend to have a good infrastructure and a well-educated workforce. They have some very large enterprises that were formerly, and may still be, partially state-owned and a group of smaller, younger and more entrepreneurial firms that have always been privately owned. The former state-owned enterprises (SOEs) tend to have hierarchical management and may be slow to react to changing market conditions. The financial sector in these countries is often dominated by banks. Countries classified as 'less developed', like much of Africa, together with parts of Latin America and Asia, face a different set of problems. Some have relatively poor infrastructure, and the workforce is likely to include people with a variety of educational backgrounds, some having received only primary education. They may rely heavily on particular sectors like agriculture and tourism, both of which give companies close ties to overseas markets and may affect the way they do business within their supply chains, as we saw in chapter 4. They tend to have small and potentially inefficient capital markets. The developing economies of the Middle East and North Africa are very different from those of the rest of Africa. The oil-rich countries have a good infrastructure and are able to attract foreign workers. Their economies are dominated by natural resources so their stock markets are small and illiquid because of the concentration of wealth in the hands of a few families.

Despite the many differences between the various parts of the developing world, in governance terms they have a lot in common. Emerging economies are dominated by small and medium-sized enterprises, so their stock markets are usually small. Income inequality means that few people consider buying shares so the ownership of listed companies is concentrated in the hands of a few families or of the state. This means that emerging stock markets are illiquid because blockholders seldom trade. They may also be inefficient due to lack of reliable and timely information. This means that it makes little sense to link remuneration to stock market measures. Equally, when managers have control which extends to accounting choices there is no point in linking payments to accounting profit. Illiquidity in the stock market also means that it cannot function as a market for corporate control, and regulation is often weak, which means that minority shareholders are poorly protected. This helps to explain why some companies from emerging markets choose to list their shares overseas in markets with stronger protection of minority shareholders and more stringent governance requirements. Wójcik and Burger (2009) report that by the end of 2008, 20 per cent of overseas listings originated from the BRIC countries discussed in Box 9.1. Not surprisingly, the companies that choose to list abroad tend to be large or to belong to the technology sector and therefore to need access to a large pool of funds.

Box 9.1 BRICs

The term 'BRIC' was coined in 2001 by Jim O'Neill, the chief economist at Goldman Sachs. It stands for Brazil, Russia, India and China, the four emerging markets which Goldman Sachs believes will dominate the world economy by 2032. While the four countries vary tremendously in terms of geography and culture, each has a large population and a government with an apparently welcoming attitude to globalisation. This makes them interesting to western economies both as a huge potential market for goods and services and as a threat to western economic and political influence. As an indicator of the success of the BRICS, between 2000 and 2009 the average annual rate of GDP growth in the EU was just 1.5 per cent. The corresponding figures for Brazil, Russia, India and China were 3.3, 5.5, 7.1 and 10.3 per cent, respectively (World Bank, 2009).

Despite this success, challenges remain. The public sectors of BRIC countries are perceived as corrupt, as we will see in a later section of this chapter, yet individual companies and stock markets are striving to introduce meaningful reforms, as illustrated in the Natura case study at the end of this chapter.

Boards are dominated by insiders due to the interplay of structural factors like concentrated ownership which allows dominant shareholders to appoint board members, the prevalence of business groups whose companies have interlocking directorships and simply because the pool of potential non-executive directors is small. Corporate governance initiatives in these economies must be seen as part of a package of reforms which may include new or improved securities legislation, improvements to accounting and auditing practices and the introduction of corporate governance codes. All this requires cooperation between governments, stock markets, companies and professional bodies.

INTERNATIONAL ORGANISATIONS AND CORPORATE GOVERNANCE

The World Bank has its roots in 1944 when the International Bank for Reconstruction and Development (IBRD) was founded in order to assist in the reconstruction of Europe after the Second World War. Today the World Bank is owned by 187 member countries, and operates through two institutions, the IBRD which offers loans to middle-income and creditworthy low-income countries, and the International Development Association (IDA) which gives grants to low-income countries. The work of these two institutions is complemented by four others which are part of the World Bank Group. Of most interest here is the International

Finance Corporation (IFC), which offers advisory services, including advice on corporate governance, to private sector companies in developing countries.

The OECD was founded in 1961 by a group of 20 developed countries in Europe and North America. They agreed that they needed to cooperate in order to promote their own growth and help less developed countries to develop and take part in international trade. The OECD now works on initiatives in six areas; the economy, society, development, finance, governance, innovation and sustainability. Within the governance area the organisation works in four distinct but overlapping fields: public governance, corporate governance, fighting corruption and regulatory reform. Its best-known contribution to corporate governance is its Principles of Corporate Governance, which are discussed in more detail below. The implementation of the Principles is monitored by the World Bank, whose Reports on the Observation of Standards and Codes (ROSCs) explain the extent to which these Principles are being used in developing countries. It is worth noting that each country can choose whether or not to be the subject of a ROSC. If they decide to go ahead, a ROSC team will go to the country and benchmark existing regulation and corporate practices against the Principles, then make recommendations on changes to the law, code or practice. The fact that the ROSCs are then made publicly available via the World Bank website makes it easy for interested investors to judge the extent to which subsequent changes are in line with the ROSCs.

OECD Principles of Corporate Governance

The council of the OECD set up a task force on corporate governance in 1998. A year later it published the OECD Principles of Corporate Governance, which were updated in 2004. The Principles cover six areas; the basis of an effective governance framework, shareholders' rights, the equitable treatment of shareholders, the role of stakeholders, disclosure and transparency and board responsibilities. The Principles are not designed to be prescriptive; instead they offer a general framework which can be tailored to meet the particular needs of individual countries. In 2006 the OECD published its methodology for the implementation of the Principles. Until this time the World Bank and IMF used their own criteria for judging how the Principles were being used. The OECD hopes that its methodology will help inspectors to judge the strengths and weaknesses of individual governance systems so that they can enter a dialogue with regulators and help to establish standards that are locally meaningful and useful.

According to the Principles an effective corporate governance framework should promote the development of transparent and efficient markets, be consistent with the country's legal system and should make clear the division of responsibilities between different regulatory authorities. The framework will include a mix of laws, regulations, self-regulation and business practices chosen by companies themselves. The Principles recognise that it would be wrong to impose a specific mix of these elements, since developing countries differ in their legal traditions and cultures, so each should find the best way forward for itself. The OECD encourages countries to monitor the corporate governance framework as it develops and to consult both within the country and internationally with a view to improving the system over time.

Shareholders have the right to systems that ensure that their ownership of equity is securely registered and easily transferred. They should have access to corporate information, be able to vote on a range of matters at general meetings and to elect and remove company directors. In order to facilitate voting, companies should introduce systems that allow voting in person or by proxy. They must also ensure that all shareholders understand what classes of equity exist, and how voting rights differ between them, but there is no pressure on companies to implement a 'one-share-one-vote' system. Institutional investors should not be obliged to vote, but they are encouraged to disclose their policy on voting to their retail investors. The Principles aim to stimulate active markets for corporate control and therefore discourage anti-takeover devices, such as poison pills that would render ineffective shareholders' attempts to monitor management.

Shareholders should be treated equally whatever the size of their holding and whether they are domestic or foreign. This does not imply that there should be a single class of equity; rather that within each class all owners should be treated equally, and all shareholders should be fully informed about their own rights and those of the holders of other types of shares. In the event that the management proposes a change in voting rights, the resolution should go to a general meeting. Minority investors need cost-effective ways of protecting their rights, which may include the ability to litigate against companies, as well as more routine methods, such the ability to bring issues to the general meeting. Shareholders should be protected from insider trading and *self-dealing*, especially in countries where pyramid ownership is usual, and board members should disclose any interest they have in the company's transactions.

Companies should respect the legal rights of their stakeholders, and when those rights are violated the law should step in to rectify the situation. Stakeholders should be reassured that if they spot ethical or legal problems in the company they can approach the board without any fear of reprisals, and that when they have a specific governance role they will be provided with the information they need to fulfil that role. The two stakeholding groups that are specifically mentioned in the Principles are employees and creditors. The Principles encourage companies to develop employee participation systems that contribute to improved corporate performance. These could operate through governance channels such as representation on works councils or the board, or through incentive schemes like employee share-ownership programmes or profit-sharing. The Principles also encourage regulators to formulate a framework for insolvency and creditors' rights alongside the governance framework. This is another area where the World Bank is also active and publishes ROSCs on insolvency and creditor rights.

A sound corporate governance system should provide timely and accurate information on the firm's financial performance as well as on the governance system itself. Without such disclosure unethical behaviour can go unchecked, markets lose their integrity and prices become uninformative. The financial data should include audited financial statements, together with management's commentary on the statements and a statement of the foreseeable risk factors affecting the company. The key aspects of the governance system which must be revealed are ownership and voting information, details on board composition, remuneration and nomination procedures and related party transactions.

The final section of the Principles concerns the board and its leadership and monitoring functions. In line with their aim of providing a non-prescriptive framework that can be applied anywhere, the Principles make no recommendation about the structure of the board. Instead they stress the need for the members of a unitary or supervisory board to act with care and loyalty towards all shareholders. In assessing the effectiveness of the board a reviewer will look at the way the board enforces the other areas covered by the Principles. Unlike the individual country codes discussed in chapter 7, which are designed to be implemented by companies, the OECD Principles have a wider audience, which includes regulators who are encouraged to develop their own codes based on them.

Recalling those national codes discussed in chapter 7, 17 of the 36 were issued in the emerging markets analysed here. Without wishing to duplicate material, it is worth mentioning some of those findings again. As we have already seen, one common problem shared by emerging economies is the fact that their stock markets are small because few companies are eligible or choose to seek a listing. This means that the pool of potential independent directors is also very small. This is the most likely explanation of the observation that none of the countries analysed in this chapter has a corporate governance code that requires the majority of board members to be independent. The codes in operation in Turkey, Bahrain, Egypt and South Africa do, however, require the majority of directors to be non-executives, which brings an external perspective to bear on corporate issues. As in other parts of the world, it is usual in emerging markets to require the roles of the CEO and chair of the board to be held by two different people. The use of board subcommittees is also widespread. Each of the emerging market codes analysed in chapter 7 requires companies to have audit committees, while 11 of the 17 also require remuneration and nomination committees. Where fewer than three subcommittees are recommended it is usually the nomination committee that is missing. This may again reflect that fact that few independent directors are available, so it is not worth having a separate subcommittee to consider how new directors can be recruited. A slim majority of the emerging market codes require boards to undertake regular evaluations of their performance.

A year after publishing its Principles the OECD produced separate 'Guidelines on Corporate Governance of State-owned Enterprises'. These Guidelines recognise that the state sector is an important part of the economy in many developing countries, and that some aspects of the existing Principles need to be modified to cover the special case of the SOE. That said, the Guidelines follow the same pattern as the Principles, and cover the same six areas. One of the themes that runs through the Guidelines is the necessity to separate the ownership and policy functions of the state. The OECD argues that in the absence of this separation the state becomes either a passive or an interfering owner, so it suggests that the state should set up an ownership entity that holds shares in SOEs. The ownership entity would take responsibility for voting its shares and for reporting on the performance of SOEs, both individually and as a group. The ownership entity should act as an owner, not as an arm of government, for example when voting it should consider the best interests of the company rather than wider economic policy. The OECD recognises that some SOEs are governed by complex or special legal arrangements such as protection from bankruptcy. While this might be desirable if the SOE is a provider of certain public services, in most cases the OECD advocates that SOEs should be organised according to company law. As part of this, they should compete on equal terms with private companies when dealing with other state organisations, like banks and the procurement sections of government departments. Finally, the state should not fill the boards of SOEs with its own officials. In addition to the usual exhortation to appoint professional boards, the guidelines indicate that smaller boards are more effective than larger ones, but do not define 'small'. Just as private companies should use a range of subcommittees, the Guidelines suggest that the boards of SOEs should have audit, remuneration and risk-management committees.

Box 9.2 World Bank ROSC on corporate governance in Azerbaijan

Azerbaijan is a former member of the Soviet Union. In recent years it has seen strong economic growth thanks to its oil revenues. Despite having a poor image as far as corruption is concerned, the country had shown a commitment to corporate governance by inviting the World Bank to undertake two ROSCs in the space of five years. The 2009 report is one of the most recently available on the World Bank website.

While the 2009 report notes some improvements in legislation since the previous report in 2005, the country has failed to implement many aspects of the OECD Principles. It has no company law, no laws to protect whistleblowers and has a range of problems concerning financial reporting and the availability of information to shareholders and other stakeholders. Only 5 per cent of companies disclose any information about their governance structures, some do not publish financial statements, and the quality of auditing is patchy, so that it is hard for investors to trust the information that is made available. This is a particular area of concern to the World Bank, which has asked for immediate action to speed the adoption of IFRS to enforce disclosures and to complete work on the country's Corporate Governance Code.

Many emerging markets have developed their own codes of corporate governance based on the OECD Principles, but only in Bangladesh, Egypt, Morocco and South Africa have regulators formulated separate codes for SOEs or included specific arrangements for them in the general code. The authorities in Brazil, Lebanon, Morocco and Tunisia have also recognised that family firms produce a governance challenge, and have written codes with them in mind.

The International Finance Corporation (IFC)

The IFC offers a range of investment and advisory services to its clients. Of interest here are the services it offers under the corporate governance heading and the rationale behind the provision of these services. In working with its clients the IFC uses a variety of governance tools tailored to fit companies in each of five categories: listed companies, family-controlled unlisted companies, privatised companies in transition economies, financial institutions and SOEs. The rationale behind the provision of these services is that they enable companies to get better access to capital and to improve their value. This in turn should lead to benefits for the economies in which these companies operate, such as capital market development, improved relationships with stakeholders and reduced financial and reputational risks. In the next section, where we look at the development of, and effectiveness of corporate governance in emerging markets, we will use these projected benefits as the basis for the discussion of the promise of improved governance.

When the IFC works with individual companies it focuses on five areas of governance which correspond closely to the OECD Principles. The areas are: commitment to good governance, the board of directors, control environment and processes, transparency and disclosure and finally shareholders' rights. It measures the extent to which companies comply with good practice in each area then writes an action plan giving very specific targets which the company must meet by a certain date. These might involve setting up board subcommittees, allowing shareholders to vote on remuneration policies or giving minority shareholders the right to bring resolutions to the AGM. This kind of tailor-made advice is invaluable to companies that are trying to improve their governance. The IFC's annual report for 2010 explains that during the previous year it gave corporate governance advice to 5,986 businesses across the world. One example is Asnova Holding, a Ukrainian company whose company secretary was given advice which, when implemented, enabled the business to increase productivity and attract new joint-venture partners. In the next section we will consider the extent to which the improvements envisaged by the IFC are realised in practice.

THE BENEFITS OF IMPROVED CORPORATE GOVERNANCE

Access to capital and capital market development

From the point of view of companies, one of the major benefits of improved governance should be better access to capital. The idea is simple. As companies improve their governance they become more trustworthy in the opinion of both lenders and potential equity holders. This means it is easier and cheaper for them to borrow and to issue new shares. This of course assumes that banks have sufficient funds to meet the demand for loans, and that there are sufficient investors in the market to buy new equity and debt instruments. When local banks and investors cannot fund companies, overseas institutions and investors may step in to fill the gap provided they are made welcome by the regulatory authorities. As more financial deals are done, capital markets grow and become more efficient, and the cost of capital falls, allowing companies to raise yet more funds for their own growth, so a virtuous circle develops.

Developing countries may have relatively small and concentrated banking markets. Economic theory implies two possible outcomes from such a situation. On the one hand the *structure-conduct-performance paradigm* often used in industrial economics implies that firms in markets where there are few competitors are able to exploit their market power by charging higher prices for a smaller volume of output than they would if they faced more competition. Applied to banking, this suggests that a concentrated banking sector will impede economic growth by restricting access to funds, and charging high interest rates. On the other hand, the information-asymmetry approach implies that a concentrated banking system is good because those few banks operating in the country have the ability and incentive to carefully screen borrowers, ensuring that only the best borrowers get access to funds. This suggests that loans will go to high-growth companies that can have the quickest and largest impact on economy-wide growth. Beck *et al.* (2004) use survey data from companies in both developing and developed countries to try to find out if concentrated banking is harmful or beneficial. They find that for companies in developing countries, a concentrated banking sector is associated with the perception that lack of finance hampers their growth. Given that less developed countries tend to have highly concentrated banking sectors, this is clearly an important issue.

Bank ownership may also affect the growth of companies. One remedy for concentration in the banking sector is to encourage the entry of foreign banks. Again this may be beneficial, encouraging competition leading to lower interest charges and a better range of products; or it may be harmful because foreign banks will find it harder than local ones to assess the creditworthiness of potential borrowers, and so may starve smaller businesses of the funds they need. Clarke *et al.* (2003) survey the literature on the impact of foreign banks and conclude that they make a positive difference to banking in developing countries. This is borne out by Beck *et al.* (2004), who report that the problems associated with concentrated banking markets are eased when foreign banks are present, but made worse by state-owned banks.

While improved corporate governance should make it easier for companies to borrow, if the banking system does not operate effectively they will be unable to gain the funds they need. The evidence discussed above suggests that governments in developing countries should encourage the entry of foreign banks which can improve the efficiency of the sector and enable well-governed companies to expand. Of course, banks are businesses and will only enter markets where they will make a profit. For this reason they tend to follow their large clients as they invest in overseas markets (Clarke *et al.*, 2003), which means that countries that are already developing because of foreign direct investment are more likely to get the banking boost they need, while other less fortunate countries will see fewer foreign banks entering. This is borne out by Van Horen (2007), who finds that banks from developed countries are less likely to operate in small developing countries than are banks from other developing nations.

Table 9.1 offers an indication of the development of the banking sector in a range of emerging markets in 2008, the latest year for which data on all variables were available for this group. The countries shown are those identified as 'emerging' by *Emerging Markets Monitor*. You may not agree with this classification, especially given that the footnotes indicate the per capita gross national income of the countries and nine of the 48 are classified by the World Bank as 'high-income'. The description 'developing' is usually given to low- and middle-income countries. Rather than enter a debate on the merits of the classifications and definitions offered by different organisations, here we simply offer the data together with comments on how they link to the themes of this chapter.

Table 9.1 includes two indicators of the health of the banking sector. The first, DC, is the value of domestic credit provided by the banking sector expressed as a percentage of gross domestic product. The higher the number, the more developed is the banking sector. SL is an index of the strength of legal rights, designed to measure the extent to which both borrowers and lenders are protected by laws on collateral and bankruptcy. The index ranges from 0 to 10, with higher scores indicating better protection. Banking in Asia appears to be more developed than in the other regions, given that this area has the highest average DC. Notice that this average masks wide variation that is not as one might have expected, related to per capita income in the region. Hong Kong and Singapore are both high-income countries yet banks in Hong Kong offer credit whose value is greater than the country's GDP, while bank credit offered in Singapore is less than the country's GDP. Thailand is classified as a lower-middle-income country yet its DC value is even higher than Hong Kong's. It achieves this despite the fact that its legal rights are lower than the average for the region. Other countries with legal rights of this level or lower, Sri Lanka and Indonesia, have relatively undeveloped banking sectors. The Philippines also has low legal rights, but data on the development of its banking sector are not available. The best legal rights are enjoyed by lenders and borrowers in the high- and upper-middle-income countries in the area; that is, Hong Kong, Malaysia and Singapore. The two Asian BRICS are quite different in terms of the development of their banking sectors. India has a below-average DC but higher than average legal rights, probably as a result of its colonial past. In China the situation is reversed; while legal rights are relatively low, the country's level of domestic credit as a proportion of GDP is higher than the average for the region.

The Middle East and Africa ranks next in terms of average banking sector development as measured by the proportion of bank credit to GDP. The range of individual country scores is even higher than in Asia, ranging from 215 per cent for South Africa to just 9 per cent for Saudi Arabia. While South Africa has a high level of domestic credit underpinned by good legal protection, with SL equal to nine, the other countries in which credit is greater than GDP, Bahrain and Lebanon, manage this despite lower-than-average legal protection. In this region legal protection is not necessarily related to economic development. Kenya achieves the maximum score for legal protection yet has per capita national income in the lowest range; both Ghana and Nigeria, which are also low-income countries, enjoy better-than-average legal rights. This can be explained by the fact that all three were British colonies and still operate according to the English common-law system. However, good legal protection does not lead to a developed banking sector, while there are no data available for Ghana, both Kenya and Nigeria have relatively poorly developed banking sectors despite the strength of their legal systems.

With an average domestic credit to GDP ratio of 64 per cent, emerging Europe comes third in terms of the development of its banking sector. Interestingly this is the only region in which no country has bank credit that is higher than GDP, at least for this year. Estonia has the highest value of DC, at 97 per cent, while Russia has the lowest at 26 per cent. Russia also has the lowest legal protection index. Intuitively it makes sense for these two characteristics to move together like this, but as we have already seen, in most cases the two features appear unrelated. This region is the most uniform of the four considered in the table, in that most countries have good legal protection and the range of DC values is lower than in other areas. Russia's relatively low scores mean that it stands out not just in comparison with the rest of emerging Europe, but also among the BRIC countries.

Table 9.1 Indicators of banking sector development, 2008

Asia	DC (%)	SL	Emerging Europe	DC (%)	SL	Latin America	DC (%)	SL	Middle East and Africa	DC (%)	SL
China[3]	121	6	Bulgaria[2]	67	8	Argentina[2]	24	4	Bahrain[1]	115	4
Hong Kong[1]	125	10	Croatia[2]	75	6	Brazil[2]	118	3	Côte d'Ivoire[4]	20	3
India[4]	68	8	Czech Republic[1]	58	6	Chile[2]	116	4	Egypt[3]	78	3
Indonesia[3]	37	3	Estonia[1]	97	6	Colombia[3]	43	5	Ghana[4]	n/a	7
Malaysia[2]	116	10	Hungary[2]	81	7	Ecuador[3]	20	3	Israel[1]	82	9
Pakistan[4]	n/a	6	Kazakhstan[2]	34	5	Jamaica[3]	54	8	Kenya[4]	40	10
Philippines[3]	n/a	3	Latvia[2]	89	9	Mexico[2]	46	4	Kuwait[1]	75	4
Singapore[1]	79	10	Montenegro[2]	88	9	Peru[3]	19	7	Lebanon[2]	169	3
Sri Lanka[3]	43	4	Poland[2]	60	8				Morocco[3]	96	3
Thailand[3]	146	4	Romania[2]	41	8				Nigeria[4]	27	8
Vietnam[4]	95	8	Russia[2]	26	3				Saudi Arabia[1]	9	4
			Serbia[2]	39	8				South Africa[2]	215	9
			Slovakia[2]	54	9				Tunisia[3]	72	3
			Slovenia[1]	n/a	6				Turkey[2]	53	4
			Ukraine[3]	82	9						
Average	92	7	Average	64	7	Average	55	5	Average	81	5

Notes:
1 High income (at least $11,116 per capita)
2 Upper-middle income ($3596–$11,115 per capita)
3 Lower-middle income (($906–$3,595 per capita)
4 Low income (less than or equal to $905 per capita)
n/a = not available

Source: World Bank, http://data.worldbank.org/topic/financial-sector

Latin America has the lowest average value of DC, but again the individual values are dispersed. Both Brazil and Chile have values over 100 per cent, despite having than lower than average legal protection indices. At the other end of the scale, Peru has the lowest ratio of bank credit to GDP, which is perhaps not surprising, given that it is a lower-middle-income country, but it has the second best legal protection in the area with a score of seven, beaten only by Jamaica with an index of eight. In relation to the other BRIC countries, Brazil ranks second in terms of the availability of domestic credit, while tying with Russia in having the lowest level of legal protection for borrowers and lenders.

Clearly the banking sector is not the only source of funds for business, so regulators should not be too concerned if a country has weak banks but a thriving stock market, so we should also consider the ability of markets to finance growth in emerging markets. Table 9.2 offers three indicators of stock market development: MC is the ratio of the stock market capitalisation of listed companies to GDP, ST is the ratio of stocks traded to GDP and TR is the ratio of the value of stocks traded to the average market capitalisation for the period. MC therefore indicates the relative size of the stock market while ST and TR measure liquidity. For each indicator higher values mean greater development.

Table 9.2 Indicators of stock market development, 2008

Asia	MC	ST	TR
China[3]	62	121	121
Hong Kong[1]	617	755	82
India[4]	53	86	85
Indonesia[3]	19	22	71
Malaysia[2]	85	39	33
Pakistan[4]	14	33	116
Philippines[3]	31	10	22
Singapore[1]	93	140	101
Sri Lanka[3]	11	3	17
Thailand[3]	38	43	78
Vietnam[4]	11	5	29
Average	94	114	69

Emerging Europe	MC	ST	TR
Bulgaria[2]	18	3	11
Croatia[2]	39	5	7
Czech Republic[1]	23	20	70
Estonia[1]	8	3	25
Hungary[2]	12	20	93
Kazakhstan[2]	23	3	12
Latvia[2]	5	<1	2
Montenegro[2]	63	2	n/a
Poland[2]	17	13	82
Romania[2]	10	2	11
Russia[2]	24	34	75
Serbia[2]	24	3	n/a
Slovakia[2]	5	<1	<1
Slovenia[1]	22	3	7
Ukraine[3]	14	1	4
Average	21	7	31

Latin America	MC	ST	TR
Argentina[2]	16	4	19
Brazil[2]	36	44	74
Chile[2]	78	21	21
Colombia[3]	36	5	13
Ecuador[3]	8	<1	4
Jamaica[3]	51	2	4
Mexico[2]	21	10	34
Peru[3]	43	4	6
Average	36	11	22

Middle East and Africa	MC	ST	TR
Bahrain[1]	97	14	12
Côte d'Ivoire[4]	30	1	4
Egypt[3]	53	43	62
Ghana[4]	20	1	5
Israel[1]	67	54	59
Kenya[4]	36	5	12
Kuwait[1]	72	83	83
Lebanon[2]	32	2	7
Morocco[3]	74	25	31
Nigeria[4]	24	10	29
Saudi Arabia[1]	52	110	138
South Africa[2]	178	145	61
Tunisia[3]	16	4	25
Turkey[2]	16	33	119
Average	55	38	46

Notes:
1 High income (at least $11,116)
2 Upper-middle income ($3596–$11,115)
3 Lower-middle income (($906–$3,595)
4 Low income (less than or equal to $905)
n/a = not available

Source: World Bank, http://data.worldbank.org/topic/financial-sector

Based on the average values of all these indicators, Asian markets emerge as the most developed. However, if we were to ignore Hong Kong, which has a huge market capitalisation and ratio of stocks traded to GDP, this region would still be relatively well developed but more comparable to the other regions, with an MC of 42, an ST of 50 and a TR of 67. To illustrate just how extreme the situation is in Hong Kong, the market capitalisations relative to GDP for the UK and US are just over 70 and 54 per cent, respectively, while their ST values are 227 and 237 per cent and their turnover ratios were 277 and 237 in 2008. It is fair to say that the Hong Kong stock market is highly developed and offers excellent opportunities for companies to raise new funds. While China's stock market is smaller than its GDP in this year, it is highly liquid, with both ST and TR valued over 100 per cent, making it more developed than India, the other Asian BRIC. Pakistan has a small but liquid market while the markets in Sri Lanka and Vietnam are both very small and illiquid, indicating that they can offer very little financing for growth. This is a particular problem for Sri Lanka since, as table 9.1 shows, it also has a small banking sector and relatively poor protection for lenders and borrowers.

Relative to its national income, South Africa has the largest stock market in the Middle East and Africa. If it is excluded, the reported average value of MC falls to 45. The Middle East tends to have larger stock markets than Africa, with the exception of Morocco, but their markets vary tremendously in terms of liquidity. Both liquidity measures for Saudi Arabia are over 100 per cent, 83 per cent for Kuwait but less than 15 per cent for Bahrain. The African markets tend to be small and illiquid while the Turkish market is small but liquid. If we read tables 9.1 and 9.2 together, markets are more important than banks in Saudi Arabia, while the reverse is true in Bahrain and Lebanon. South Africa has a developed stock market and a developed banking sector. Countries like Côte d'Ivoire, Kenya and Nigeria suffer because both parts of the financial sector are not well developed.

Stock markets in emerging Europe and Latin America are small relative to GDP, and none have turnover ratios over 100 per cent, but the markets in the Czech Republic, Hungary, Poland, Russia and Brazil turned over at least 70 per cent of their market value in 2008. The others were much less liquid. In Europe, Estonia, Hungary, Latvia, Slovakia and Ukraine have particularly weak markets; however their banking sectors are relatively strong. Most Latin American countries with the exception of Brazil and Chile face liquidity constraints in their stock markets, and some, like Argentina, Ecuador and Peru, have banking sectors offering credit that is less than one-quarter of the value of GDP, indicating that companies with good ideas face major problems in financing growth, which can only hinder wider economic development. The data on stock market indicators illustrate that Brazil and Russia are more highly developed that their regional counterparts, even though they lag behind the other BRICs.

These observations on financing are important because they highlight the fact that corporate governance reforms in developing countries can only aid economic development if they are part of a package of reforms to the financial sector. There is evidence that even in a small stock market like that of Côte d'Ivoire, stock market development drives economic progress (N'Zué, 2006), but other evidence from Africa (Adjasi and Biekpe, 2006) indicates that this effect is felt only in higher-income countries. Other studies of both bank finance and stock market development indicate that both are important in promoting economic growth (Arestis *et al.*, 2001; Beck and Levine, 2004), but bank development may have a larger impact (Arestis *et al.*, 2001). This evidence shows that improved corporate governance can have little impact if companies with good monitoring systems make high-quality disclosures to small, illiquid stock markets and a highly concentrated banking industry. Regulators in emerging markets must introduce reforms to the financial sector to accompany improvements in corporate governance.

Improvements in performance

As we saw in the previous section, improved governance should imply better access to capital, allowing growth and enhanced value. Improvements in monitoring should also lead to greater efficiency and higher profits, so better corporate governance should be associated with better performance, whether measured in terms of operating or market returns. You might question the likelihood of this given the rather mixed evidence on the relationship between governance in performance in developed economies that we discussed in earlier chapters. However, in the case of emerging markets, improvements in governance do seem to lead to better corporate performance.

Following interest in corporate governance and shareholder rights indices in the US, many researchers have applied a similar methodology in developing countries. There is no need to say too much here about the construction of indices because we have already discussed it in chapter 1. The key point to recall is that governance indices bring together various items of information about how a company is governed, for example whether or not the CEO is also the chair, whether or not there is a majority of independent directors on its board, and so on. They assign points for the adoption or omission of certain governance practices so as to build up a general picture of how well or how badly a company is governed. If, having taken account of other variables that are likely to affect performance, there is a significant relationship between corporate performance and the index, then we can conclude that governance matters, but not that any individual governance practice is responsible for improving performance. Klapper and Love (2004) and Morey *et al.* (2009) use indices calculated by financial institutions for companies in a range of developing markets around the world. They agree that better governance leads to higher market valuation. In addition, Klapper and Love (2004) find that operating performance is also improved by stronger governance. Bai *et al.* (2004), Cheung *et al.* (2007) and Garay and González (2008) create their own indices for companies in China, Hong Kong and Venezuela and also find that better governance leads to higher market value. These findings are in line with a survey by McKinsey & Co. (2002), which indicates that investors are prepared to pay a premium for well-governed companies, and that premium is higher in emerging than in developed markets. The strength of the relationship between governance and performance in emerging markets as compared with developed markets is not surprising. Companies in developed markets tend to have very similar governance practices which have evolved over time as new regulations have been introduced. Companies in emerging markets vary more in their practices which tend to change in discrete 'jumps'. A company that introduces new practices to improve its monitoring, disclosure or accountability will stand out from its competitors and be rewarded in terms of better stock market performance.

Reduced reputational and other risk

The relationship between corporate governance and reputation is often discussed in the context of the decision to list overseas. It is well documented that when a company makes the decision to obtain a listing in an overseas market with tougher listing requirements than those found at home, this acts as a signal of corporate quality. This can be particularly important for companies that come from countries with a reputation for corruption. Corruption is detrimental to economic growth. Taking bribery as an example, if it necessary to bribe officials to ensure that imported raw materials clear customs and reach their destination or to secure government contracts, the practice of bribery diverts funds from real economic activity.

The best known measure of corruption is the Corruption Perceptions Index (CPI), which has been published by Transparency International since 1995. The index is based on surveys of business leaders and country experts from a variety of organisations including the Economist Intelligence Unit and the World Bank. Participants respond to questions concerning the extent to which public-sector officials can use their office for private gain and on the way in which regulators react to cases of corruption. Countries are then given a rank between 0, indicating that corruption is perceived to be very high, and 10, which signifies very low levels of perceived corruption. In 2008 Denmark, New Zealand and Sweden shared the highest score of 9.3, indicating that they were perceived to be the least corrupt that year, while Somalia had the lowest score of 1, revealing it to be perceived as the most corrupt country. Table 9.3 presents data on the 2008 CPI for the regions we have been considering in this chapter.

If we were to take the average CPI indices reported in table 9.3 at face value, we would classify Asia and emerging Europe as the least corrupt regions and the Middle East and Africa as the most corrupt region. However, the regional averages are very close to one another, while there is huge variation within each region. The Asian data has the largest range, with CPI varying from a high of 9.2 in Singapore to a low of 2.3 in the Philippines. Looking across all regions, Singapore and Hong Kong with an index of 8.1 are the outliers. The next highest index value of 6.9 is achieved by Chile. The other Latin American countries are a long way behind Chile, with Ecuador having the lowest score of 2, which is also the lowest in the table. We see similar variability in the other regions, with scores in emerging Europe ranging from 6.7 for Slovenia down to 2.1 for Russia and in the Middle East and Africa, Israel achieves the highest score of 6 while Kenya gets a score of 2.1, making it the most corrupt country in its region. As we hinted in box 9.1, the BRIC countries are perceived as relatively more corrupt than others in their regions.

Garmaise and Liu (2005) use the CPI in their empirical work on the financial impact of corruption. They find that country-level corruption raises firm-level betas. This means that companies in corrupt countries are more risky and hence must pay a higher return to equity holders. Their relatively high cost of capital impacts on the profit they make from any investment. This is not, however, the end of the story. Garmaise and Liu (2005) go on to report that the effect of corrup-

Table 9.3 Corruption Perceptions Index, 2008

Asia	CPI	Emerging Europe	CPI	Latin America	CPI	Middle East and Africa	CPI
China[3]	3.6	Bulgaria[2]	3.6	Argentina[2]	2.9	Bahrain[1]	5.4
Hong Kong[1]	8.1	Croatia[2]	4.4	Brazil[2]	3.5	Côte d'Ivoire[4]	n/a
India[4]	3.4	Czech Republic[1]	5.2	Chile[2]	6.9	Egypt[3]	2.8
Indonesia[3]	2.6	Estonia[1]	6.6	Colombia[3]	3.8	Ghana[4]	3.9
Malaysia[2]	5.1	Hungary[2]	5.1	Ecuador[3]	2.0	Israel[1]	6.0
Pakistan[4]	2.5	Kazakhstan[2]	2.2	Jamaica[3]	3.1	Kenya[4]	2.1
Philippines[3]	2.3	Latvia[2]	5.0	Mexico[2]	3.6	Kuwait[1]	4.3
Singapore[1]	9.2	Montenegro[2]	3.4	Peru[3]	3.6	Lebanon[2]	3.0
Sri Lanka[3]	3.2	Poland[2]	4.6			Morocco[3]	3.5
Thailand[3]	3.5	Romania[2]	3.8			Nigeria[4]	2.7
Vietnam[4]	2.7	Russia[2]	2.1			Saudi Arabia[1]	3.5
		Serbia[2]	3.4			South Africa[2]	4.9
		Slovakia[2]	5.0			Tunisia[3]	4.4
		Slovenia[1]	6.7			Turkey[2]	4.6
		Ukraine[3]	2.5				
Average	4.2	Average	4.2	Average	3.7	Average	3.6

Notes:
1 High income (at least $11,116)
2 Upper-middle income ($3596–$11,115)
3 Lower-middle income ($906–$3,595)
4 Low income (less than or equal to $905)
n/a = not available

Source: Transparency International, http://www.transparency.prg/policy_research/surveys_indices/cpi/2008

tion on beta is reduced when shareholders have strong rights, in other words, when there is good corporate governance. Wu (2005) looks at the causal relationship between the CPI and two corporate governance indices, one measuring the effectiveness of boards in protecting shareholders' interests, the other measuring the quality of accounting information, using data from a panel of developed and developing nations. The results show that both higher-quality accounting practices and better shareholder protection lead to lower perceived corruption. Taken together, these papers imply, as one would expect, that country-level corruption affects company-level performance, but is also affected by companies' actions. Once again this indicates that improvements to corporate governance practices are just one aspect of a package of measures that governments in emerging markets must take to improve the reputation of their nations and reduce the risks of investing in them.

CONCLUSION

Developed markets vary considerably in the way their corporate governance systems work. Despite variations in terms of board structure, the roles of financial institutions and of the market for corporate control, there are certain features which all regulators agree must form part of a sound governance system. These include boards with a substantial independent element, specialist board subcommittees and detailed disclosure of financial information and control systems as well as of governance practices. Companies in some emerging markets find it difficult to adopt these practices. Some countries have small stock markets. With few listed companies there is a very small pool of directors to draw from when appointing independent board members. If this small group of directors were to sit on one another's boards that would lead to conflicts of interest as well as to huge pressures on their time. Both would militate against their ability to contribute to good monitoring practices. In some countries a lack of educational opportunities means that the accountancy profession is small or poorly trained. This affects both the quality of financial reporting and the quality of audits, both of which make corporate disclosures unreliable and potentially misleading. This may hamper improvements in stock market efficiency.

These considerations mean that attempts to improve corporate governance cannot be made as a stand-alone project in emerging markets. Governance reforms must be seen as part of a package of reforms to financial markets and reporting requirements. There is a body of evidence that shows the importance of governance to corporate performance in emerging markets. Improvements in governance lead to higher company valuations. This is good for investors and will encourage more people to enter the stock market as well as prompting companies to raise more finance in the markets or to seek a stock market listing. These developments will contribute to the overall growth of the economy. Without improved growth in the developing world the economic, social, health and educational inequalities we see today cannot be reduced. In 2000 the United Nations launched a set of Millennium Development Goals which it hoped to achieve by 2015. None of these goals can be met unless the developing world achieves sustained economic growth. Improved corporate governance can make a contribution to this growth, hence the interest in governance issues from international organisations like the World Bank and the OECD. These organisations cannot impose good governance practices. It is up to investors and regulators to demand better governance and to companies to recognise that it is in their interests to supply it.

KEY POINTS

- Empirical evidence from emerging economies shows that improved corporate governance leads to higher corporate value. This gives companies a clear incentive to improve their governance practices.
- Corruption is a problem in emerging markets. It raises firms' cost of capital, but this effect is tempered by good corporate governance which also improves perceptions of corruption in the country.
- The OCED Principles of Corporate Governance encourage regulators and companies to introduce local reforms. They do not prescribe the adoption of specific practices.
- The World Bank monitors the local implementation of the OECD Principles and the International Finance Corporation advises companies on how to improve governance. This is because improvements in governance contribute to economic growth.

CASE STUDY Natura and Brazil's Novo Mercado show how governance can be improved through partnership

Natura is Brazil's largest cosmetics company. It develops, manufactures and distributes a range of cosmetics, mainly through direct sales channels, but it also sells through duty-free stores at Brazilian airports and through its shop in Paris. It has won many awards, including *Carta Capital* magazine's Most Admired Company in Brazil, 2004 and 2005, Fundação Getúlio Vergas's Chemical Industry Company of the Year, 2005 and 2006 and of most relevance here, *IRMagazine* Brazil's Best Corporate Governance award, 2006 and 2007. Its success is based on its founders' commitment to all its stakeholders, and its reputation has been enhanced by its listing on Brazil's Novo Mercado.

The company was founded in 1969 and remained privately owned until 2004 when it was listed on the Novo Mercado. Even before its listing the company's founders were keen to establish the kind of corporate governance practices that are required of listed companies, so that when the IPO finally came the company would be well prepared. Brazilian companies typically feature many of the negative characteristics associated with companies in emerging markets. Most issue dual-class shares, and pyramids are common, which means that founding families are able to keep control of business empires. The stock market is relatively illiquid because only a small proportion of each company's equity is in free-float; this deters interest from individuals and overseas investors. The Brazilian authorities sought to change this by introducing a new market segment, the Novo Mercado. In order to obtain a listing in this part of the market firms have to agree to abide by a stricter set of regulations than those that apply elsewhere. They must float at least 25 per cent of their equity, issue only common stock with voting rights, produce quarterly financial information, use internationally accepted accounting standards and publish their financial statements in English as well as in Portuguese. The market can apply sanctions to companies that do not abide by the stricter rules, in the most extreme case removing them from this sector of the market. By introducing the Novo Mercado the regulators hoped to encourage companies to voluntarily adopt better governance practices so as to differentiate themselves from weaker firms. This would then lead to greater investor interest in this group, thereby encouraging their competitors to see the benefit of adhering to tighter regulations.

The new market opened cautiously. At first companies were unable to comply with the tough regulation, so the authorities introduced two intermediate sections with less stringent requirements, levels 1 and 2, the idea being that they would act as stepping stones to the Novo Mercado. In June 2001 15 companies attained a level 1 listing, and by the end of the year a further 4 had joined them. The first Novo Mercado listing came in 2002, but the turning point came in 2004, a year which saw more IPOs than usual, including that of Natura. In January 2010 the IGC index, which includes only those companies that comply with the additional listing requirements of Levels 1 and 2 and the Novo Mercado, contained 174 companies.

Natura's corporate governance is clearly good by Brazilian standards. It has some features in common with companies in more developed countries, but has other distinctive features that are valuable in its situation. The company has a seven-person board. The three executives are the company's co-founders Antonio Luiz de

Cunha Seabra and Guilherme Peirão, together with Pedro Luiz Barreiros Passos, who joined Natura in 1983. These three men are the co-chairs of the board. The remaining members are non-executives who bring the independence which makes the board as a whole comparable with boards in more developed countries. The company also has a board of executive directors which includes the CEO, Alessandro Giuseppe Carlucci. The board has four subcommittees which, with the exception of the strategy committee, are coordinated by board members, but include other members from outside the board. The audit, risk management and finance committee includes one board member, one member of the board of executive directors and four others. The organisation and people committee includes three board members, the CEO and two others, while the corporate governance committee includes two board members and three others. In terms of subject coverage these subcommittees are comparable with those found in American and European companies, but they differ in that they include people from outside the board. Given that the pool of independent directors is relatively small in emerging markets in makes sense to make use of expertise from outside the boardroom. Natura's corporate governance mechanisms include three other features which illustrate the prominence given to stakeholders. Since 1995 the company has shown its commitment to its employees by using an independent company to conduct employee satisfaction surveys. Ten years later it initiated a programme of Natura Relationship Principles. The group responsible for this has so far completed two sets of principles, one dealing with relationships between the company and its employees, the other covering relationships with the direct sales force. Finally it has created an ombudsman's office headed by the CEO to deal with issues of communications with all stakeholders. The company does not forget the welfare of its shareholders. Its by-laws commit Natura to pay 30 per cent of the company's net profit as a dividend.

Natura's corporate governance is exemplary in the context of an emerging market. Just under 60 per cent of its equity is owned by the controlling shareholders, which in other contexts could lead to self-dealing. The listing requirements of the Novo Mercado mitigate against this by requiring that all shares carry equal votes, but even before it was listed this firm took governance seriously and introduced measures which would ease its transition to a publicly listed company. It looks after the interests of its shareholders and stakeholders and is an example to other companies considering a listing on the Novo Mercado.

CASE-STUDY QUESTIONS

1 What are the key differences between the board subcommittees established by Natura and the ones discussed in chapter 4 of this book?

2 Is Natura focusing too much on its stakeholders at the expense of its shareholders?

3 What benefits do you believe the Novo Mercado has brought to the companies listed on it and to the market as a whole?

REVISION QUESTIONS

1 How do the OECD Principles of Corporate Governance differ from the corporate governance codes considered in chapter 7?

2 Why has the OECD prepared separate Guidelines for SOEs?
3 How might improvements in corporate governance contribute to greater or quicker economic growth in developing economies?
4 How does corruption affect firms' financing decisions?

REFERENCES

Adjasi, C.K.D. and Biekpe, N.B. (2006) 'Stock Market Development and Economic Growth: The Case of Selected African Countries' *African Development Review* 18 (1) 144–161

Arestis, P., Demetriades, P.O. and Luintel, K.B. (2001) 'Financial Development and Economic Growth: The Role of Stock Markets' *Journal of Money, Credit and Banking* 33 (1) 16–41

Bai, C.E., Liu, Q., Lu, J., Song, F.M. and Zhang, J. (2004) 'Corporate Governance and Market Valuation in China' *Journal of Comparative Economics* 32 (4) 599–616

Beck, T., Demirgüç-Kunt, A. and Maksimovic, V. (2004) 'Bank Competition and access to Finance: International Evidence' *Journal of Money, Credit and Banking* 36 (3) 627–648

Beck, T. and Levine, R. (2004) 'Stock Markets, Banks, and Growth: Panel Evidence' *Journal of Banking and Finance* 28 (3) 423–442

Cheung, Y., Connelly, J.T., Limpaphayon, P. and Zhou, L. (2007) 'Do Investors Really Value Corporate Governance? Evidence from the Hong Kong Market' *Journal of International Financial Management and Accounting* 18 (2) 86–122

Clarke, G., Cull, R., Peria, M.S.D. and Sánchez, S.M. (2003) 'Foreign Bank Entry: Experience, Implications for Developing Economies and Agenda for Further Research' *World Bank Research Observer* 18 (1) 25–59

Garay, U. and González, M. (2008) 'Corporate Governance and Firm Value: The Case of Venezuela' *Corporate Governance: An International Review* 16 (3) 194–209

Garmaise, M.J. and Liu. J. (2005) 'Corruption, Firm Governance, and the Cost of Capital' Anderson Graduate School of Management, Finance Working paper 1'05

Klapper, L.F. and Love, I. (2004) 'Corporate Governance, Investor Protection, and Performance in Emerging Markets' *Journal of Corporate Finance* 10 (5) 703–728

McKinsey and Company (2002) 'Global Investor Opinion Survey: Key findings' McKinsey & Co.

Morey, M., Gottesman, A., Baker, E. and Godridge, B. (2009) 'Does Better Corporate Governance Result in Higher Valuations in Emerging Markets? Another Examination Using a New Data Set' *Journal of Banking and Finance* 33 (2) 254–262

N'Zué, F.F. (2006) 'Stock Market Development and Economic Growth: Evidence from Côte D'Ivoire' *African Development Review* 18 (1) 123–143

OECD (2004) 'Principles of Corporate Governance' OECD

Van Horen, N. (2007) 'Foreign Banking in Developing Countries; Origin Matters' *Emerging Markets Review* 8 (2) 81–105

Wójcik, D. and Burger, C. (2009) 'Listing BRICs: Stock issuers from Brazil, Russia, India and China in New York, London and Luxembourg' http://ssrn.com/abstract= 1431511

World Bank (2009) 'Corporate Governance Country Assessment: Azerbaijan September 2009' World Bank

Wu, X. (2005) 'Corporate Governance and Corruption: A Cross-Country Analysis' *Governance: An international Journal of Policy, Administration, and Institutions* 18 (2) 151–170

SUGGESTIONS FOR FURTHER READING

Barton, D. and Wong, S.C.Y. (2006) 'Improving Board Performance in Emerging Markets' *McKinsey Quarterly* 1, 35–43. This short paper looks at the main problems experienced by corporate boards in emerging economies and suggests practical ways of improving the way they operate.

Claessens, S. (2003) 'Corporate Governance and Development' Global Corporate Governance Forum Working Paper, World Bank. This paper by a renowned author gives a useful overview of the relationship between corporate governance and economic growth.

http://www.oecd.org/topic/0,3373,en_2649_37439_1_1_1_1_37439,00.html The corporate governance section of the OECD website allows access to a number of useful publications on the governance issues faced by companies in developing economies.

http://www.transparency.org/ This website offers a wealth of resources on corruption including access to data on the Corruption Perceptions Index.

CONCLUSION

> ### ◉ LEARNING OBJECTIVES
>
> - To review the contributions to corporate governance made by different disciplines and theoretical approaches
> - To recall the dramatic changes in corporate governance that have taken place since the 1980s
> - To consider the limitations of some of the early empirical evidence on the relationship between governance and corporate value

INTRODUCTION

In this short, final chapter we will briefly remind ourselves of some of the important developments in corporate governance that have been encountered in earlier chapters of this book. The first section will consider how corporate governance has drawn on theories developed by scholars from a variety of academic disciplines. The second will consider how practices have changed dramatically in the last 30 years in response to changing market conditions, shareholder attitudes and financial scandals. The third will discuss the practical problems in carrying out empirical work in this area, and offer possible explanations for some of the inconclusive results reported in earlier chapters.

THE THEORY BEHIND CORPORATE GOVERNANCE

The first chapter of this book used Denis (2001) to trace the history of corporate governance to 1976, the year in which Jensen and Meckling published their seminal paper on agency theory. We have seen throughout this book that agency theory has had a huge influence on the way scholars have approached the subject of governance. It has drawn attention to the potential for managers to make decisions that make themselves better off at the expense of shareholders. This has led to the search for governance mechanisms capable of solving the type I agency problem through monitoring by independent boards or auditors and the alignment of incentives through the use of performance-related remuneration or reliance on the market for corporate control.

The type I agency problem is associated with situations in which share ownership is dispersed. Other authors like Villalonga and Amit (2006) have recognised that this is not the case in all parts of the world. When share ownership is concentrated, blockholders can use the company to make themselves better off at the expense of minority shareholders. This is the type II agency problem which can be alleviated through regulation that changes the rights of the different shareholder groups. This may involve giving minorities the right to elect board members with a specific remit to represent their interests, or it might cap the voting rights of blockholders.

The agency-theoretic approach is associated with finance theory, but other disciplines have made important theoretical contributions to the study of governance. New institutional economists like Williamson (1979) have made us aware of the importance of transactions costs in determining which activities take place within companies and which take place between companies in the market. This in turn has implications for the relationships between companies, especially those in vertical supply chains. It suggests that when simple products are traded contracts can fully describe the nature of the transaction and govern the relationship between the supplier and purchaser. In the case of more complex products more complicated governance mechanisms are needed, these include but are not limited to forcing suppliers to use specific types of equipment, having surprise inspections of production facilities and exchanging personnel between companies in the supply chain.

While both agency theory and transactions costs economics are compatible with the idea that shareholders have a unique place in corporate governance because they are owed a fiduciary duty by corporate management, ethicists like Boatright (2004) have questioned this. They have offered reasons to extend the concept of fiduciary duty to other groups and thereby promoted a stakeholder-theoretic approach espoused by sociologists and management scholars. This approach encourages an exploration of the trade-offs involved in managing companies made up of several different interest groups, and implies that employees and other groups should play an active role in governance.

Stewardship theory provides a unique way of bringing together the self-centredness of decision-makers implied by agency theory and the ethical duty that underpins stakeholder theory. In this approach, managers aim to make themselves as well off as possible, but recognise that the way to do this is to keep their shareholders happy. If managers think in this way there is no need for costly monitoring and it is quite safe indeed desirable to concentrate power in the hands of a few key decision-makers. Stewardship theory is linked to fundamental ideas about how people are motivated. It relies on the notion that intrinsic motivation is very powerful and can thereby explain why performance-based rewards that rely on the need for extrinsic motivation can sometimes produce perverse incentives.

As we have seen, it is impossible to point to a single theory of corporate governance. The subject has drawn on a variety of theories each of which can contribute to our understanding of the complex relationships that exist between the stakeholders who together make up the listed company. This can be a source of frustration. Over the years this author has had many conversations which started with the words 'I am interested in governance, too' only to discover that one person's idea of governance is very different from another's. One of the benefits of writing, and we hope reading a book like this one is to discover that each academic discipline has something to offer to our understanding of governance problems and potential solutions.

DEVELOPMENTS IN PRACTICE

As we have already seen, there is no single corporate governance problem that plagues all countries equally. For this reason, some of the practical developments we have seen over the years are related to particular countries. In the US, a key development in corporate governance has been a shift from the belief that governance problems are best solved by shareholder exit via the market for corporate control, to the view that more independent boards can both protect shareholders and give them opportunities to use voice. Alongside changes in the boardroom we have seem improvements in the information available to shareholders and in the independence of the auditors who attest to the quality of that information. These diverse initiatives were brought together in the Sarbanes–Oxley Act, 2002.

There can be little doubt that the rise of private equity during the 1980s was one of the causes of this sea-change in attitudes towards governance. The wave of leveraged buyouts created leaner, fitter private companies in which there was a close relationship between boards and shareholders. The shareholders in listed companies could see that while the boards of their companies were able to protect themselves from hostile takeover by the implementation of poison pills, the managers of LBO targets were vulnerable because of the huge amounts of debt that had financed the acquisitions. That threat of financial distress was a great motivator that encouraged management to work hard and create shareholder value. Not surprisingly the shareholders in listed companies became more vocal and lobbied for change. It was not just success stories that encouraged change. In the early 2000s financial scandals at Enron, WorldCom and Tyco to name but a few, added to shareholders' discontent and prompted the passage of the Sarbanes–Oxley Act, 2002.

In the UK we have witnessed major changes in corporate boards thanks to the Cadbury Report (Financial Reporting Council, 1992) and subsequent corporate governance codes. While companies have never been forced to adhere to every provision of these codes, they have been obliged to explain to their shareholders why they choose to diverge from the code on any specific practice. This approach has led the majority of companies to comply with the codes which have encouraged them to ensure that their CEOs no longer chair the board, that the majority of directors are independent and sit on the audit, remuneration and nomination committees. While non-financial companies have been subject to codes of governance since 1992, today institutional investors (Financial Reporting Council, 2010), financial entities (HM Treasury, 2009) and audit firms (Institute of Chartered Accountants in England and Wales, 2010) have their own codes.

A series of financial scandals prompted this surge of interest in corporate governance. A common feature of the frauds at Mirror Group Newspapers and Polly Peck in the late 1980s was the presence of a powerful and charismatic chief executive who was also the chair of the board. This may explain why the emphasis of reform in the UK has been on board composition, the introduction of more independent directors and the rejection of duality.

The appetite for codes of corporate governance has spread around the world, encouraged in part by the OECD's decision to recommend that all countries produce a code based on their 'Principles of Corporate Governance'. These principles reach beyond the boardroom, and encourage the development of better investor protection, improved disclosure and the involvement of stakeholders in corporate decision-making. Better comparability of financial statements has been encouraged by the introduction of International Financial Reporting Standards which are now in operation throughout the EU and in many other parts of the world thanks to the efforts of the World Bank.

The EU's adoption of IFRS is just one aspect of its objective to harmonise company law and corporate governance in Europe in order to facilitate the operation of the single market. Among other initiatives it has produced a directive on cross-border mergers, issued a statement on proportionality in capital and control, in other words the debate on whether each share should carry one vote and established the European Corporate Governance Forum. This forum has in turn issued statements on a variety of governance topics including takeovers, voting rights and remuneration.

The importance of corporate governance has been recognised in the formation of many governance networks involving academics and practitioners. These networks together with professional associations and publications have instituted an array of prizes for corporate governance awarded to both individuals and companies around the world. These include the ICSA-Hermes award for transparency in governance, the Hawkamah-Union of Arab Banks award, the *Corporate Secretary Magazine* award and the International Corporate Governance Network awards. Of course, all awards are controversial and sometimes subsequent events show that better decisions could have been made. In 2002 the World Council for Corporate Governance and the Centre for Corporate Governance gave a Golden Peacock award for excellence in corporate governance to Satyam Computer Services, a company which had to be rescued in 2009 in the wake of a massive fraud initiated by the founder and chair of the board. Despite sorry tales like this one, the fact that so many awards now exist is a testimony to the importance of good governance in corporate life.

EMPIRICAL ISSUES

The theoretical and regulatory interests in governance issues have combined to encourage a huge interest in empirical research on corporate governance. Much of it can be interpreted as an attempt to answer the question 'do improvements in governance lead to improvements in performance?' Such a broad question can be answered in many ways. Early empirical work focussed on particular governance mechanisms such as the avoidance of duality, the proportion of independent directors on the board or the use of board sub-committees and their impact on corporate performance. Most papers concentrated on market performance, choosing Tobin's q or a variant as their measure of performance. In Tobin's original formulation (Tobin, 1978) q is the ratio of the market value of a firm's assets to their replacement cost. When q is greater than one it is sensible to invest in new capital, while if it is less than one it is cheaper to acquire assets through the acquisition of the firms that own them. Given the difficulties involved in measuring replacement cost the concept has been implemented by substituting book value for replacement cost. This reduces q to the market to book value of the company. Many researchers used Tobin's q as the dependent variable in a regression equation whose independent variables included one or more measures of the strength of corporate governance and a list of control variables such as size and leverage which would normally be expected to drive stock market value.

At first glance such a formulation seems entirely sensible, but in fact it is open to question. The first issue that arises is over the point at which the variables are measured. The variables are often measured contemporaneously, that is at the same point in time. To illustrate the potential problem here, suppose the governance measure used is the proportion of independent directors on the board. If the proportion is measured at the same time as q we are assuming that today's board is responsible for today's market value. This ignores the history of the board and the fact that it takes time to have an effect on the company. The composition of the board might have changed during the year causing the proportion of independent directors to jump. The company would look good in governance terms, but those new independent directors might still know little about the business and so may not yet be effective monitors or be able to affect strategy. This suggests that board composition is likely to affect performance with a lag, so it would be more sensible to regress this year's performance on last year's board composition.

A second problem with this formulation is that it assumes that causation flows in one direction only, from board composition to performance. The board of a poorly performing company might react to poor performance by inviting new independent directors to join it. This means that there is a relationship between performance and board structure, but it flows from performance to structure, not the other way round. This might be too simplistic a view. Causation might flow in both directions, that is, the board might react to poor performance by improving governance, and that tighter governance might in the future lead to better performance. A single equation model in which all variables are measured at the same point in time cannot capture these interactions.

A further problem with this type of model is that it assumes that the presence of a particular governance mechanism is enough to ensure that it works properly. Again we can take the predominantly independent board as an example. It is not enough simply to bring a group of well-qualified, experienced individuals together and to expect them to work together effectively to solve complex problems. Successive England football managers can testify to this. A good board must include individuals who are given access to high-quality information, who get on well together and have sufficient time to devote to the problems faced by the company. A simple observation that a company has a high proportion of independent directors does not guarantee that they are working well. The classic example of this was the board of Enron at the time of its collapse.

These lines of reasoning might explain why so much American and British evidence on the relationship between board composition and corporate performance yields results that either inconclusive or contrary to expectations. Researchers using different methodologies like Rosenstein and Wyatt (1990) who use an event study methodology to look at the impact of announcements of changes in board composition on stock prices, and Perry and Peyer (2005) who take account of previous board structure when looking at the impact of the addition of independent directors find clear cut results that support the premise that shareholders react positively to additional independence on the board.

A rather different issue is the early focus on individual measures of corporate governance. Regulation whether through codes or laws introduces many measures at one time, indicating that the various mechanisms work together to produce the desired outcome. This suggests that research that focuses on looking for statistical significance in individual explanatory variables takes too simplistic a view and ignores the fact that mechanisms work together to create a climate in which investors believe they are protected from self-serving managers or blockholders. This explains why some researchers have created indices of corporate governance or shareholder rights, or have used commercially-available measures of the kind described in the case study in chapter 1. Research based on governance indices applied in a variety of countries indicates that the market value of companies is improved by stronger governance (Bai *et al.*, 2004; Cheung *et al.*, 2007; Garay and González, 2008; Klapper and Love, 2004; Morey *et al.*, 2009).

Despite the fact that so much evidence is available on the relationship between corporate governance and performance, there is still scope for more good quality empirical research in this area. As regulators around the world introduce additional codes and laws affecting not just companies themselves but also their shareholders and auditors, it is important that corporate life is not over-regulated. So we need to know which mechanisms are vital and which are peripheral to economic success. In order to provide convincing evidence on this, researchers must use best-practice econometric techniques that take account of lags and endogeneities within systems of equations. In addition to statistical research we also need more high-quality survey and interview-based research on how boards work and how their operation can be improved. This could then feed into director training and ensure that future boards exercise their responsibilities effectively.

This emphasis on boards is based on the fact that so much empirical work has used board data, but has not always taken account of the complex interrelationships between board composition and corporate performance. We need better evidence on all aspects of corporate governance. This includes evidence on the cultural and legal aspects of governance. As we saw in the previous section, within the EU there is a desire to harmonise regulation on accounting, governance and takeovers. Yet within the region there are different legal traditions, and as the EU is enlarged there are also increasingly different cultural backgrounds of member countries. There is a danger that inappropriate governance mechanisms will be imposed on new member states and that this will lead to worse rather than better governance and performance.

CONCLUSION

Corporate governance is a vibrant and exciting subject, partly because it draws on so many academic disciplines and partly because it is an area where policy is changing rapidly. It is up to the next generation of researchers and practitioners that is to the readers of this book, to ensure that future policy is based on solid foundations. This means that you must be willing to accept ideas from outside your narrow academic discipline, to use best practice techniques in your work and to realise that a system that works well in one country cannot necessarily be exported to another.

REFERENCES

Bai, C.E., Liu, Q., Lu, J., Song, F.M. and Zhang, J. (2004) 'Corporate Governance and Market Valuation in China' *Journal of Comparative Economics* 32 (4) 599–616

Boatright, J.R. (2004) 'Employee Governance and the Ownership of the Firm' *Business Ethics Quarterly* 14 (1) 1–21

Cheung, Y., Connelly, J.T., Limpaphayon, P. and Zhou, L. (2007) 'Do Investors Really Value Corporate Governance? Evidence from the Hong Kong Market' *Journal of International Financial Management and Accounting* 18 (2) 86–122

Denis, D. (2001) 'Twenty-five Years of Corporate Governance Research … and Counting' *Review of Financial Economics* 10 (3) 191–212

Financial Reporting Council (1992) 'The Financial Aspects of Corporate Governance' FRC

Financial Reporting Council (2010) 'The UK Stewardship Code' FRC

Garay, U. and González, M. (2008) 'Corporate Governance and Firm Value: The Case of Venezuela' *Corporate Governance: An International Review* 16 (3) 194–209

HM Treasury (2009) 'A Review of Corporate Governance in UK Banks and other Financial Industry Entities: Final Recommendations' HM Treasury 16 July

Institute of Chartered Accountants in England and Wales (2010) 'The Audit Firm Governance Code' Financial Reporting Council

Jensen, M.C. and Meckling, W. (1976) 'Theory of the Firm: Managerial Behavior, Agency Costs and Ownership Structure' *Journal of Financial Economics* 3 (4) 305–360

Klapper, L.F. and Love, I. (2004) 'Corporate Governance, Investor Protection, and Performance in Emerging Markets' *Journal of Corporate Finance* 10 (5) 703–728

Morey, M., Gottesman, A., Baker, E. and Godridge, B. (2009) 'Does Better Corporate Governance Result in Higher Valuations in Emerging Markets? Another Examination Using a New Data Set' *Journal of Banking and Finance* 33 (2) 254–262

Perry, T. and Peyer, U. (2005) 'Board Seat Accumulation by Executives: A Shareholder's Perspective' *Journal of Finance* 60 (4) 2083–2123

Rosenstein, S. and Wyatt, J.G. (1990) 'Outside Directors, Board Independence, and Shareholder Wealth' *Journal of Financial Economics* 26 (2) 175–191

Tobin, J. (1978) 'Monetary Policies and the Economy: The Transmission Mechanism' *Southern Economic Journal* 44 (3) 421–431

Villalonga, B. and Amit, R. (2006) 'How Do Family Ownership, Control and Management Affect Firm Value?' *Journal of Financial Economics* 80 (2) 385–417

Williamson, O.E. (1979) 'Transaction-Cost Economics: The Governance of Contractual Relationships' *Journal of Law and Economics* 22 (2) 233–261

SUGGESTIONS FOR FURTHER READING

Bhagat, S. and Jefferis, R.H. (2005) *The Econometrics of Corporate Governance Studies* MIT Press. This slim volume offers an excellent assessment of the problems involved in empirical research on corporate governance. You will need a good background in econometrics in order to fully appreciate it.

http://ec.europa.eu/internal_market/company/ecgforum/index_en.htm. This section of the European Commission website offers information on how work on corporate governance contributes to the single market for goods and services in the EU. It includes links to reports and statements issued by the European Corporate Governance Forum.

http://projects.exeter.ac.uk/RDavies/arian/scandals/ This fascinating website provides information on corporate scandals of all kinds, and should help you to appreciate why regulation has changed so much during the last 30 years.

NOTES

1 The Germanic group of countries includes Germany, the Netherlands, Switzerland, Sweden, Austria, Denmark, Norway and Finland.

2 The Latin group includes France, Italy, Spain and Belgium.

3 All the codes referred to in this chapter are available from the European Corporate Governance Institute website (http://www.ecgi.org/). At the end of October 2010 this part of the site listed codes issued in 77 countries. This does not mean to say that other codes are not available through different sources.

4 The Sarbanes-Oxley Act of 2002 includes 11 'titles' which are public company accounting oversight board, auditor independence, corporate responsibility, enhanced financial disclosures, analyst conflicts of interest, commission resources and authority, studies and reports, corporate and criminal fraud accountability, white collar crime penalty enhancements, corporate tax returns and corporate fraud and accountability.

5 Emerging Europe is defined to include Bulgaria, Croatia, the Czech Republic, Estonia, Hungary, Kazakhstan, Latvia, Montenegro, Poland, Romania, Russia, Serbia, Slovakia, Slovenia, Tajikistan and Ukraine.

6 Asia includes China, Hong Kong, India, Indonesia, Malaysia, North Korea, Pakistan, the Philippines, Singapore, South Korea, Sri Lanka, Taiwan, Thailand and Vietnam.

7 Latin America includes Argentina, Brazil, Colombia, Costa Rica, Chile, the Dominican Republic, Ecuador, Guatemala, Jamaica, Mexico, Paraguay, Peru, Uruguay and Venezuela.

8 The Middle East and Africa is defined to include Algeria, Bahrain, Côte D'Ivoire, Egypt, Ghana, Iran, Iraq, Israel, Kenya, Kuwait, Lebanon, Mali, Morocco, Nigeria, Oman, Qatar, Saudi Arabia, South Africa, Tunisia, Turkey, Uganda, the United Arab Emirates, West Bank and Gaza and Zambia.

GLOSSARY

Agency theory: a theory which looks at what happens when a principal delegates decision-making authority to an agent. The agent is likely to make decisions in their own interest instead of the interests of the principal. In companies this means that managers may not make decisions that lead to the maximisation of shareholder value.

Agent: A person who has been given the authority to make decisions on behalf of, and in order to benefit another person or group. The board of directors can be thought of as the agent acting on behalf of company shareholders.

Affiliated non-executive: a director who is brought in from outside this company (making them a non-executive) to sit on the board but has business links to it so is not independent. The American literature sometimes uses the term 'gray' (*sic*) director.

Anti-trust law: the law relating to the control of monopolies and near-monopoly situations. In most countries governments can use this law to prevent mergers that would create near-monopolies; in some cases the law can be used to break up existing companies that dominate their market.

Articles of Association: a legal requirement in the UK. The Articles form an internal constitution for limited liability companies. Companies can choose to write their own Articles or to adopt the Model Articles of Association offered by the 2006 Companies Act. These cover matters such as directors' responsibilities and the conduct of general meetings.

Asset-stripping: the practice of buying a company in order to sell its assets for profit rather than to operate the business as a going concern. Many acquisitions involve some asset-stripping but the term is usually used in connection with the decision to close the acquired company not just certain divisions.

Audit committee: a sub-committee of the board of directors, usually made up of independent or non-executive directors. It has a wide-ranging remit including the management of the relationship between the external auditors and the company, oversight of financial controls and in some cases risk management.

Auditor: an accountant responsible for verifying the procedures used to compile financial statements and to attest to the reliability of those statements. Governance normally focuses on the external auditor who works for an accounting firm, but companies also employ their own internal auditors who review procedures before the external audit takes place.

Blockholder: a shareholder who owns a 'large' proportion of the equity in a company and can therefore exert control over it. The size of the block needed to take control varies between markets.

Board of directors: the highest level of management in any company. It is a group of executive and non-executive directors which forms corporate strategy and is responsible for monitoring performance on behalf of the shareholders.

Bonding: a form of agency cost. Bonding activities are chosen by management as a sign of good faith to the shareholders. Such activities are costly to the managers in that they restrict their autonomy and hence their ability to make decisions that are not in shareholders' best interests; by incurring bonding costs managers reduce the residual loss to shareholders.

Bounded rationality: a term associated with transactions costs economics. It describes a situation in which a person finds decision-making difficult because they lack information or understanding of the problem in hand.

Brand champion: a consumer or employee who is so enthusiastic about a brand that they create free word-of-mouth advertising for it.

Bridging: a term associated with stakeholder theory. Bridging is any form of intensive interaction with stakeholders who have a major influence over the company.

Buffering: a term associated with stakeholder theory. It describes interactions with those stakeholders whose influence over the firm is transitory.

Cash-flow rights: the right of a shareholder to receive cash from the company, usually in the form of dividend payments.

Chaebol: at term used in Korea to describe a group of companies which is run as a single business despite the fact that each company is a separate legal entity.

Civil law: a body of law based on statutes and codes.

Codetermination: the practice of giving employees the right to sit on the board of directors of listed companies.

Common law: a body of law built upon judgements made in previous legal cases.

Comply or explain: an approach to regulation in which companies are asked to respect a governance code, but allowed to choose different practices as long they give a public explanation for their deviation from the code.

Conglomerate merger: a merger that takes place between companies in unrelated industries.

Control rights: the right of a shareholder to vote on issues raised at a company's general meeting.

Covenant: part of a loan agreement in which the borrower agrees to additional conditions demanded by the lender.

Cronyman: a term used in some Asian countries to describe a CEO or company chair who is also a blockholder.

Cross-shareholding: a situation in which two or more companies own one another's shares. In some countries this happens because firms are part of corporate groups, in others it is a strategy used in order to prevent hostile takeover bids.

Crowding-in: a situation in which people make more effort in response to monetary rewards.

Crowding-out: a situation in which people make less effort when they receive monetary rewards.

Derivative stakeholder: a stakeholder with little direct contact with a company, but who has the power to influence stakeholders who have a strong relationship with the company.

Diversification discount: the name given to a situation in which the shares of a conglomerate company trade at a discount to those of more focussed businesses. It is usually associated with control problems.

Dual board: a form of corporate board which assigns the responsibilities for forming strategy and for monitoring to two separate committees made up of different members. They are sometimes known as two-tier boards.

Dual-class shares: company shares which give their holders the same cash-flow rights but different control rights. The shares with greater voting rights might be held by management or some other controlling group, but where they are traded they are priced at a premium.

Duality: a situation in which a single person is both chief executive of a company and the chair of its board.

Endogenous: a way of describing a variable whose value is determined by a model. For example, corporate value may depend on the composition of the board of directors. In this case corporate value is endogenous.

Enlightened shareholder value maximisation: a management philosophy which recognises that all stakeholders are valuable and so creates processes which empower them to make decisions in line with the over-arching aim of maximising shareholder wealth.

Entrenchment: a term which may be used to describe the adverse effects of having either a strong CEO or a major shareholder. An entrenched CEO might pursue their own aims due to having served in that position for a long time or through force of personality. An entrenched blockholder can use the company for purposes that other shareholders do not accept.

Executive director: a director who works for a company and sits on its board.

Exogenous: a way of describing a variable that determines the value of another. For example, if corporate value depends on the presence or absence of duality, duality is exogenous.

Expectations gap: the difference between the public's expectations and the reality of what auditors do. Many people believe that auditors are supposed to detect all frauds or to check every transaction; in reality their role is more limited.

Extrinsic rewards: rewards, usually in the form of money offered to compensate someone for undertaking a task.

Factors of production: a generic term used in economics to describe the inputs that are needed to produce a company's product. Land, labour and capital are the factors most frequently mentioned, some economists would add entrepreneurship to the list.

Fiduciary duty: a duty of care which is established when one person manages assets on behalf of another. The duty must be discharged with honesty, care and loyalty. Corporate law states that company directors have a fiduciary duty their company. This is usually interpreted as a duty to shareholders, but some authors believe it should be extended to other stakeholders.

Financial distress: a situation in which a company has to divert spending on other activities in order to meet its interest payments. It may lead to bankruptcy if cash flows are not improved.

Firm-specific human capital: human capital is the sum total of all the skills and experience gained by an employee. Firm-specific human capital relates to employment in a particular company and so is not useful in other employment.

Fog index: a way of describing the complexity of a written document by measuring the number of years of education required in order to understand it. The index is based on the proportion of words made up of three or more syllables.

Free-rider: a person who is able to share the benefits of a group activity without contributing effort to the activity. In governance terms this might be a shareholder who does not vote at general meetings but benefits from the activism of other shareholders.

Genre analysis: a way of analysing text in order to classify it by genre or type. It has been applied to corporate statements in order to decide if they are optimistic or pessimistic.

Greenmail: a defence against a hostile takeover bid in which the target company pays a premium in order to repurchase the shares already acquired by the bidding company. This defence is available in the US but is not permitted in most other countries.

Horizontal merger: a merger between two companies in the same industry, operating at the same stage in the production process.

Independent director: a non-executive board member who has no formal links to the company or its shareholders. The criteria for independence are laid down by regulators.

Institutional investor: a financial institution such as a pension fund, insurance company or unit trust which uses its members' contributions to buy shares and other financial securities then uses the proceeds from trading to meet its liabilities. In some stock markets financial institutions are the major holders of equity; in these markets regulators are keen to persuade the institutions to play an active role in corporate governance.

Inter-locking directorship: a situation in which executive directors from two or more boards sit on one another's boards as non-executives. This is viewed as bad practice in countries where board independence is prized.

Intrinsic reward: a feeling of achievement based on successfully accomplishing a task. This feeling is not related to a payment for completion of the task.

Kantian ethics: the approach to ethics advocated by Immanuel Kant. For Kant the key difference between man and other animals is that man can choose how to achieve goals while animals achieve their goals by relying on instinct. In addition, man can also incorporate the idea of duty to others in deciding how achieve goals.

Keiretsu: a term used in Japan to describe a group of companies which are run separately, but are linked through cross-directorships and are thereby encouraged to cooperate with one another.

Limited liability company: a company in which shareholders' liability is limited to the value of their shares. This means that if the company is liquidated they lose the value of their initial investment only.

Majoritarian voting system: a voting system in which candidates are elected in geographical areas. The winning party is the one that wins in the most areas.

Management board: in a two-tier board system this board is made up of executives and responsible for making strategic decisions.

Managerial power approach: a way of thinking about remuneration systems where pay packages are seen as part of the agency problem in that managers are rewarded for pursuing goals other than value maximisation.

Managerial slack: a term used by some economists to describe a situation where managers are not working so as to optimise an objective function. Managers may enjoy 'slack' in the form of an easy life.

Managerial utility: the non-monetary gains that managers enjoy as part of their job; this can include the consumption of perks or managerial slack.

Managerial utility maximisation: a corporate aim in which the board looks after its own interests rather than those of shareholders.

Merger wave: a period of time during which the number of company acquisitions rises before tailing off again. Waves may be associated with changes in technology or regulation and often form when the stock market is performing strongly.

Monitoring: a form of agency cost. Monitoring activities are undertaken at shareholders' expense to oversee the decisions taken by management. The aim of monitoring is to reduce the residual loss associated the existence of an agency relationship.

Morning-after pill: a security with the rights like those of a poison pill. While a conventional poison pill must be in place before a hostile bid is made, a morning-after pill, which could be in the form of discretionary warrants, can be implemented in response to a bid.

Nomination committee: a sub-committee of the board of directors, which is responsible for finding new board members. Good practice suggests that most members should be independent directors.

Non-executive director: a board member who works for another organisation.

Normative stakeholder: a stakeholder to whom the company has an ethical obligation because of their close relationship with the company.

Opportunism: a behavioural trait according to which people are happy to take advantage of other people's lack of information or understanding of a situation.

Optimal contracting approach: a way of designing remuneration contracts so that managers are rewarded for improving shareholder value. It is used to solve the agency problem.

Partnership: a form of business organisation in which two or more partners share the profits of the enterprise. They are jointly responsible for the liabilities of the business.

Path-dependency: the idea that institutions or practices are determined by pre-existing conditions. Different conditions lead to different outcomes.

Poison pill: formally known as a shareholder rights plan. It gives shareholders the right to buy shares at a discount in the event that a hostile bid is launched for their company.

Pre-emption rights: a right offered to a group of shareholders allowing them to buy securities before they are offered to other investors.

Primary stakeholder: a stakeholder who makes frequent transactions with a company.

Principal: a person who delegates decision-making authority to an agent.

Propping: any method by which cash is transferred between the companies within a pyramid ownership structure. The aim is to improve the cash flows of a struggling company by diverting cash from another which is performing well.

Pyramid ownership: a situation in which one company is owned by another which may in turn be owned by another.

Rationality: a concept from finance theory which is used to describe the motivation of investors. Investors are assumed to seek the highest possible returns given the level of risk they are prepared to take.

Relational contract: a contract which cannot cover all eventualities because it relates to a situation in which one party has the power to make discretionary decisions.

Relationship marketing: a marketing technique whose aim to increase the loyalty of existing customers rather than to attract new ones.

Remuneration committee: a board sub-committee usually made up of independent directors, whose role is to advise on the type of remuneration packages to be awarded to executive directors. It may also be called the compensation committee.

Resolution: a proposal brought to a general meeting of shareholders.

Revenue maximisation: a corporate objective based on the maximisation of sales revenue. Economic theory shows that a revenue maximising firm will produce more output than a profit maximising firm.

Risk aversion: a general dislike for risk which means that a decision-maker will only accept more risk if they believe it will lead to higher rewards.

Satisficing: the practice of doing enough work to 'get by', rather than to maximise an objective function.

Secondary stakeholder: a stakeholder who rarely transacts with a company.

Self-actualisation: the highest goal in Maslow's hierarchy of needs. An individual achieves self-actualisation when they have met lower-level needs.

Self-dealing: any transaction in which a fiduciary acts in their own interests rather than to benefit their client.

Sole trader: an organisational form in which one person owns and runs the business. The sole trader is completely responsible for the liabilities of the business.

Staggered board: a board of directors in which a proportion of members resign each year; this ensures that the board is constantly refreshed while maintaining some continuity.

Stakeholder: a person or group that can affect or is affected by an organisation.

Stakeholder theory: an approach to management in which decisions are made to benefit all interested parties rather than to achieve the ends of one particular group.

Stewardship theory: an approach to management in which decision-makers are assumed to maximise their own utility or satisfaction, where satisfaction is dependent on pleasing another group. In the context of companies that other group is the shareholders.

Structure-conduct-performance paradigm: an approach used in industrial economics. It relies on the idea that the structure of an industry predicts the way in which companies behave, and their behaviour leads to particular outcomes for the industry.

Supervisory board: in a two-tier board system the supervisory board monitors the decisions made by the management board.

Supply chain: a group of companies in which one company supplies another with components which it uses to manufacture another product which may in turn act as input to some other product.

Toe-hold: a 'small' proportion of a company's equity acquired in open market transactions by a potential hostile acquirer.

Transactions costs economics: a branch of economics in which companies are assumed to make optimal decisions by considering the costs of transacting in markets as well as the costs of producing output. It also known as 'new institutional economics'.

Transfer pricing: the practice of setting prices within a vertically-integrated company or between companies in a group so as to move profit from one part of the group to another.

Tunnelling: a means of moving cash flows between the companies within a pyramid ownership structure. The aim is to move cash to the company over which the ultimate owner of the pyramid has the highest cash flow rights.

Unitary board: a board structure in which a single board both makes and monitors decisions.

Variety index: a way of judging the style of a piece of text based on the number of different words used.

Vertical merger: a merger between two companies in the same industry that operate at different stages in the production process.

Voting cap: a limit on the number of votes that can be cast by a blockholder, it implies that a majority owner may not hold a majority of votes.

Warrant: a derivative security issued by a company and giving the holder the right to buy new equity at some future date. It can be used as defence against a hostile takeover bid.

Whistle-blowing: the situation when an employee breaks a confidentiality agreement with their employer so as to warn a regulator or the general public about a problem at their business.

INDEX